Deep Learning and
Its Applications Using Python

Scrivener Publishing
100 Cummings Center, Suite 541J
Beverly, MA 01915-6106

Publishers at Scrivener
Martin Scrivener (martin@scrivenerpublishing.com)
Phillip Carmical (pcarmical@scrivenerpublishing.com)

Deep Learning and
Its Applications Using Python

Niha Kamal Basha

*Department of Information Security, School of Computer Science
and Engineering, Vellore Institute of Science and Technology, India*

Surbhi Bhatia Khan

*Department of Data Science, School of Science, Engineering and Environment,
University of Salford, Manchester, United Kingdom*

Abhishek Kumar

*Department of Computer Science & Engineering, Chandigarh University,
Punjab, India*

and

Arwa Mashat

*Faculty of Computing and Information Technology, King Abdulaziz University,
Rabigh, Saudi Arabia*

Scrivener
Publishing

WILEY

This edition first published 2023 by John Wiley & Sons, Inc., 111 River Street, Hoboken, NJ 07030, USA and Scrivener Publishing LLC, 100 Cummings Center, Suite 541J, Beverly, MA 01915, USA
© 2023 Scrivener Publishing LLC
For more information about Scrivener publications please visit www.scrivenerpublishing.com.

Wiley Global Headquarters
111 River Street, Hoboken, NJ 07030, USA

For details of our global editorial offices, customer services, and more information about Wiley products visit us at www.wiley.com.

Limit of Liability/Disclaimer of Warranty
While the publisher and authors have used their best efforts in preparing this work, they make no representations or warranties with respect to the accuracy or completeness of the contents of this work and specifically disclaim all warranties, including without limitation any implied warranties of merchantability or fitness for a particular purpose. No warranty may be created or extended by sales representatives, written sales materials, or promotional statements for this work. The fact that an organization, website, or product is referred to in this work as a citation and/or potential source of further information does not mean that the publisher and authors endorse the information or services the organization, website, or product may provide or recommendations it may make. This work is sold with the understanding that the publisher is not engaged in rendering professional services. The advice and strategies contained herein may not be suitable for your situation. You should consult with a specialist where appropriate. Neither the publisher nor authors shall be liable for any loss of profit or any other commercial damages, including but not limited to special, incidental, consequential, or other damages. Further, readers should be aware that websites listed in this work may have changed or disappeared between when this work was written and when it is read.

Library of Congress Cataloging-in-Publication Data

ISBN 978-1-394-16646-6

Cover image: Pixabay.Com
Cover design by Russell Richardson

Set in size of 11pt and Minion Pro by Manila Typesetting Company, Makati, Philippines

Printed in the USA

10 9 8 7 6 5 4 3 2 1

Contents

Preface

Research into deep learning has come a long way across multiple domains, such as healthcare, marketing, banking, manufacturing, education, and so on. Notable applications within these domains are trending, like visual recognition, fraud detection, virtual assistance, NLP, etc. Deep learning models are used to implement these applications. Those models include Convolutional Neural Network (CNN), Recurrent Neural Network (RNN), Long Short-Term Memory (LSTM), and others. To deploy these application-based deep learning models, Python programing is ideal, with its open source software libraries like keras, tensorflow, and soon.

This book thoroughly explains deep learning models and how to use Python programming to implement them in applications such as NLP, face detection, face recognition, face analysis, and virtual assistance (chatbot, machine translation, etc.). This book provides hands-on guidance to using Python for implementing deep learning application models. It also identifies future research directions for deep learning.

Chapter 1 deals with the history of deep learning. The origin tracks back to 1943, when Walter Pitts and Warren McCulloch computed a model (computer model) that supported the human brain (the neural networks). To mimic the thought processes of humans, Pitts and McCulloch used a collection of algorithms and arithmetic concepts, called *threshold logic*. Since then, deep learning has continuously evolved.

TensorFlow and Keras play a major role in the implementation of deep learning models. Therefore, Chapter 2 explains TensorFlow fundamentals, based on a deep learning framework. TensorFlow plays a major role in pattern recognition, specifically in regards to language, images, sound, and time-series data. Classification, prediction, clustering, and feature extraction occurs, too, with the help of deep learning.

Chapter 3 explains how a Python library called Keras has been used for deep learning. The chapter outlines the objective and focus of Keras to create neural networks layers and mathematical models. Chapter 4 continues the presentation of intelligent learning algorithms, explaining how multilayer perceptron is one of the supervised learning algorithms and is an example of artificial neural network with a feedback loop. Among other deep learning models, Chapter 5 delves into CNN algorithms, which act as an artificial neuron (neural network). This neural network is widely used to deal with image input for image processing, recognition, and classification.

A Chapter 6 deals with RNN and LSTM, which are deep learning algorithms that can be used for sequencing numerical inputs to enable tasks, such as handwritten recognition without segmentation or speech recognition. In Chapter 7, the importance of artificial intelligence and its vital role in communicating with humans and machines, as shown in the form of text or voice. Programs that can converse naturally with humans are called *chatbots,* and this chapter explores have chatbots can be automated to perform user-performed tasks.

Chapter 8 discusses different advanced models of deep learning algorithms that are used frequently. Upgrades or modifications are possible because of the flexible nature of neural network, which can lead to the design of an end-to-end model. Therefore, this advancement allows researchers to build simple to complex structures that align need with imagination. Some advanced deep learning algorithms include AlexNet, VGG, NiN, GoogLeNet, ResNet, DenseNet, GRU, LSTM, D-RNN, and Bi-RNN. These advanced deep learning algorithms are discussed in detail, along with code for implementation using Python's Keras library on the TensorFlow platform.

Chapter 9 includes a detailed discussion on new trends in deep learning, current and future challenges, and its prospects. The chapter is supported by a practical case study and working proofs. Some notable works highlighted in this chapter come from different domains, such as semantic intelligence, quantum AI, cyber security, the LAMSTAR system, epilepsy seizure onset prediction, etc.

We hope this book will expand your knowledge on this expanding subject. Our thanks go to the prestigious Wiley and Scrivener Publishing for their continuous kind support and guidance.

Editors
Niha Kamal Basha
Surbhi Bhatia Khan
Abhishek Kumar
Arwa Mashat

Introduction to Deep Learning

The deep learning history is often tracked back to 1943 when Walter Pitts and Warren McCulloch computed a model (computer model) which support the human brain (the neural networks). To mimic the thought process of human, they used a collection of algorithms and arithmetic concepts which is called as *threshold logic*. Since 1943, Deep learning [1] is evolving without break. As it utilizes multiple algorithm in multiple layers to mimic the thought process by processing the data, understanding the human speech and visually recognizing objects. Here the information is processed by passing it into multiple layers, where each layer's output act as an input for the next layer. The first layer in a network is called the input layer, while the last is called an output layer. All the layers between the two are referred to as hidden layers. Each layer is typically a simple, uniform algorithm containing one kind of activation function. Deep learning's other aspect is feature extraction. It uses an algorithm to automatically construct meaningful "features" from the data which will be used for training, learning, and understanding. Mostly, a data scientist, or a programmer, is responsible for this process.

1.1 History of Deep Learning

Right now, the world is seeing a global *Artificial Intelligent* revolution across all industry with the driving factor as deep learning. Google and Facebook using deep learning now, and it has not appeared overnight, rather it evolved slowly and steadily over several decades. There are so many machine learning researchers worked with great determination behind this evaluation. All might be surprised to know the key discoveries of deep learning made by our researchers from 1940s has been illustrated in Table 1.1.

For the evolution of deep learning, many researcher's contributions directly or indirectly, would have influence in the growth. Here, to present the history of deep learning with the help of some key moments have

Niha Kamal Basha, Surbhi Bhatia Khan, Abhishek Kumar and Arwa Mashat (eds.) Deep Learning and Its Applications Using Python, (1–24) © 2023 Scrivener Publishing LLC

Table 1.1 Key discoveries of deep learning.

Year	Inventor name	Invention/technique
1943	Warren Mcculloch and Walter Pitts	Computer Model based on human brain [2]—Threshold Logic (combination of algorithms and mathematics)
1957	Frank Rosenblatt	Perceptron (Binary Classifier) [3]—has true learning ability.
1960	Henry J. Kelley	Neural Network [4]—Continuous Back Propagation Model. Used to recognize the kinds of patterns.
1962	Stuart Dreyfus	Updated the Neural Network back propagation model with chain rule [5].
1965	Alexey Grigoryevich Ivakhnenko and Valentine Grigor'evich Lapa	Multilayer Neural Network with activation function and GMDH (Group Method of data Handling)
1969	Marvin Minsky and Seymour Papert	Frank Rosenblatt perceptrons are proposed with multiple hidden layers.
1970	Seppo Linnainmaa	Generated and implemented the automatic differnceable back propagation method in computer code.
1971	Alexey Grigoryevich Ivakhnenko	8 Layer Deep Neural Network with GMDH (Group Method of data Handling)
1980	Kunihiko Fukushima	Convolutional Neural Network with Neocognitron.
1982	John Hopfield	Recurrent Neural Network (Hopfield Network)—it acts as a content addressable memory system.
1982	Paul Werbos	Proposed the steps to use Back propagation

(Continued)

Table 1.1 Key discoveries of deep learning. (*Continued*)

Year	Inventor name	Invention/technique
1985	David H. Ackley, Geoffrey Hinton and Terrence Sejnowski	Stochastic Recurrent Neural Network (Boltzmann Machine).
1986	Terry Sejnowski	NeTalk—Talking Neural Network.
1986	Geoffrey Hinton, Rumelhart and Williams	Implemented back propagation in neural network [6].
1986	Paul Smolensky	Updated the Boltzmann Machine to Restricted Boltzmann Machine with connection between input and hidden layer.
1989	Yann LeCum	Implemented back propagation in Convolutional Neural Network.
1989	George Cybenko	Implemented Feed Forward Neural Network [7] to approximate continuous function.
1991	Sepp Hochreiter	Identified the vanishing gradient problem in deep neural network.
1997	Sepp Hochreiter and Jurgen Schmidhuber	LSTM [8]—Long short-term memory
2006	Geoffrey Hinton, Ruslan Salakhutdinov, Osindero and Teh	Deep Belief Network [9]
2008	Andrew NG's	Implemented GPU with Deep Neural Network
2009	Fei-Fei Li	Launches ImageNet dataset with deep learning.

(*Continued*)

Table 1.1 Key discoveries of deep learning. (*Continued*)

Year	Inventor name	Invention/technique
2011	Yoshua Bengio, Antoine Bordes, Xavier Glorot	Implemented ReLU activation function in Neural Network as Rectified Neural Network to solve vanishing gradient problem.
2012	Alex Krizhevsky	AlexNet—Implemented GPU with Convolutional Neural Network (CNN) for image classification.
2014	Ian Goodfellow	Created Generative Adversarial Network (GAN)
2016	Deep Mind Technology	AlphaGo—Deep reinforcement Learning Model
2019	Yoshua Bengio, Geoffrey Hinton and Yann LeCun	Turing Award 2018

been attempted. Work has been made to present the chronological events of deep learning history as accurately as possible. For more information on the above chronological events, refer to the links given in the references. All these inventions incorporate mathematics that quantify uncertainty by probability. Introducing probability concept to deep learning helps deep learning–based system to act like a human with common sense. Which mean when dealing with real world, these systems make decisions with incomplete information. Using probability in deep learning helps to model components of uncertainty.

1.2   A Probabilistic Theory of Deep Learning

Using probability in science quantify uncertainty. When lots of data are utilized by machine learning and deep learning for training and testing a model to find patterns, only data is utilized by the system instead of logic. At that time uncertainty increases with relevant probability. In deep learning, most of the models like Baysian model, Hidden Markov model, probability graphical model completely depend on the concepts of probability. Since these system using real world data they have to handle chaoticness with the help of tools. The simplified versions [10] of probability and statistics are

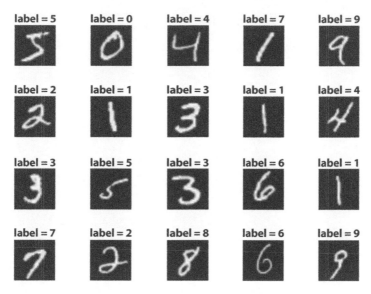

Figure 1.1 MNIST data set.

presented here in terms of deep learning. In Figure 1.1, the MNIST digit recognition dataset have been shown, which is a hello world program of deep learning. This explains the foundation of probability concept in terms of deep learning. This data set is used to classify the handwritten digits and label them.

To do this classification task, the system which planned to create using machine learning is not going to be an accurate one. To do this task, the below neural network in Figure 1.2 has been used to process the input images of 28*28 pixel.

The input image of size 28*28 is feed into input neural network layer. In this layer input image is computed by multiplying with weights (w) and bias (b). Each neural network layer has ten neurons in which each digit processed to proceed further with activation function. At the end, probability of each digit of length 10 along with the vector value is obtained as output. Here in the output vector, the highest values index with its probability have been obtained using argmax. The detailed explanation of neural networks and its layers will be discussed in detail in chapter 4. The purpose of using neural network example in this chapter is to understand how some basic probability concepts used in deep learning. Consider a given vector below in Eq. 1.1.

$$\text{vector a} = [a0, a1, a2, a3, a4, a5, a6, a7, a8, a9] \qquad (1.1)$$

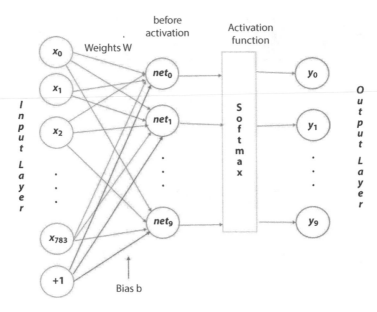

Figure 1.2 Structure of neural network.

The hidden probability and distribution concepts, such as sample space, random variable, probability distribution, discrete distribution, conditional probability, normalization, joint probability, marginal probability, continuous distribution, binomial distribution, uniform distribution, normal distribution, and softmax distribution along with how these concepts correlate with input data used by neural network have been explained below.

Sample Space—All the set of possible data used in a procedure to test a hypothesis.

In terms of MNIST data set, the input used to compute sample space is in the form of image, and the output can be predicted out of 0 to 9 digits which is considered as sample space to predict the output.

Random Variable—Variable which have been randomly chosen among the values of different sample space.

An input x as vector and the output as prediction along with its weights as random variable in neural network are initialized randomly with the help of probability distribution.

Probability Distribution—The random variable have to be taken among different sample space values.

Here the probability distribution have been used to initialize weights and the output y (vector) depends on the probability of X by using different digit from 0 to 9. Here the distribution of y is discrete (discrete distribution). It provides the probability using PMF (Probability Mass Function) and denoted as $P(X = x)$ is called as discrete distribution.

Note: some of the output vector (y) which is all adding up of 1.0 and falls between 0 and 1 is called as normalization. The event which is impossible is denoted as 0 and the possible event as 1. The same applicable for continuous variables

A frequently used probability concepts are listed below:

Joint Probability—The probability of occurrence of two events simultaneously is called joint probability and is denoted as given below in Eq. 1.2.

$$P(l = m, \text{m} = \text{m}) \text{ or } p(m \text{ and } l) \tag{1.2}$$

Conditional Probability—The probability of occurrence of some event y, because of the event x occurred is called conditional probability and is denoted as given below Eq. 1.3.

$$P(m = l|l = l) = P(m, l)/P(l) \tag{1.3}$$

Marginal Probability—It is to find the probability among the subsets of random variable form a superset of random variable. It is denoted as below in Eq. 1.4.

$$P(L = l) = \sum_m P(L = l, M = m) \tag{1.4}$$

Bayes Probability—The current event probability depends on previous knowledge of conditions related to current event. It is denoted as below in Eq. 1.5.

$$P(M|L) = P(L|M) . P(M)/P(L) \tag{1.5}$$

Binomial Distribution—A random variable which have two outcomes (Yes/No), is called as binomial distribution. It is applicable for discrete random variables and denoted as below in Eq. 1.6.

$$P(L = l) \; nD_{l . d^l q^{n-l}} \tag{1.6}$$

In programing context the implementation of binomial distribution have been shown below.

```
import numpy as np
g=10
h=0.5
e=1000
np.random.binomial(g,h,e)
```

Continuous Distribution—This is defined using continuous random variables and explained with the help of probability density function (PDF). Its integral is equal to 1 and is denoted as below in Eq. 1.7.

$$\int p(l)dx = 1 \qquad (1.7)$$

Uniform Distribution—A simple form of distribution with an item of equal sample space. It is denoted as below in Eq. 1.8.

$$f(l) = 1/j\text{-}i, l \text{ belongs to } [i,j] \qquad (1.8)$$

In programing context the implementation of uniform distribution have been shown below.

```
import numpy as np
np.random.uniform(Lw=1, Hgh=10, Siz=100)
```

Normal Distribution—This is also known as Gaussian distribution and is an important distribution for random, generated and independent variables. It is symmetric about the mean which shows that the occurrence of data are more frequent near the mean than the data far away from mean. While presenting the data in graph, it appears as bell curve as shown in Figure 1.3. Here, as standard normal distribution the mean is equal to zero and the standard deviation is equal to one.

The mathematical representation of normal distribution is denoted as below in Eq. 1.9.

$$f(l)=1/\sigma\sqrt{2\pi} \cdot e^{-1/2(l-\mu/\sigma)^2} \qquad (1.9)$$

In programing context the implementation of normal distribution have been shown below.

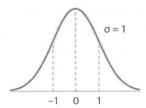

Figure 1.3 Bell curve.

```
import numpy as np
m=0
sig=1
np.random.normal(m, sig,siz=100)
```

The frequency of usage of words "normalization" and "standardization" are more in deep learning. The process of obtaining normal distribution is known as standardization and the process of converting the data values to the range of 0.0 to 1.0 is known as normalization. In programing context the implementation of normalization and standardization have been shown below.

```
from sklearn.preprocessing import StandardScaler
import numpy as np
data = no.array([1,2,3,4,5])
scaler = StandardScaler()
scaler.fit_transform(data)
```

Softmax Distribution—The most used probability distribution (categorical distribution) in deep learning to represent 1 out of N class. The mathematical representation of softmax is denoted as below in Eq. 1.10.

$$s(x_j) = e^{x_{zj}} / \sum_{k=1}^{K} e^{x_{zk}} \quad \text{where } j = 1,2,3,\ldots,K \qquad (1.10)$$

In programing context, the implementation of softmax distribution have been shown below.

```
def softmax(x):
    a_i = np.max(i)
    return a_i / a_i.sum(axis=0)
```

The most commonly used statistical measures [5] are Mean, Median, Mode, Variance, Covariance and Standard deviation are explained below.

Mean—It is the average of input data, which is mathematically represented as below in Eq. 1.11.

$$\mu = x1 + x2 + x3 + \dots + xn \ / \ n \qquad (1.11)$$

In programing context, the implementation of mean have been shown below.

```
Import numpy as np
p = np.array([[2,8,4,5,6]])
np.mean(p,axis=0)
```

Median and Mode—The middle value of the data is called as median and the frequently occurring value is called as mode. In programing context, the implementation of median and mode have been shown below.

```
import numpy as np
from scipy import stats
stats.mode(p)
np.median(p,axis=0)
```

Variance—It is a measure of difference among an input from the mean value. The mathematical representation is denoted as given below in Eq. 1.12.

$$\sigma^2 = \sum_{i=1}^{n} \frac{(xi - \mu)^2}{n} \qquad (1.12)$$

For random variable the variance is denoted as given below in Eq. 1.13.

$$\text{Var}[X] = E[[(x - E(x))^2] \qquad (1.13)$$

Co-variance is used to measure how variables related (linearly) to each other. In programing context, the implementation of variance and co-variance have been shown below.

```
import numpy as np
L = np.array([[1,3,4,8,6]])
```

np.var(p)
np.cov(p)

Standard Deviation—The square root of the variance is called as standard deviation. The mathematical representation of standard deviation is denoted as below in Eq. 1.14.

$$\sigma = \sqrt{\sum_{i=1}^{n} \frac{(xi - \mu)^2}{n}} \qquad (1.14)$$

In programing context, the implementation of standard deviation have been shown below.

import numpy as np
np.std(i)

To measure the working of models in terms of performance [11], the list of metrics have been used. They are, accuracy, confusion matrix, precision and recall, F1 Score, mean absolute error, mean square error, ROC curve, Markov chains. For example, if the network predicts 95 out of 100 inputs correctly, then its accuracy is 95% and this will be done with the help of sklearn python library. The discussion on these metrics are given below.

Accuracy—It is a measure which provide wrong insights based on its value. Some times this value provide wrong insights. The high accuracy doesn't mean the model is right. To check the following metrics in Figure 1.4, have to be calculated with the help of confusion matrix.

$$\text{Accuracy} = (TP + TN)/(TP + FP + TN + FN) \qquad (1.15)$$

Confusion Matrix—This is the matrix which includes True Positive, False Positive, True Negative and False Negative values which have been shown in Figure 1.5.

If a binary classifier have outputs as 0 or 1, in that case if it is normal with unbiased model then the accuracy of the model will be obtained. The working of confusion matrix have been shown below.

```
from sklearn.metrics import confusion_matrix
m_true = [2,0,2,2,1]
m_pred = [0,0,2,2,2]
confusion_matrix(m_true, m_pred)
```

| True Positives (TP) - Total of positive examples labeled as such. |
| False Positives (FP) - Total of negative examples labeled as positive. |
| True Negatives (TN) - Total of negative examples labeled as such. |
| False Negatives (FN) - Total of positive examples labeled as negative. |

Figure 1.4 Metrics to calculate accuracy.

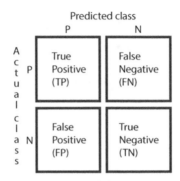

Figure 1.5 Representation of confusion matrix.

But if the model is tuned to through 0 always (or 1 always), even then the accuracy of the model is high (prediction of the model is none). To get the clarity on the performance of the model, the below Figure 1.6 have to be observed.

It is observed in the above figure that the performance of the model as poor because, the positive class incorrectly classified with 83% accuracy. To know a valid output the metrics, precision, recall and F1 score have been used.

Precision and Recall—This metric is used to check the selected objects as correct. A recall to check correct objects where selected or not. The precision and recall value is 0 in the above example. Which means the model is extremely poor. The mathematical notation have been shown in Eq. 1.16 and Eq. 1.17.

$$\text{Precision} = \text{TP/TP+FP} \qquad (1.16)$$

$$\text{Recall} = \text{TP/TP+FN} \qquad (1.17)$$

	Classified positive	Classified negative
Positive class	0 (TP)	25 (FN)
Negative class	0 (FP)	125 (TN)

Figure 1.6 Output for the confusion matrix.

F1 Score—The average of precision and recall is F1 score. Here, F1 score is 0, which mean worst model and 1 means best model. Based on these metrics the chaotic behavior of accuracy metric will be resolved. The mathematical notation have been shown in Eq. 1.18.

$$F1 \text{ score} = 2. \text{ Precision. Recall/Precision} + \text{Recall} \qquad (1.18)$$

The working of precision, recall and F1 score have been illustrated in Figure 1.7 with the help of Sklearn classification report function.

Mean Absolute error and Mean squared error—The average difference among values of original and predicted values is called as mean absolute error. The average of square have been used. The mathematical notation have been shown in Eq. below. An implementation of mean squared error is shown in below line of code.

```
from sklearn.metrics import mean_squared_error
m_true -= [3,-0.5,2,6]
m_pred = [2.5,2,8]
mean_squared_error(m_true, m_pred)
```

Receiver Operating Characteristic (ROC) curve—It is used to find the performance of classification model. It depend on two parameters they are, TPR—True Positive Rate which is similar to recall and FPR—False Positive Rate. TPR is called as sensitivity and FPR is also called as specificity. The mathematical notation have been shown below in Eq. 1.19 and Eq. 1.20, these equation have been plotted to obtain the graph in Figure 1.8. Here measure of accuracy is obtained below the cure is the ROC.

$$\text{TP rate} = \text{TP/TP} + \text{FN} \qquad (1.19)$$

$$\text{FP rate} = \text{FP/FP} + \text{TN} \qquad (1.20)$$

```
from sklearn.metrics import classification_report
y_true = [0, 1, 2, 2, 2]
y_pred = [0, 0, 2, 2, 1]
target_names = ['class 0', 'class 1', 'class 2']
print(classification_report(y_true, y_pred, target_names=target_names))

              precision    recall  f1-score   support

     class 0       0.50      1.00      0.67         1
     class 1       0.00      0.00      0.00         1
     class 2       1.00      0.67      0.80         3

   micro avg       0.60      0.60      0.60         5
   macro avg       0.50      0.56      0.49         5
weighted avg       0.70      0.60      0.61         5
```

Figure 1.7 Code to demonstrate the working of precision, recall and F1 score.

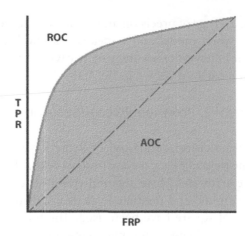

Figure 1.8 The graphical representation of TPR and FPR.

Area Under Curve (AUC)—To check whether the model is best AUC value have been used. If AUC is 1 then the model is best, if AUC is 0.5 the model is poor and If AUC is 0.0 then the model results with reverse output. (i.e., classify 1 as 0 and 0 as 1). The working of ROC and AUC is shown in below line of code.

```
import numpy as np
from sklearn.metrics import roc_auc_score
m_true = np.array([0,0,0,1,1,1])
m_scores = np.array([0.1,0.4,0.35,0,1,0.8])
roc_auc_score(m_true, m_scores)
```

1.3   Back Propagation and Regularization

Both back propagation and regularization [12] have been used to improve the working of neural network. Back propagation is the important part of training the neural network. This step is applied to fine-tune the weight of neural network based on the error occurred during the previous iteration. Doing this will reduce the error rate. Also by increasing the models regularization increases the reliability of the model. The working of the back propagation have been illustrated in Figure 1.9.

Initially the input enters the pre-connected network as X. The weights are modeled using real value as W and in general the weights are randomly selected. After this, calculate the neurons output from all the three layers.

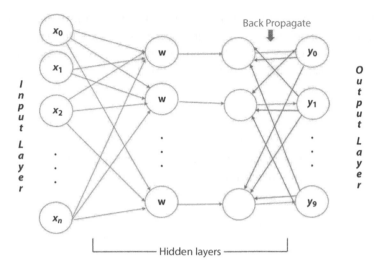

Figure 1.9 Working of back propagation.

The layers are input, hidden and output layer. To compute the output error, the below Eq. 1.21 have been used. With this computed error, fine tune the weights based by back propagation. Which have been done by traversing from output layer to hidden layer by tuning the weights to decrease the error.

$$\text{Error} = \text{Actual Output} - \text{Desired Output} \qquad (1.21)$$

This back propagation have two types, they are static and recurrent back propagation.

Static back propagation—It maps the static input for static output and also solves the problem like optical character recognition which is a static classification issue.

Recurrent back propagation—It fed forward until it achieve a fixed value, then it computes the error and back propagate. The main difference between the static and recurrent back propagation is mapping. In static, it has a static mapping where as in recurrent mapping is non-static.

Similar to back propagation, regularization has been used to improvise the neural network. Regularization has been used to overcome the over fitting. If the model learn well from the data and training data obviously that models have a poor performance on the unknown data. On the other hand, the models complexity increases with decrease in the error rate but the testing error remains the same.

In deep learning, regularization means which penalize the weight matrix of the node. If the coefficient of regularization is high, then the weight matrix is nearly equal to zero. It results as a normal linear network with less under fitting on the training data. In case if the use of higher coefficient of regularization is not useful then an optimized values of regularization coefficient is used in order to obtain well-fitted model. There are L2 and L1 regularization, dropout regularization, data argumentation regularization, and early stopping regularization.

L2 and L1 regularization—It is a widely used method which update cost function. The value of weighted matrix decreases due to the addition of this regularization term because the simpler models will have a smaller weight matrix. The regularization term differs in L1 and L2.

$$\text{In L2, cost function} = \text{loss} + \frac{\lambda}{2m} * \sum \|W\|^2 \qquad (1.22)$$

$$\text{In L1, cost function} = \text{loss} + \frac{\lambda}{2m} * \sum \|W\| \qquad (1.23)$$

Here, in Eq. 1.23 and Eq. 1.24, lambda (λ) is the regularization parameter. These values are optimized to get better results, which are also known as weight decay. L1 is used when the model undergo for compression, otherwise L2 is used.

Dropout—It is the important regularization technique which is used frequently to get good results. At each iteration, it selects the node randomly and removes all incoming and outgoing connections.

Data Augmentation—By using this technique, the over fitting is reduced by increasing the amount of data using data augmentation. For example, in handwritten digital data example, increasing the size of training data, following transformation applied. The transformations are rotating the image, flipping the image, scaling the image, shifting the image, etc. which have been shown in Figure 1.10. This improves the accuracy of the model.

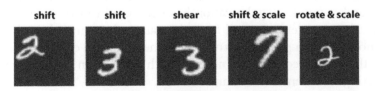

Figure 1.10 Transformation of handwritten digit data.

Early Stopping—It is the cross-validation strategy which keeps the training set as validation set. When the validation set's performance is getting worse, the training on the model immediately stop.

1.4   Batch Normalization and VC Dimension

It is a technique [13] used for a standardization of the data in a network, i.e., transforming the data to have a mean value as zero and standard deviation as one. It is applied either to a prior layer or applied directly to the input. It accelerates training, in some cases by halving the epochs or better, and provides some regularization, reducing generalization error. By using this, the models performance increases with its accuracy. The mathematical representations are given below in Eq. 1.24 and Eq. 1.25.

$$\mu = \frac{1}{m} \sum h_i \qquad (1.24)$$

$$\sigma = \left[\frac{1}{m} \sum (h_i - \mu)^2 \right]^{\frac{1}{2}} \qquad (1.25)$$

Here, μ and σ—mean & standard deviation
m is the number of neurons at layer h.

Once these values are computed then by using these values, the hidden activation has been normalized. For that the mean value is subtracted from the input and divided by the sum of standard deviation and smoothing value (ϵ). It is used to assume the stability within the operation by stopping a division by a zero value. The mathematical representation of smoothing term is shown in Eq. 1.26.

$$h_{i(norm)} = \frac{(h_i - \mu)}{\sigma + \Delta} \qquad (1.26)$$

At last, the re-scaling and offsetting of the input have to be done. Here γ (gamma) and β (beta) are the components used as notation for re-scaling and shifting, which is used to batch normalize the values from the previous operations. These components are learnable parameters used during training neural networks to ensure the optimal values and for each batch it will enable accurate normalization. The mathematical representation is presented in Eq. 1.27.

$$h_i = Yh_{i(norm)} + \beta \tag{1.27}$$

The Vapnik–Chervonenkis (VC) dimension is related to the number of training inputs which are needed to train network (N) to compute a target function $h : D \rightarrow \{0, 1\}$. It is used to find the error boundaries of infinite class by measuring the capacity of a function class. Based on this VC dimension value, the complexity of the classifier will be measured. If the VC dimension is large, then the classifier is more complex and vice versa. The mathematical representation of VC dimension is shown in Eq. 1.28.

$$\text{Test error} \leq \text{Training error} + \frac{1}{\sqrt{n}} \cdot \sqrt{v \, log\left(\frac{2n}{v}\right) + v - log \, log\left(\frac{\delta}{4}\right)}$$

with probability $1 - \delta$

$$\tag{1.28}$$

Here, v is the VC complexity and n is the sample size.

From this, it is interpreted that there is a trade-off in standard bias variance. If the model is more complex then it will be because of higher VC complexity, and there will be more variance in value. The test error and training error is analogous to the model risk and its bias. Here the variance is related to the VC dimension. All these methods and techniques are used to improvise the performance of the model.

1.5   Neural Nets—Deep and Shallow Networks

Neural Nets [14] are the back born of deep learning. It is the series of algorithms that mimics the working of human brain to identify the relationship amount of input data. The neural nets are categorized into perceptron, feed forward neural networks, convolutional neural networks (CNN), and recurrent neural networks (RNN).

Perceptron is the oldest neural network with single neuron. Feed forward neural network is also called as multilayered perceptron (MLPs) comprises of input layer, hidden layer and output layer. In this to note that it actually consists of sigmoid neurons, not a perceptron because most of the problems are nonlinear. This neural network is a base for computer vision, natural language processing where the input is feed in to the network to train them to get the desired output. Similar to feed forward network CNN [15] is widely used for computer vision, pattern detection, and image processing. These networks follow linear algebra that too matrix multiplication to get the desired output based on pattern detection on image input. RNN is a network which have feedback loop, primarily used on time series data to make prediction on future outcome, eg, sales forecast, stock market prediction. These networks are broadly divided into shallow and deep networks.

Shallow network is a normal neural network which has a structure with artificial neuron consisting of machine learning algorithms that perform computation on the dataset like the human brain to make decision. Under machine learning, deep learning is a branch with a set of nonlinear processing unit that consists of multiple layers for feature transformation and extraction. Initially, the input is fed into the first layer, after processing, it passes information to the second layer where the obtained information is processed further by adding additional information and pass it to the next layer. This process continues until the desired output is achieved.

In shallow network [16] based on the structure it consist of neurons, connection and weight, propagation function, linear rate as components. When the amount of data increases then we move on to deep learning structure for processing the input. In deep learning model, it consists of motherboard, processors, RAM, PSU as its components for processing the input. The choose of usability of these networks are completely user dependent and also based on the input going to be consider for training the model and testing the model.

Based on the architecture, the neural network include feed forward network, recurrent neural networks, symmetrically connected neural networks, and the deep learning model consists of unsupervised pre-trained networks, convolutional neural network, recurrent neural networks, recursive neural networks. The detailed description and usage of shallow and deep learning models will be discussed in upcoming chapters.

1.6   Supervised and Semi-Supervised Learning

A supervised and semisupervised learning [17] in general perform a learning/training on the input data to obtain the desired output. Among these two learning, supervised learning work with both input (x) and output (y) data in hand (labeled data) to creating a mapping function between them.

Here to well approximate the mapping function a new input (x) is introduced for learning algorithm which can predict the output (y) on the data. The process involved in this supervised learning is related to an example, a teacher supervising the learning process of the students, i.e., for training an algorithm to determine the important feature with supervision. The problems based on the supervised learning are grouped further into regression and classification problem.

Regression—It is a problem that deals with the relationship between an output variable i.e. a variable is a real value. E.g. dollars or weights.

Classification—It is a problem which deals with process of classifying an output variable is a category, e.g., disease or no disease.

Most widely used supervised learning algorithm linear regression, random forest, and support vector machines.

A semi-supervised learning [18] is trained on the labeled and unlabeled data. Unlabeled data are used by unsupervised learning for training to determine the important feature on its own. The unsupervised learning problems are categorized into clustering and association problem.

Clustering—It is a problem that deals with finding a pattern or structure on unlabeled data by natural grouping (if it present in the group) process on the data.

Association—It is a problem that deals with creating a rules on learning the data to describe about its relationship among them.

The most widely used unsupervised learning algorithms are k-means, a priori algorithm. The application of these supervised and unsupervised learning is limited. To overcome this problem semi-supervised learning is used. The combination of these two learning contains small amount of labeled and large amount of unlabeled data. Initially the process of labeling the data for supervised learning will consumes lots of time. When the unlabeled data are used for training, the accuracy of the model increases with less time and cost. With this, the model has been trained to obtain a structure in the data. Then the supervised learning have been used by feeding the data back to model for training and use them to get best prediction on unlabeled data to find the desired output. Some of the application of semi-supervised learning are speech analysis, Internet connect, and protein sequence classification. This is how the supervised and semisupervised learning have been used to improvise the performance of the model.

Apart from these learning, for prediction self-supervised learning algorithm have been used which is also called as predictive learning. It is a method of machine learning which work on the unlabeled sample data to extract features/pattern on its own. These learning algorithms are

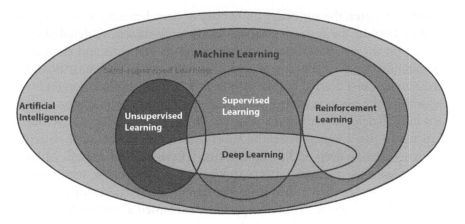

Figure 1.11 Presentation of intelligent learning algorithms in computer science.

used together to make machine learn to get an optimal output. Machine Learning is process of applying mathematics and statistics approach on the data to make machines learn. It is a type of intelligence that helps to predict more accurate results without the help of programmers. All these learnings, along with deep learning and reinforcement learning, have been illustrated in Figure 1.11.

1.7   Deep Learning and Reinforcement Learning

Deep learning [19] and reinforcement learning are the system/model which automatically learn from the input data. Deep learning learn from the input and apply its learning on the new input while the reinforcement learning change the action to improvise the rewards with its continuous feedback. For example, the robot learn to walk is based on reinforcement learning. Initially robot try long step and fall down, it learn from the outcome occurred by its action by feedback. Now it adjusts the action with small step. Now, because of this action, robots are able to move forward. Both deep learning and reinforcement learning [20] are used together by using deep learning in reinforcement learning and called it as deep reinforcement learning. It combined neural networks with reinforcement learning framework that help an agent to learn to reach its destiny. To maximize the reward, it combines approximation function, target optimization, mapping states and actions. This is how the performance of the model has been improvised by using different learning models.

In this chapter, the summary on history of deep learning from the year 1943 to 2019 in the form of pictorial chain is discussed. A detailed discussion on the use of different probability-based concepts and statistical computation for deep learning process which benefit on choosing the right model to obtain a desired output. Along with this, the explanation on how to improve the performance of a model by using back propagation, regularization, batch normalization, and VC dimension technique have been depicted in this chapter. Then the short description on neural nets with difference among deep and shallow network have been discussed. At last, different learning methods, such as supervised, unsupervised, semi-supervised, deep, and reinforcement learning, have been depicted along with its example. The basics of TensorFlow will be explained along with python-based implementation in the next chapter.

References

1. Fellow, I.G., Bengio, Y., Courville, A., *Deep learning*, MIT Press, Cambridge, United States, 2017.
2. McCulloch, W.S. and Pitts, W., A logical calculus of the ideas immanent in nervous activity. *Bull. Math. Biophys.*, 14, 5, 115–133, Maryland, US, 1943.
3. Rosenblatt, The perceptron—A perceiving and recognizing automaton, in: *Technical Report, Cornell Aeronautical Laboratory*, Buffalo, New York, 1957, 85-460-1.
4. Kelley, H.J., Gradient theory of optimal flight paths. *ARS J.*, 30, 947–954, New York, US, 1960.
5. Dreyfus, S., The numerical solution of variational problems. *J. Math. Anal. Appl.*, 5, 1, 30–45, US, 1962.
6. Rumelhart, D., Hinton, G., Williams, R., Learning representations by back-propagating errors. *Nature*, 32, 3, 533–536, United Kingdom, 1986.
7. Cybenko, Approximation by superpositions of a sigmoidal function. *Math. Control Signal Syst.*, 25, 2, 303–314, United Kingdom, 1989.
8. Hochreiter, S. and Schmidhuber, J., Long short-term memory. *Neural Comput.*, 9, 8, 1735–1780, United States, 1997.
9. Hinton, G.E. and Osindero, S., A fast learning algorithm for deep belief nets. *Neural Comput.*, 18, 7, 1527–54, United States, 2006.
10. Singh, P. and Manure, A., *Learn TensorFlow 2.0: Implement machine learning and deep learning models with python*, Apress Publisher, New York, 2019.
11. Rungta, K., *TensorFlow in 1 Day: Make your own neural network*, Amazon Digital Services LLC - KDP Print US, 2018.
12. Pattanayak, S., *Pro deep learning with TensorFlow: A mathematical approach to advanced artificial intelligence in python*, Apress Publisher, New York, 2018.

13. Atienza, A., *Advanced deep learning with TensorFlow 2 and Keras: Apply DL, GANs, VAEs, deep RL, unsupervised learning, object detection and segmentation, and more*, Pack Publishing Limited, Birmingham, United Kingdom, 2020.
14. Jain, A., Fandango, A., Kapoor, A., *TensorFlow machine learning projects: Build 13 real-world projects with advanced numerical computations using the Python ecosystem*, Packt Publishing, Birmingham, United Kingdom, 2018.
15. Glorot, X., Bordes, A., Bengio, Y., Deep sparse rectifier neural networks. *Proc. Mach. Learn. Res.*, 15, 2, 315–323, Fort Lauderdale, FL, USA, 2011.
16. Jose, J., *Introduction to machine learning*, Khanna Book Publishing Co, Delhi, India, 2020.
17. Theobald, O., *Machine learning for absolute beginners: A plain english introduction*, 2nd edition, Scatterplot Press, United States, 2017.
18. Pradhan, M. and Kumar, U.D., *Machine learning using python*, Wiley, 2020.
19. Shalizi, C.R., *Advanced data analysis from an elementary point of view*, Now Publishers, Hanover, Maryland, United States, 2013.
20. Deng, L. and Yu, D., *Deep learning: Methods and applications*, Now Publishers, Hanover, Maryland, United States, 2013.

2

Basics of TensorFlow

This chapter explains TensorFlow fundamentals based on deep learning framework. It plays a major role in pattern recognition, specifically about language, images, sound, and time-series data. Classification, prediction, clustering, and feature extraction have been done with the help of deep learning. Favorably, TensorFlow released in November 2015 by Google and its evolution are tabulated in Table 2.1.

The aim of this chapter is to explain the basic components of TensorFlow. TensorFlow [10] has a facility for performing partial sub-graph computation to agree distributed training by partitioning the neural networks. In addition to that, TensorFlow agrees model parallelism as well as data parallelism. TensorFlow also offers numerous APIs. The deepest level API has named as TensorFlow Core, which provide wide-ranging programming control. The important features of TensorFlow have been enumerated below:

- Its graph deals an illustration of computations.
- Its graph has nodes used for operations.
- It performs computation within stipulated period.
- A graph for computation must be launched in a session.
- The devices such as CPU and GPU places the graph operations in a session.
- For executing graph operations, a session, which has methods have been used.

2.1 Tensors

Initially, the basic of TensorFlow have been discussed. It is a mathematical object. A multidimensional array is used for representation. A tensor [11] of rank one is vector/array whereas tensor of rank two is matrix. Briefly, a

---

Niha Kamal Basha, Surbhi Bhatia Khan, Abhishek Kumar and Arwa Mashat (eds.) Deep Learning and Its Applications Using Python, (25–44) © 2023 Scrivener Publishing LLC

Table 2.1 Noticeable TensorFlow evolution.

Inventor	Year	Invention
Google	2011	A proprietary machine learning system (DistBelief) [1]
	2015	A googles first generation system (TensorFlow) [2]
		RackBrain backed by TensorFlow.
	2016	Tensor Processing Unit (TPU) – ASIC for machine learning [3].
	2017	A second generation system (TensorFlow 1.0.0) [4]
		TensorFlow Lite – Software stack for mobile development.
		Second generation TPU.
		Pixel Visual Core (PVC) – supports processing of image, vision and AI for mobile device [5].
		Google, Cisco, RedHat, CoreOS, and CaiCloud developed Kubeflow (to deploy TensorFlow on Kubernetes) [6].
	2018	Beta version of TPU available on Google cloud Platform [7]
		Version 1.0 of TensorFlow.js for machine learning in JavaScript.
		Third generation TPU [8].
		Edge TPU to run TensorFlow Lite machine learning model.
	2019	TensorFlow Graphics for deep Learning [9].
		Third Generation system (TensorFlow 2.0.0)

tensor can deliberated as n-dimensional array and some examples of tensors are:

- 7: Can be taken as tensor with rank 0, as it is scalar in shape.
- [4., 7., 3.]: Can be taken as tensor with rank 1, with a 1 dimensional shape.
- [[1., 2., 7.], [3., 5., 4.]]: Can be taken as tensor with rank 2, with a 2 dimensional shape.
- [[[1., 2., 3.]], [[7., 8., 9.]]]: Can be taken as tensor with rank 3, with a 3 dimensional shape.

2.2   Computational Graph and Session

Two main actions of TensorFlow Core programs are,

- The computational graph has been built in the production phase.
- The graph computation has been run in the finishing phase.

The working of TensorFlow [12] are given below,

- Program of Tensor Flow has organized as construction phase and execution phase.
- A graph has constructed with nodes (ops/operation) and edges (tensors) in construction phase.
- A graph has session for executing ops (operations) in execution phase.
- The default graph of TensorFlow library uses ops as constructors to get nodes.

The TensorFlow program structure, with its two phases, has been depicted in Figure 2.1.

A computational graph consists of operations on TensorFlow layout into a nodes (graph). In Numpy, first, the matrices have to be created and then multiply the two matrices. While in TensorFlow [13], a graph has to be set up and subsequently initialize the variables once the session has been created. Finally, the data have been feed into placeholders to invoke any action. The evaluation of the nodes is completed when the session is run by the computational graph. This finally completes the process of control and also the state of tensorflow runtime is achieved. The two methods called as "run" is executed for the evaluation purposes of two nodes as

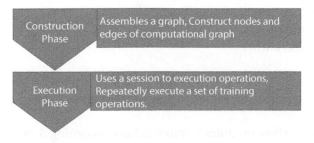

Figure 2.1 The program structure of two-phase TensorFlow with description.

node1 and node2. This function explains the computation mechanism as neither computes nor holds anything. It basically defines the operations that are mentioned in the code. The process starts by initiating the creation of the default graph. Multiple purposes can be achieved by this task. The graphs or parts of graphs can be executed with a session. The resources are also allocated for the execution purposes like CPUs/GPUs, as it keeps the values of the intermediate operations as result for different variables used in executing the program. During the process created in Tensorflow, the value defined by a variable will remain valid in only one session, else will return an error in a second session because the variable is not initialized there a session have to be created for the graph in order, to run any operation. This will also store the current value of the variable by allocating memory.

2.3   Constants, Placeholders, and Variables

Tensor data structure used to represent all data in TensorFlow [14] program. Only tensors were passed among operations in computational graph. A TensorFlow is considered as tensor with n-dimensional array/list, which has a static type, a shape, and a rank. A constant result was produced by graph.

The different deep learning algorithms have been associated with several mages, where the pixel values are assigned to each image and iterations are performed on the image pixel values. The training of the model is achieved by constructing the graph and optimization and tuning is done on the objects notified as weight and bias. The weight is assigned to the objects, adjusting the bias for best results. In summary, variables have been enabled to add trainable parameters in a graph. The code to demonstrate is given below.

```
import tensorflow as tf
L = tf.constant(10, dtype='float')
ses = tf.Session()
print(ses.run(L))
```
10.0

The code has been explained in simple steps given below:

1. Tensorflow modules is imported and assigning it as tf.
2. A constant value (L) is also assigned.

3. A numerical value 10 is assigned.
4. A Session is created for computation.
5. A variable L is run and current value is printed.

The construction phase have been used in first three steps belong, and the execution phase used in last two-step. The previous code has been rewritten as shown below.

```
import tensorflow as tf
L = tf.const(10, dtype='float')
with tf.Ses() as ses:
    print(ses.run(L))
```
10.0

To create a variable and initialize it have been shown in below line of code.

```
import tensorflow as tf
L = tf.const(10, dtype='float')
M = tf.Var(L+10)
mod = tf.glb_var_initiz()
with tf.Ses() as ses:
    ses.run(mod)
    print(ses.run(M))
```
20.0

The code is explained in the given steps below:

1. TensorFlow module can be imported first.
2. Then call it like tf.
3. L was created as constant variable and assigned value 10.
4. Define a equation 10+10 to a new variable M.
5. Initializing the variable by tf.global_variables_initializer().
6. Creation of session to compute the values.
7. Run the model which was created in step 5.
8. Run and print the value of M.

A below lines shows the code for using variable using array.

```
import tensorflow as tf
L = tf.const([14.0, 23.0, 40.0, 30.0])
```

```
M = tf.Var(L*2 + 100)
mod = tf.Var(L*2 + 100)
with tf.Sess() as ses:
    ses.run(mod)
    print(ses.run(M))
```

[128.0 146.0 180.0 160.0]

Placeholder was a container to store value that can be used later. It can accept input from user. Dimension of placeholder was one or multiple dimensions, which can store n-dimensional arrays. Below line of code demonstrate the working of placeholder.

```
import tensorflow as tf
L = tf.placeholder("float", None)
M = L*10 + 500
with tf.Sess() as ses:
    placeL = ses.run(M, fed_dict={L: [0.0, 5.0, 15.0,25.0]})
    print(placeL)
```

[500.0 550.0 650.0 750.0]

The code is explained as follows:

1. TensorFlow module can be imported first.
2. Then call it like tf.
3. A tensor y is created, attained by the operation of multiplication followed by addition (L * 10 + 500).
4. Check initial values for x are not defined
5. To compute the values create a session.
6. Run and print the value of M.

The code given below describe the way to create 2D array to store few numbers. The first dimension is declares as None, which means that it can accept any number of rows. Here, each element in placeholder was multiplied by 10 and incremented by 1.

```
import tensorflow as tf
L = tf.placeholder("float", [None, 4])
M = L*10+1
with tf.Sess() as ses:
```

```
datL = [[12.0, 2.0, 0.0, -2.0],
         [14.0, 4.0, 1.0,  0.0]]
placeL = sess.run(M, fed_dict=[L: datL])
print(placeL)
```

```
[[121.0 21.0  1.0 -19.0]
 [141.0 41.0 11.0   1.0]]
```

In the above code, if none was replaced by 2 in line no: 2 then also we obtain the same output. Size of the matrix was 2×4 which is shown below.

```
import tensorflow as tf
L = tf.placeholder("float", [2, 4])
M = L*10+1
with tf.Sess() as ses:
    datL = [[12.0, 2.0, 0.0, -2.0],
            [14.0, 4.0, 1.0, 0.0]]
    PlaceL = ses.run(M, fed_dict=[L: datL])
    print(placeL)
```

```
[[121.0 21.0  1.0 -19.0]
 [141.0 41.0 11.0   1.0]]
```

Later, there was a need to create a placeholder of [3,4] shape. If the previous code was used and changed the size to [3,4], there occurs an error which is shown in below line of code.

```
import tensorflow as tf
L = tf.placeholder('float', [3,4])
M = L*10+1
with tf.Sess() as ses:
    datL = [[12.0, 0.0, -2.0],
            [14.0, 1.0,  0.0]]
        placeL = ses.run(M, fed_dict={L: datL)
        print(placeL)
ValueError                        Tracback (most recent call last)
<ipython-input-10-c70a14b67c27> in <module>()
      5        datL = [[12.0, 0.0, -2.0],
      6                [14.0, 1.0, 0.0]]
      7        placeL = ses.run(L, feed_dict={L: datL})
      8        print(placeL)
```

This error can be solved by applying linear model. The procedure to implement linear model in placeholder have been shown below line of code.

```
V = tf.Variable([2], dtype=tf.float32)
c = tf.Variable([3], dtype=tf.float32)
l = tf.placeholder(tf.float32)
y = V * l + c
```

The values of constants were never change, and they were initialized as tf.constant. However, in the case of variable, they were not initialized when tf.Variable was used. A function should explicitly call for initializing all the variables in a TensorFlow program which was shown below.

```
sess.run(tf.global_variables_initializer())
```

2.4   Creating Tensor

An image is a tensor [15] with order three as dimensions of width, height, and no.of channels (R,B,G).

How the image input will be handled by tensor network is shown in Figure 2.2 and its code was shown below.

```
img = tf.img.decode_jpeg(tf.read_file("./Desktop/input.jpg"),
    chan=3)
ses = tf.InteractiveSession()
print(ses.run(tf.shape(img)))
```

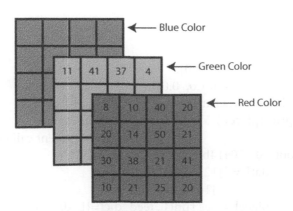

Figure 2.2 Representation of image as tensor.

```
        [218.0 178.0 3.0]
        print(ses.run(img[10:15,0:4,1]))
```

```
[[47.0 48.0 48.0 47.0]
 [45.0 45.0 45.0 44.0]
 [43.0 43.0 43.0 42.0]
 [41.0 42.0 42.0 41.0]
 [41.0 41.0 41.0 40.0]]
```

Different types of tensors have been created. They are sequential tensors, fixed tensors, and random tensors.

Fixed Tensors
A tensor was created with fixed value. Below the line of code shows the tensor creation with 1 as well as 0.

```
    import tensorflow as tf
    ses = tf.Session()
    L = tf.zeros([2,3])
    print(ses.run(L))
```

```
[[0.0 0.0 0.0]
 [0.0 0.0 0.0]]
```

```
        M = tf.ones([4,3])
        print(ses.run(M))
```

```
[[1.0 1.0 1.0]
 [1.0 1.0 1.0]
 [1.0 1.0 1.0]
 [1.0 1.0 1.0]]
```

tf.fill is used to create a shape (2×3) of tensor which has a unique number 13 which is shown below.

```
    P = tf.fil([2,3],13)
    print(ses.run((P))
```

```
[[13 13 13]
 [13 13  13]]
```

tf.diag used to create a tensor of shape (2×3) having elements only in diagonal which was shown below.

```
Q = tf.diag([4,-3,2])
print(ses.run(Q))
```

```
[[ 4  0 0]
 [ 0 -3 0]
 [ 0  0 2]]
```

tf.constant used to create a constant tensor which was shown below.

```
R = tf.constant([5,2,4,2])
print(ses.run(R))
```

Sequence Tensors
tf.range used to create tensor with a sequence of numbers (initiated by a certain value with an increment value) It was shown below.

```
S=tf.range(start=6,limit=45,delta=3)
print(ses.run(S))
```

```
[6 9 12 15 18 24 27 30 36 39 42]
```

tf.linspace used to create a sequence of values with equal line space which was shown below.

```
T=tf.linspace(10.0,92.0,5)
print(ses.run(T))
```

```
[10.  30.5  51.   71.5  92.]
```

Random Tensors
tf.random_uniform used for random value generation in uniform distribution format within the specific range which was shown below.

```
U1=tf.random_uniform([2,3],minval=0,maxval=4)
print(ses.run(U1))
```

```
[[0.7450636  1.957832   3.112966]
 [2.35518    2.10438    2.6589   ]]
```

tf.random_normal used for random value generation with normal distribution, which has the specific mean along with the value of standard deviation. The example is shown below.

```
U2=tf.random_normal([2,3],mean=5,stddev=4)
print(ses.run(U2))
```

```
[ [-1.896243  3.251744  5.962127]
[ 8.30709   4.84437    6.846846]]
```

```
print(ses.run(tf.diag([3,-2,4])))
```

```
[[3  0 0]
[0 -2 0]
[0  0 4]]
```

2.5   Working on Matrices

The following code explain the steps for creating three matrices A, B and C, which was shown below. Matrix A was created with 3×2 dimension using tf.random_uniform() and matric B was created with 2×4 dimension using tf.fill(). Matrix C was created as output matrix with 3×4 dimension using tf.random_normal().

```
import tensorflow as tf
import numpy as np
ses=tf.Session()
P=tf.random.uniform([3,2])
Q=tf.fill([2,4],3.5)
R=tf.random_normal([3,4])
print(sess.run(P))
```

```
[[0.31633115  0.71407604]
[0.18088198  0.36230946]
[0.34481096  0.6156665 ]]
```

```
print(sess.run(Q))
```

```
[[3.5 3.5 3.5 3.5]
[3.5 3.5 3.5 3.5]]
```

The following code explain the steps to perform PxQ+R, which was shown below. Matrix P and Q was multiplied using the function tf.matmul(P,Q)and then it was added with matrix R.

```
print(ses.run(tf.matmul(P,Q)))
```

[[0.9450191 0.9453191 0.9453191 0.9453191]
[4.4488316 4.4488316 4.4488316 4.4488316]
[3.308284   3.308284   3.308284   3.308284]]

```
print(ses.run(tf.matmul(P,Q)+R)
```

[[4.6027136 4.5958595 6.9527874 4.413632]
[3.3000264 4.4702578 5.0858393 5.168917]
[3.1176403 4.626109   4.1446424 3.7285264]]

2.6   Activation Functions

The activation function [16] depicted the working of human brain. The active stage of neuron above threshold is known as activation potential. The output was reached to small range in many situation. The activation function was shown in Figure 2.3.

The most popular activation functions were Sigmoid, hyperbolic tangent (tanh) and ReLU.

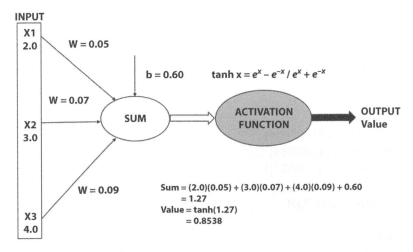

Figure 2.3 An activation function.

Tangent Hyperbolic and Sigmoid

Tangent hyperbolic and sigmoid activation functions were shown in Figure 2.4 and Figure 2.5.

tf.nn.tanh and tf.nn.sigmoid [17] were used to generate tangent and sigmoid value respectively which was shown below.

```
T=tf.nn.tanh([10,2,0.5,-0.5,-1.,-2.,-10.])
print(ses.run(T))
```

```
[ 1.   0.964276   0.765942     0.4621717   0.   -0.4621717
 -0.765942 -0.964276 -1.  ]
```

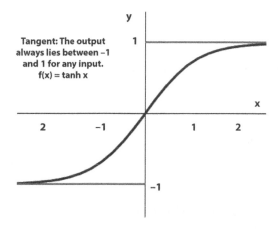

Figure 2.4 Tangent activation function.

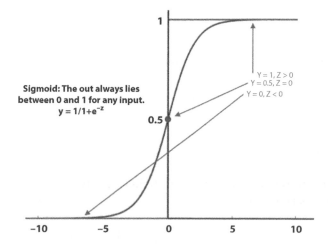

Figure 2.5 Sigmoid activation function.

```
W=tf.nn.sigmoid([10,2,1,0.5,0,-0.5, -1., -2., -10.])
print(ses.run(W))
```

[9.995458e-01 8.807973e-01   7.310586e-01 6.245935e-01 5.000000e-01
 3.775468e-01   2.689443e-01 1.192392e-01   4.537872e-05]

ReLU
The code to produce ReLU was shown below.

```
Z=tf.nn.relu([-2,1,-3,13])
print(ses.run(Z))
```

[0 1 0 13]

ReLU6
ReLU6 is same as ReLU other than maximum limit of output cannot be more than six ever which was shown below.

```
Z1=tf.nn.relu69[-2,1,-3,13])
print(ses.run(Z1))
```

[0 1 0 6]

```
Z2=tf.nn.relu([[-2,1,-3],[10,-16,-5]])
print(ses.run(Z2)
```

[[0 1 0]
[10 0 0]]

The code for SoftPlus and ReLU have been shown below.

```
Z3=tf.nn.relu([10,2,0.5,-0,-0.5,-1.,-2.,-10.])
print(ses.run(Z3))
```

[10. 2. 1. 0.5 0. 0. 0. 0.]

```
Z4=tf.nn.soft plus([10,2,1,0.5,-0,-0.5,-1.,-2.,-10.])
print(ses.run(Z4))
```

[1.000046e+01 2.169281e+00 1.312616e+00 9.707699e-01 6.934718e-01
  4.747699e-01 3.132663e-01 1.269285e-01 4.541776e-05]

2.7   Loss Functions

The loss function [18] value should be minimized for getting a good value
for every parameter in the model. For example, for getting a good output
on weight and bias (weight represent slope and bias represent y-intercept),
there was a need to describe target (y) with respect to predictor (X). The
best output of the slope was achieved by this method to minimize the cost
of loss function. There can be use of numerous parameters for any model
like the parameters of model structure for prediction or classification. The
need is to define the cost function to evaluate the model. The loss function minimization is used for finding the optimum value of each parameter. L1 or L2 be the useful loss function for regression/numeric prediction
and Softmax or sigmoid cross entropy be the popular loss functions for
classification.

2.8   Common Loss Function

The list of common loss functions were shown below.

    tf.cotrib.loses.absolute_difference
    tf.cotrib.loses.add_loss
    tf.cotrib.loses.hinge_loss
    tf.cotrib.loses.compute_weighted_loss
    tf.cotrib.loses.cosine_distance
    tf.cotrib.loses.get_losses
    tf.cotrib.loses.get_regularization_losses
    tf.cotrib.loses.get_total_loss
    tf.cotrib.loses.log_loss
    tf.cotrib.loses.mean_pairwise_squared_error
    tf.cotrib.loses.mean_squared_error
    tf.cotrib.loses.sigmoid_cross_entrophy
    tf.cotrib.loses.softmax_cross_entrophy
    tf.cotrib.loses.sparse_softmax_cross_entropy
    tf.cotrib.loses.log(predictions,labels,weight=2.0)

2.9 Optimizers

Initially the values are computed based on bias and weight of the model (linear regression, etc.) then improvise the parameters using optimizer to obtain the best result. Initially a set have a value of weight as sixteen and biases as four. With the goal of minimization every bias and weight are assigned to be zero (or one or any number). The optimizer will suggests whether to increase weight or decrease weight in the next iteration. The weight would be stabilize to get the good parameters, after many iterations.

Optimizers [19] work on bias and weight for each iteration as well as to the next iteration (I.e., TensorFlow, and deep learning framework, provides optimizers that slowly change each parameter in order to minimize the loss function). Selecting the best optimizer is a tricky task for each model it all depends on how to converge, learn weights and biases. For converging faster models, adadelta, adagrad, etc. have been used as adaptive techniques which will be the good optimizers. For most cases, Adam is the best optimizer. Even though it was computationally costly, it also outperforms other adaptive techniques. Figure 2.33 shows the code to use optimizer using tf.train.GradientOptimizer().

```
import tensorflow as tf
l=tf.variable(3,name='l',dtype=tf.float32)
log_l=tf.log(l)
log_l_squared=tf.square(log_l)
optim=tf.train.GradientDescentOptimizer(0.7)
trn=optim.minimize(log_l_squared)
```

Common Optimizers
The list of common optimizers such as gradient based and delta based were shown below.

```
tf.train.Optimizer
tf.train.GradientDescentOptimizer
tf.train.AdadeltaOptimizer
tf.train.AdagradOptimizer
tf.train.AdagradDAOptimizer
tf.train.MomentumOtimizer
tf.train.AdamOptimizer
tf.train.FtrlOptimizer
tf.train.ProximalGradientDescentOptimizer
```

tf.train.ProximalAdagradOptimizer
tf.train.RMSPropOptimizer

2.10   Metrics

Metrics [20] have been used to give idea to design a model as well specify the evaluation time of model. The models have to be evaluated to perform classification/regression. There were various metrics for evaluation, such as accuracy, logarithmic loss, and ROC curve. Classification accuracy was defined as the ratio of the number of correct predictions to the number of all predictions. Accuracy was considered as a good metric because the observations for every class were not skewed properly and the code have been shown below.

tf.contrib.metrics.accuracy(actual_labels, predictions)

Metrics Examples
Accuracy was checked for the created actual values(x) as well as predicted values(y). The term accuracy was defined as the ratio of number of times actual values equals predicted values to total number of occurrences. The coding part was shown below.

```
import numpy as np
import tensorflow as tf
l=tf.plcholdr(tf.int32,[5])
m=tf.plcholdr(tf.int32,[5])
ac, ac_op=tf.metrc.ac(labl=l, predct=m)
Ses=tf.InterSesn()
Ses.run(tf.glob_var_initialz())
Ses.run(tf.loc_var_initialz())
val=ses.run([ac,ac_op],feed_dict={l:[1,1,0,1,0], m:[0,1,0,0,1]})
val_ac=ses.run(ac)
print(val_ac)
```

0.4

In this chapter, the tensor flow basics along with graph creation, session computation, placeholder creation, constant creation, and variable creation have been explained along with creation of overall tensor component for computation. Then matrix computation has been illustrated with implementation. To improvise each tensor performance, activation function, loss function, and optimizers have been used. Lastly, the metric implementation has been shown to evaluate the model.

References

1. Dean, J. and Monga, R., *TensorFlow: Large-scale machine learning on hetero-geneous systems*, TensorFlow.org, US, 2015.
2. Metz, C., *Google just open sourced TensorFlow, its artificial intelligence engine*, Wired, San Francisco, California, 2015.
3. Jouppi, N., *Google supercharges machine learning tasks with TPU custom chip*, Google Cloud Platform Blog, Moncks Corner, South Carolina, USA, 2016.
4. Dean, J. and Holzel, U., *Build and train machine learning models on our new Google Cloud TPUs*, Google Blog, Mountain View, California, United States, 2017.
5. Vincent, J., *Google's new machine learning framework is going to put more AI on your phone*, Thevergi Blog, Washington, District of Columbia, 2017.
6. TensorFlow, *TensorFlow lite now faster with mobile GPUs (Developer Preview)*, Medium, San Francisco, 2019.
7. Kundu, K., *Google announces edge TPU, Cloud IoT Edge at cloud next*, Beebom Blog, Delhi, India, 2018.
8. Barras, J. and Stone, Z., *Cloud TPU machine learning accelerators are now available in beta*, Google Cloud Platform Blog, Moncks Corner, South Carolina, USA, 2018.
9. He, H., The state of machine learning frameworks, The Gradient, Boston, Massachusetts, United States, 2019.
10. Singh, P. and Manure, A., *Learn TensorFlow 2.0: Implement machine learning and deep learning models with python*, Apress Publisher, New York, United States, 2019.
11. Rungta, K., *TensorFlow in 1 Day: Make your own neural network*, Amazon Digital Services LLC - KDP Print US, 2018.
12. Pattanayak, S., *Pro deep learning with TensorFlow: A mathematical approach to advanced artificial intelligence in python*, Apress Publisher, New York, United States, 2018.
13. Atienza, R., *Advanced deep learning with TensorFlow 2 and Keras: Apply DL, GANs, VAEs, deep RL, unsupervised learning, object detection and segmentation, and more*, Pack Publishing Limited, Mumbai, India, 2020.
14. Jain, A., Fandango, A., Kapoor, A., *TensorFlow machine learning projects: Build 13 real-world projects with advanced numerical computations using the Python ecosystem*, Packt Publishing, Mumbai, India, 2018.
15. McClure, N., *TensorFlow machine learning cookbook: Explore machine learning concepts using the latest numerical computing library - TensorFlow - with*

the help of this comprehensive cookbook, Packt Publishing, Mumbai, India, 2017.

16. Hope, T., Resheff, S., Lieder, I., *Learning TensorFlow: A guide to building deep learning systems*, 1st Edition, O'Reilly, USA, 2020.

17. McClure, N., *TensorFlow machine learning cookbook: Over 60 recipes to build intelligent machine learning systems with the power of Python*, 2nd Edition, Packt Publishing, Mumbai, India, 2018.

18. Géron, A., *Hands-on machine learning with Scikit-Learn and TensorFlow: Concepts, tools, and techniques to build intelligent systems*, 1st Edition, O'Reilly Media, California, United States, 2018.

19. Abrahams, S., Hafner, D., Erwitt, E., Scarpinelli, A., *TensorFlow for machine intelligence: A hands-on introduction to learning algorithms paperback*, Bleeding Edge Press, Santa Rosa, California, USA, 2016.

20. Shukla, N., *Machine learning with TensorFlow*, 1st Edition, Manning, United Kingdom, 2018.

3

Understanding and Working with Keras

A python library called Keras has been used for deep learning which work over TensorFlow. The objective and focus of Keras on deep learning with perceptions of creating neural networks layers and its mathematical models. The backend of Keras is TensorFlow. The advantage of this is Keras can run applications independently. Keras is simple, flexible, and powerful. A sequential and functional API's are two frameworks of Keras. Among these, sequential API has been used at initial stage, which is working on linear stack of layers. The added advantage of using sequential model is easy-to-insert layers. The main features [1] are shown in Figure 3.1

The history of Keras is shown in Table 3.1.

3.1 Major Steps to Deep Learning Models

The number of steps involved in Keras are four [3] in relation with deep learning models, which is shown in Figure 3.2.

Define the model—This is used for creating the model and adding the layers (convolution layer, pooling layer, and fully connected layer), which perform different functions. They are convolution layer, pooling layer, batch normalization layer, and activation function layer.

The model to Compile—The compilation have been done using compile () function before that the loss function, as well as an optimizer are applied.

Fit the model—This is used for training the model with set of test data. The training task is executed by calling fit () function.

Make predictions—The functions used for prediction is evaluate () and predict (). These functions are used to make predictions on new data set.

In Keras, eight steps have been used to process data using deep learning [4] and are depicted in Figure 3.3, which include steps to load the data, pre-process the data, define the model, compile the model, fit the model, evaluate the model, make prediction, and save the model.

Niha Kamal Basha, Surbhi Bhatia Khan, Abhishek Kumar and Arwa Mashat (eds.) *Deep Learning and Its Applications Using Python*, (45–56) © 2023 Scrivener Publishing LLC

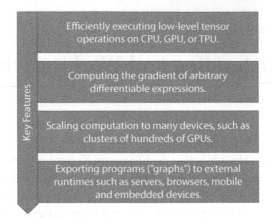

Figure 3.1 Key features of Keras.

Table 3.1 Notable Keras evolution.

Sl.No	Year	Invention
1	2015	Keras—initial version
2	2017	Keras 2.0.1
3	2019	Keras 2.2.5 API
4	2019	Keras 2.3.0 API—it supports tensorflow and theano [2].
5	2020	Keras 2.4—it supports only tensorflow

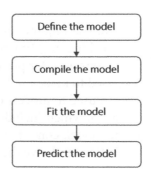

Figure 3.2 Four steps in deep learning model.

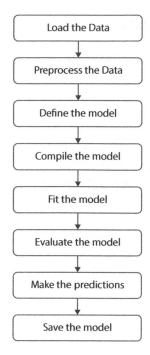

Figure 3.3 Steps involved in deep learning to process data using Keras.

3.2 Load Data

The steps [5] to import the Keras module are shown below. The major modules imported for Keras are cifar10, Sequential, Dense, Droupout, Activation, adam and np_utils. The load_data() used for loading the data from dataset. Below code shows the steps to load the image from cifar10. Cifar10 which has images like airplane automobile, bird, cat, deer, etc. with unique label.

```
import numpy as np
import os
from keras.datasets import cifar10
from keras.models import Sequential
from keras.layers.core import Dense, Dropout,Activation
from keras.optimizers import adam
from keras.utils import np_utils
np.random.seed(100)
(l_train, m_train),(l_test,m_test)=cifar10.load_data()
```

3.3   Pre-Process Data

The need of pre-processing [6] the data is to structure the data from one form to another form which is shown below. In this example, Gaussian normalization is applied for both training and test data. Also, np_utils. to_categorical() function is used to convert vector form to matrices form.

```
L_train+L_train.reshape(50000,3072)
L_test+L_test.reshape(10000,3072)
L_train=(L_train - np.mean (L_train))/np.std(L_train)
L_test=(L_test - np.mean (L_test))/np.std(L_test)
labels=10
M_train =np_utils.to_categorical(m_train,labels)
M_test =np_utils.to_categorical(m_test,labels)
```

3.4   Define the Model

This is used for creating [7] the model and adding the layers. When creating the model, it is necessary to specify the correct number of inputs. As shown below, the number of input variables used in the given example is 3072. The node needed in each hidden layers are given. In first hidden layer, 512 nodes have been used. In second hidden layer, 120 nodes are used. The output layer of this model can use 10 nodes. Each node in output layer represents the probability of mapping to image label.

```
model Sequential()
model.add (Dense(512, input_shape-(3072,)))
model.add (Activation( 'relu'))
model.add (Dropout (0.4))
model.add (Dense(120))
model.add(Activation( 'relu'))
model.add(Dropout (0.2))
model.add (Dense (labels))
model.add(Activation('signoid'))
```

An image has three channels; they are Red, Green and Blue. Each image has 1024 pixels (32×32) in each channel. As total, an image has 3072 pixels (3x1024). From the 3072 pixels (features), predication carried out for each label. The resultant prediction of model gives ten outputs from digit 0 to

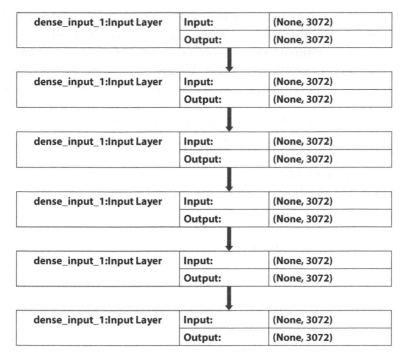

Figure 3.4 Defining the model with input and output.

digit 9, when using sigmoid as activation function which yield output 0 for nine label and 1 for one label. Figure 3.4 shows the model with input and output. For example 3072->512->120->10 nodes.

The next goal is to find count of layers and its parameters of network structure. That network structure should capture the problem and it is identified by trial-and-error practice. For an example, a network is structured with fully connected network structure and has three layers. This fully connected layers are defined by dense class. Now, there is a need to assign network weight. The network weight is generated from uniform distribution with less random value between 0 and 0.05. Also, the network weight generated using Gaussian distribution is small random value.

3.5   Compile the Model

The defined model [8] should have additional usage of loss function, optimizer, and evaluation metrics in layers. After the creation of model, weight, as well as bias values, should be initialized. The initialization can take place by random distribution of values 0 or 1. The weight and bias value of the model is not the best for reaching target/labels. Therefore, there is a need to acquire optimal value. This can be achieved with motivation that leads to reduce the cost/loss function. The created model can be compiled using model.compile(). This function takes three parameters, such as loss function, optimizer, and evaluation metrics. The below code shows that compilation model with loss function as categorical_crossentropy, adam optimizer, and metrics as accuracy.

```
adam = adam(0.01)
model.compile(loss='categorical_crossentropy',optimizer=adam,
    metrics=["accuracy"])
```

Different loss functions used in created model that is listed in Figure 3.5. During the compilation of model, an optimizer is also used as one parameter that is shown in Figure 3.6. The list of evaluation metrics is shown in Figure 3.7 which is also used a parameter in model.compile().

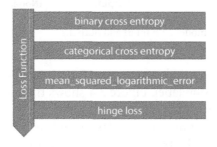

Figure 3.5 List of loss functions.

Figure 3.6 List of optimizers.

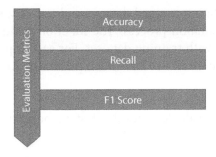

Figure 3.7 List of evaluation metrics.

3.6 Fit and Evaluate the Mode

After the compilation [9] of model, it needs to be executed with few data for making predictions. Then state the count of epoch; that means no. of iteration have been used for training over data set, as well as with batches with different size. Size of batch means number of instances, which was evaluated before updating weight.

The function used to fit the model is model.fit() with five parameters, which are shown in below line of code. This problem takes the following data; the number of images used in training set is 50,000, number of epoch defined is 1,000. So the iterations taken place is 50 (50000/1000). The rule for selecting batch size should be less than the size of training samples.

> Model.fit(L_train, M_train, batch_size=1000, nb_epoch=10,
>   validation_data=(L_test,M_test)
> Train on 50000 samples, validate on 10000 samples
> Epoch 1/10
> 1000/50000 [...............] – ETA: 6s – loss: 2.3028 – acc 0.1060

By considering some data, the model has been defined and compiled to make prediction. For that the epochs have to be specified along with that the no. of iterations and size of each batch. The number of instances has to be evaluated along with updating weights. Here, the program consists of 10 number of epochs to complete 50 iterations with 1000 as size of batch and 50,000 instances as training data set.

The modeled data set has to be evaluated to know the networks performance (measuring the accuracy of training). However, it cannot measure the performance of algorithm on new set of data. Therefore, it is necessary to segregate the data into trained data set and test data set before the start of training and evaluation process. The function evaluation () is used to evaluate the model with training data set. For each input and output pair, average loss and other metrics have been predicted. An example is shown in below line of code.

```
score = model.evaluate(L_test,M_test, verbose=0)
print('Test accuracy:',score[1])
```

3.7   Prediction

The evaluated model [10] must undergo the prediction process for unknown data set. The function used to achieve this is Tpredict_classes(). The example code for prediction is shown in below line of code with data set used is L_test.

```
model.predict_classes(L_test)

9888/10000[=============> ] – ETA; 0s
array([3,8,8,....3,4,7], dtype=int64)
```

3.8   Save and Reload the Model

It is the final step where the function used have been to save and load the model is save() and load_weights() respectively which is shown in below line of code.

```
model.save('model.h5')
jsonModel = model.to_json()
model.save_weights('modelWeight.h5')
modelWt = model.load_weights('modelWeight.h5')
```

The summary report of the created model can be generated by the summary () function. It will illustrate type of layer, output shape and its parameter value, total parameters with trainable, and non-trainable values which are shown in Figure 3.8.

```
#Summary of the model
model.summary()
```

Layer (type)	Output Shape	Param #
dense_7 (Dense)	(None, 512)	157337
activation_7 (Activation)	(None, 512)	0
dropout_5 (Dropout)	(None, 512)	0
dense_8(Dense)	(None, 120)	61560
activation_8(Activation)	(None, 120)	0
dropout_6 (Dropout)	(None, 120)	0
dense_9(Dense)	(None, 10)	1210
activation_9(Activation)	(None, 10)	0

Total params: 1,636,146
Trainable params: 1,636,146
Non-trainable params: 0

Figure 3.8 Summary of model.

3.9   Additional Steps to Improve Keras Models

The steps to improve the designed model are:

1. Due to vanishing or exploding gradient value, the creation of model does not complete. To complete the creation of model perfectly, it is necessary to add the code which is shown below to the model.

2. from keras.callbacks import EarlyStopping
   early stopping monitor = EarlyStopping(patience=2)
   model.fit(l_train,m_train,batch_size=1000,epochs=10,
   validation_data=(l_test,m_test),
   callback=[early_stopping_monitor])

3. Modeling the output shape.
   The output_shape is used to shape the n-dimensional array which is shown below.

   model.output_shape

4. Modeling the summary representation.
   The summary of the designed model can be displayed using summary() which is shown below.

   model.summary()

5. Modeling the configuration.
   The get_config() is used to get the configuration of the designed model which is shown below.

   model.get_config()

6. In the model a weight of tensors have to be listed.
   The get_weights() is used to specify the weight of tensors in the designed model which is shown below.

   model.get_weights()

The following code shows the complete deep learning model with Keras. The major steps used here is loading data, creating a model, compiling a model, fit, and evaluate a model, finally predict a model.

```
import numpy as np
from keras.models import Sequential
from keras.layers import Dense
data np.random.random((500,100))
labels np.random.randint(2,size=(500,1))
model.Sequential()
model.add(Dense(12, input dim 8, activation='relu'))
model.add(Dense(8, activation 'relu'))
model.add(Dense(1, activation sigmoid'))
model.compile(loss binary crossentropy', optimizer 'adam',
                            metrics ['accuracy'])
model.fit(Litrain), Mltrain), epochs 150, batch size 10, verbose 0)
scores model.evaluate(Litesti, Mitest), verbose-0)
print("%s:/i6" % (model metrics_names[1], scores[1]*100)
cvscores.append(scores11 100) print("/%6% (+/- !%%*%
(numpy meantevscores), numpy std(cvscores)))
prediction=model.predict(data)
```

3.10   Keras with TensorFlow

High-level neural networks are offered to Keras with great and simple deep learning library over TensorFlow/Theano. Keras provides a considerable accumulation with TensorFlow also it perform well along with other TensorFlow libraries.

The steps for using Keras foe TensorFlow is listed below:

1. Create the Tensor Flow session and register it with Keras. It will lead to using the registered session for initializing the variables, which created internally. The code is shown below.

   Import TensorFlow as tf sess = tf.Session()
   From keras import backend as p p.set_session(sess)

2. The modules of Keras are used to build a model. These modules are needed to be converted into equivalent script of TensorFlow by Keras engine.
3. The back end of Keras are Theano and CNTK.
4. The input shape in depth where depth means number of channels, height and width order are created at the back end of TensorFlow.
5. The back end of TensorFlow is configured by keras.json file.

The structure of file look like as shown below.

```
{
"backend": "theano",
"epsilon": 1e-07,
"image_data_format": "channels_first", "floatx": "float32"
}
```

In this chapter, Keras is used for deep learning which run over TensorFlow which is a high-level python library. It can be stated as simple, flexible and powerful among other python libraries. It uses two frameworks such as sequential API and functional API which are mainly used for creating neural network layer and its mathematical models. The steps used for creating model follows eight steps such as load the data, pre-process the data, define the model, compile the model, fit the model, evaluate the model, make prediction and save the model. Also, it provides considerable accumulation with TensorFlow because its models and different layers are well suited with pure tensors.

References

1. Chollet., F., Xception: Deep Learning with depthwise separable convolutions. *Comput. Vision Pattern Recognit.*, 16, 23–57, 2016. *arXiv*:1610.02357.
2. Jakhar, K. and Hooda, N., Big data deep learning framework using Keras: A case study of pneumonia prediction. *International Conference on Computing Communication and Automation (ICCCA)*, pp. 1–5, 2018.
3. Atienza, R., *Advanced deep learning with TensorFlow 2 and Keras: Apply DL, GANs, VAEs, deep RL, unsupervised learning, object detection and segmentation, and more*, Pack Publishing Limited, Mumbai, India, 2020.
4. Jouppi, N., *Google supercharges machine learning tasks with TPU custom chip*, Google Cloud Platform Blog, Moncks Corner, South Carolina, USA, 2016.
5. Dean, J. and Holzel, U., *Build and train machine learning models on our new Google Cloud TPUs*, Google Blog, Mountain View, California, United States, 2017.
6. Vincent, J., *Google's new machine learning framework is going to put more AI on your phone*, Thevergi Blog, Washington, District of Columbia, 2017.
7. Kundu, K., *Google announces edge TPU, Cloud IoT Edge at Cloud Next*, Beebom Blog, Delhi, India, 2018.
8. Barras, J. and Stone, Z., *Cloud TPU machine learning accelerators are now available in beta*, Google Cloud Platform Blog, Moncks Corner, South Carolina, USA, 2018.
9. Horace, H., *The state of machine learning frameworks*, The Gradient, Boston, Massachusetts, United States, 2019.
10. Shukla, N., *Machine learning with TensorFlow*, 1st Edition, Manning, United Kingdom, 2018.

4

Multilayer Perceptron

As discussed in first chapter on presentation of intelligent learning algorithms, multilayer perceptron is one of the supervised learning algorithm, which is an example of artificial neural network with feedback loop. Neural network [1] is a combination of different algorithms arranged in sequence to solve the problems by training and testing the networks with input. The process involved in this network resembles the working of human brain. The structure of neuron in the human brain is shown in Figure 4.1. The neurons cell body is soma. The chemical messages are received by dendrites which are extended from soma. Axon acts as a transmitter to transfer electro-chemical signal from one neuron to another and the myelin sheath acts as an insulator. Axon terminal (bouton) acts as a convertor to pass information from one neuron to another by converting electric signal into chemical signal. The same way the neural networks pass input and process them among multiple layers. Before getting into multilayer perceptron, the working of perceptron and artificial neural network has been given shown below.

4.1   Artificial Neural Network

It is a system of nodes in different layers [2] which interconnected to each other to process information. In Artificial Neural Network (ANN), the structure of the network is layered as input, hidden and output layer. In this, first input layer receives input in the form of text, image, number, audio files etc. The middle hidden layer performs various mathematical computations on input data. Finally, the output layer [3] provides the result obtained after rigorous operations on input from the hidden layer. The representation of different layers in ANN is shown in Figure 4.2. The performance mainly relies on multiple parameters. They are batch size, learning rate, biases and weights etc.

Niha Kamal Basha, Surbhi Bhatia Khan, Abhishek Kumar and Arwa Mashat (eds.) Deep Learning and Its Applications Using Python, (57–80) © 2023 Scrivener Publishing LLC

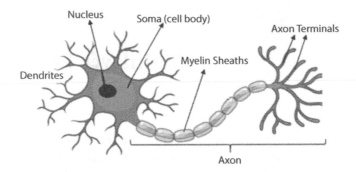

Figure 4.1 Structure of human neuron.

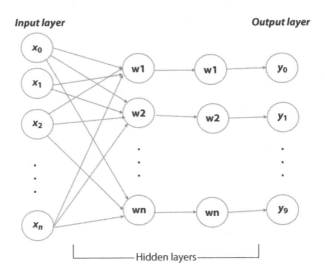

Figure 4.2 Artificial Neural Network with input, hidden and output layers.

Each node in ANN has some weight and two functions for processing input. They are transfer function and activation function. Transfer function [4] has been used for calculating the summation of weights of input and bias. The activation function fires the result from the node based on the output received and is shown in Figure 4.3. Some of the activation functions are sigmoid, softmax, tanh, and RELU. Let us consider the example as a problem to predict the output with the given set of input and output for training in Table 4.1.

Input layer

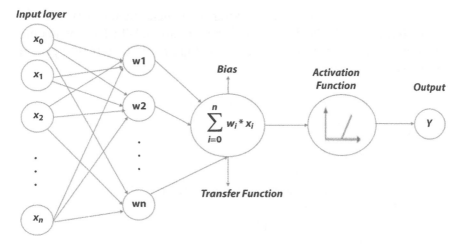

Figure 4.3 ANN with transfer function and activation function (Single layer ANN).

Table 4.1 Training example.

Input 1	Input 2	Input 3	Output
0	1	1	1
1	0	0	0
1	0	1	1

While training the network two steps to follow,

1. Forward Propagation – Pass the input to each layer by computing the input with weights and pass on to the activation function to obtain the output. In this example, sigmoid function is used to normalize between 0 and 1.
2. Back Propagation – The error have been computed by finding the difference between actual and expected output. Based on this error weights have been fine tuned to get the optimal result.

After training the network have been tested with the below inputs in Table 4.2 to predict the output.

Table 4.2 Testing example.

Input 1	Input 2	Input 3	Output
1	0	1	?

The below code explain the working of artificial neural network. The output have been obtained as 0.659 after 10 iteration. Which is not an optimal output, so the iterations are increased gradually to 10000 to get the optimal output as 0.998.

```
from joblib.numpy_pickle_utils import xrange
from numpy import *
class NeuNet(obj):
        def_init_(sel):
                randm.sed(1)
                sel.synap_weig = 2 * ran.ran((3,1)) – 1
        def_sigmd(sel, l):
                return 1/(1+exp(-l))
        def_sigmd_deriv(sel, l):
                return l*(1-l)
        def trn(sel,inp,oup,trn_iterat):
                for iterat in lrang(trn_iterat):
                        oup = sel.lrn(inp)
                        eror = oup – oup
                        fact = dot(inp.R,eror*sel._sigmd_deriv(oup))
                        sel.synap_weig += fact
        def lrn(sel, inp):
                return sel._sigmd(dot(inp, sel.synap_weig))
if_name_== "_main_":
        neu_netwk = NeuNet()
        inp = array([[0,1,1], [1,0,0], [1,0,1]])
        oup = array([1,0,1]).T
        neu_netwk.trn(inp, oup, 10000)
print(netwk_netwk.lrn(ary([1,0,1])))
```

Next to ANN, single layer perceptron and multilayer perceptron have been discussed.

4.2   Single-Layer Perceptron

A simple network [5] with input layer and output layer (no hidden layer), which is considered as one of the first artificial neural network used for binary classification task is called as single-layer perceptron. It takes the input and its respective weight for computation to get desired output. Logistic Regression model comes under single layer perceptron.

Figure 4.4 Logistic regression model with single input (single input vector).

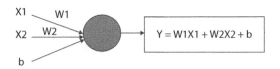

Figure 4.5 Logistic regression model with multiple input (linear model).

The working of this model with single input and multiple input are depicted in Figure 4.4 and Figure 4.5.

In this Figure 4.4 single input is processed with weight and bias to compute output. In Figure 4.5 multiple inputs are processed with their respective weights along with bias to compute output.

4.3 Multilayer Perceptron

It is a network with fully connected multilayer neural network [6] with three layers with at least one hidden layer. It is a feed forward artificial neural network. A perceptron consist of fully connected input layer and output layer where the input is processed with weights and bias and feed into the hidden layer. This computer input to the hidden layer is passed through the activation function then the values are pushed into the next layer of the perceptron to obtain the result. The illustrations and working of multilayer perceptron is shown in Figure 4.6.

4.4 Logistic Regression Model

It is a machine learning classifier which predict the probability among dependent variable. The dependent variable is a binary variable used to code date which is 1 or 0. Here one refer to Yes/success/etc. and zero refer to No/failure/etc. It also predict probability as a function of X as P(Y=1). The structure of logistic regression is shown in Figure 4.7.

Consider a binary classification problem to detect whether an email is spam or not. Here the category is labeled with 0 and 1. If an email belong to spam then it is labeled it as 1 and if it is not a spam then labeled it as 0. Before

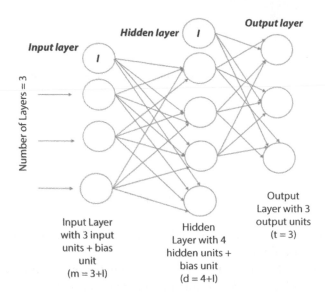

Figure 4.6 Multilayer perceptron (fully connected multilayer ANN).

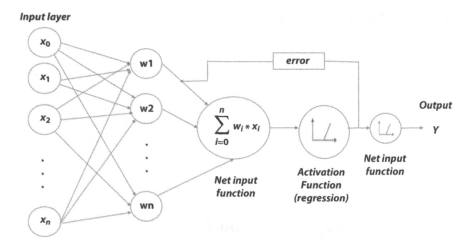

Figure 4.7 Structure of logistic regression.

applying logistic regression classifier the features have to be extracted to categories them to a respective category [7]. The features are, i) email id of the sender, ii) no. of typos used in email, iii) word/phrase occurrences. These feature vectors are used to train the model and the output will be between 0 and 1. If the output is 0.5 then it belongs to spam label.

4.5   Regression to MLP in TensorFlow

In the early stage researchers are using regression model [8] for classification which have been shown in this chapter with examples in the previous topics. Later on they started using simple neural network where one or more hidden layers have been added in between input and output layers. This model is called MLP (Multilayer Perceptron). Here using python programing with the help of TensorFlow the basic models such as linear and logistic regression models are built. Along with the description examples are explained using these models and will be discussed in upcoming topics.

4.6   TensorFlow Steps to Build Models

By using TensorFlow to build a model [9] the following steps have to be performed.

1. Initially, data have to be loaded.
2. The loaded data have to be separated into training and test set.
3. The data have to be normalized to process further.
4. The placeholder have to be initialized with target and predictor values.
5. The bias and weights have to be tuned by creating the variable.
6. Operations have to be declared along loss function and optimizer.
7. The variables and session have to be initialized.
8. The model have to be trained to get the best fit.
9. The model have been verified using test data and obtain the result.

In the next topic linear regression model have been constructed using TensorFlow and its working have been explained using Iris data.

4.7   Linear Regression in TensorFlow

The aim of the given linear regression model [10] using TensorFlow is to predict the length of petal by obtaining the value of sepal length. Here X indicates sepal length and Y indicated the petal length. The above steps to build linear regression model have been illustrated below,

Initially import the required packages, which is shown below.

```
import matpltlib.pyplt as plt
import tensorflow as tf
from sklearn import datasets
import numpy as np
from sklern.cross_valid import trn_tst_splt
from matpltlib import pyplt
```

After that the data have to be loaded which is shown below line of code.

```
ir=dataset.load_iris()
predict_vals = np.aray([predct[0] for predct in iris.dat])
target_vals=np.aray([predct[2] for predct in iris.dat])
```

The data have to be normalized [11] to process further and the place-holder have to be initialized with target and predictor values, which have been depicted below.

```
predict = tf.plchold(shp=[None, 1],dtype=tf.float32)
targt= tf.plchold(shp=[None, 1],dtype=tf.float
```

The bias and weights have to be tuned by creating the variable, which is shown below.

```
A=tf.Varb(tf.zero(shp=[1,1]))
b=tf.Varb(tf.one(shp=[1,1]))
```

Operations have to be declared along loss function and optimizer, which is shown below which have been used for declaring model operation and to declare loss and optimizer function code given have to be used.

```
mod_out = tf.add(tf.matmul(predict, A), b)
los = tf.red_men(tf.abs(trgt = mod_out))
my_opt= tf.GradntDecntOptmz(0.01)
trn_stp = my_opt.mini(los)
```

The variables and session have to be initialized and trained to get the best fit, which is shown below.

```
ses = tf.Ses()
init = tf.glb_var_ini()
ses.run(init)
losAray = []
btc_siz = 40
for k in range(200):
    rand_rw = np.rand.randint(0, len(l_trn)-1, siz=btc_siz)
    btcL=np.trans([l_trn[rand_rw]])
    batchM=np.trans([y_trn[rand_rw]])
    ses.run(trn_stp,fed_dict={predict: btcL,trgt: btcM})
    losAray.apnd(btcLos)
    if(k+1)%50==0:
        print('Step Number' +str(k+1) +'S=' + str(sess.run(S)) +'c='
            +str(ses.run(c)))
        print('L1 Los=' +str(btcLos))
[slp]=ses.run(S)
[y_intcpt]=ses.run(c)
```

The model have been verified using test data and obtain the result, which is depicted in the below line of code.

```
losAray = []
btc_siz = 30
for k in range(100):
    rand_rw = np.rand.randint(0, len(strn)-1, siz=btc_siz)
    btcL=np.tranpos([s_trn[rand_rw]])
    btcM=np.tranpos([m_trn[rand_rw]])
    ses.run(trn_stp,fed_dict={predic: btcL,trg: btcM})
    losAray.apnd(btcLos)
    if(k+1)%50==0:
        print('Step Number' +str(k+1) +'S=' + str(ses.run(S)) +'c='
            +str(ses.run(c)))
        print('L1 Loss=' +str(btcLos))
[slope]=ses.run(S)
[m_intecep]=ses.run(c)
```

To plot all the finding and the original data with predicted values and loss over time, the following code have to be used which is depicted in the below line of code.

```
plt.plt(_tst,m_tst,'o',label='actual data')
tst_fit=[]
for k in l_tst:
    tst_fit.apnd(slp*k+m_intercept)
plt.plot(l_tst,tst_fit,'r-',labl='predcted line',linewidth=3)
plt.leg(loc='lower right')
plt.tit('petal Length vs sepal length')
plt.mlabl('petal length')
plt.llabl('sepal length')
plt.shw()
plt.plt(lossArray,'r-')
plt.tit('L1 Loss per loop')
plt.llabl('Loop')
plt.mlabl('L1 Loss')
plt.shw()
```

The predicted output and graph have been plotted in Figure 4.8 and Figure 4.9.

```
Step Number50 A = [[0.57060003]] b = [[1.05275011]]
L1 Loss = 0.965698
Step Number100 A = [[0.56647497]] b = [[1.00924981]]
L1 Loss = 1.124
Step Number150 A = [[0.56645012]] b = [[0.96424991]]
L1 Loss = 1.18043
Step Number200 A = [[0.58122498]] b = [[0.92174983]]
L1 Loss = 1.20376
Step Number: 20 A = [[0.58945829]] b = [[0.90308326]]
L1 Loss = 1.18207
Step Number: 40 A = [[0.62599164]] b = [[0.88975]]
L1 Loss = 0.826957
Step Number: 60 A = [[0.63695836]] b = [[0.87108338]]
L1 Loss = 0.838114
Step Number: 80 A = [[0.60072505]] b = [[0.8450833]]
L1 Loss = 1.52654
Step Number: 100 A = [[0.6150251]] b = [[0.8290832]]
L1 Loss = 1.25477
```

Figure 4.8 Code to demonstrate output of linear regression model (weight, bias, loss at each step).

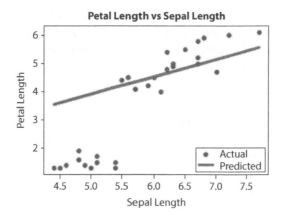

Figure 4.9 Actual and predicted values of linear model.

4.8   Logistic Regression Mode in TensorFlow

The aim of the given logistic regression model [12] using TensorFlow is to predict the species of flower by obtaining the value of sepal length and sepal width. Here out of five attributes in iris data set, sepal length and sepal width act as a predictor attribute and flower species is the target. The steps to build logistic regression model have been illustrated below, Initially, required packages have to be imported and the data have to be loaded. The code for these two steps are depicted in the below line of code.

```
import numpy as np
import tensflw as tf
from sklean import datasets
import pandas as pd
from sklearn.cros_validat import trn_tst_splt
from matplotlib import pyplot
iris = datasets.load_iris()
predict_val=np.aray([predict[0:2] for predict in iris.data])
targ_vals = np.aray([1.if predict==0 else 0.for predict in iris.
    targ])
```

The data have to be divided into training and test set as 75 percent and 25 percent. These data are normalized and initialize placeholders for target and predictor which have been used for dividing data into test and train set and normalization [13] are shown in the below line of code.

```
predict_vals_trn, predict_vals_tst,targ_vals_trn,targ_vals_tst=
    trn_tst_splt(predict_vals, targ_vals,trn_siz=0.75,rand_stat=0)
l_dat = tf.plachold(shap=[None, 2], dtype=tf.flot32)
y_targ = tf.plachold(shp=[None, 1],dtyp=tf.float32)
```

After normalization, turn network weight and bias. Later declare model operations, loss function and optimizer which have been given in the below line of code to declare the operation and to declare loss and optimization below code have to be used.

```
w=tf.var(tf.one(shp=[2,1]))
b=tf.var(tf.one(shp=[1,1]))
mod = tf.add(tf.matmul(l_dat, V), c)
los = tf.reduc_mean(tf.nn.sigmd_cros_entro_with_logt(logt=
    mod,labl
                                    =m_targt))
my_opt=tf.trn.AdmOpti(0.02)
trn_stp=my_opt.min(los)
```

The variables and session have to be initialized for the model and compute accuracy to predict the output. Then train the model [14] with batch size by tuning the weight and bias of the network. These steps are depicted in the below line of code which have been used for initialization and to train the model code given below have to be used.

```
init=tf.glb_var_ini()
ses=tf.Ses()
ses.run(init)
predict= tf.rond(tf.sigmd(mod))
predict_corect=tf.cast(tf.equ(predict,m_targt),tf.flot32)
acc=tf.reduc_mean(predict_corect)
losAray = []
trnAcc = []
tstAcc = []
for k in range(1000):
    bat_siz =4
    batInd = np.rand.cho(len(predict_vals_trn), siz=bath_siz)
    batcL=predict_vals_trn[btcIndx]
    batcM=np.trans([targ_vals_trn[batIndx]])
    ses.run(trn_stp,fed_dict={l_dta: btcL,m_targ: btcM})
    btcLos=sess.run(los,fed_dict={l_dat: bthL,m_targ: batcM})
```

```
losAray.apnd(btcLos)
btcAccTrn=ses.run(acc,fed_dict={l_dat: predict_vals_trn,m_targ:
  np.trans({targ_vals_trn])})
trnAcc.apnd(bthAccTrn)
btcAccTst=ses.run(acc,fed_dict={l_dat: predict_val_trn,m_targ:
  np.trans({targ_vals_trn])})
trnAcc.apnd(btcAccTst)
if(k+1)%50==0:
  print('Loss=' + str(btcLos) +'and Acc=' +str(btcAccTrn))
```

The models performance have been analyzed using metrics are depicted in the code for performance loss and the plot of entropy loss is shown in Figure 4.10.

```
pyplt.plt(losAray, 'r-')
pyplt.til('Logistic Regression: Cross Entropy Loss per Epoch')
pyplt.llabl('Epoch')
pyplt.mlabl('Cross Entropy Loss')
pyplt.shw()
```

Next to logistic regression, the working of multilayer perceptron using TensorFlow will be discussed along with code in next topic.

4.9   Multilayer Perceptron in TensorFlow

The aim of the given multilayer perceptron model [15] or a feedback artificial neural network using TensorFlow is to reduce the loss function by

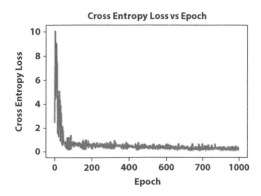

Figure 4.10 Cross entropy loss of logistic regression model.

tuning the weight and bias with one hidden layer and non-linear activation function. The steps to build multilayer perceptron model have been illustrated. Initially import all necessary library and packages. Then the data have been categorized into training set and testing set along with creating placeholder for predictor and target. Then create variable for weight and bias of the network. The code importing packages are shown in the below line of code, for categorizing input data these line of code have to be used. Also these line of code used for initialization as well as to define weigh and bias of the model.

```
import matpltlib.pyplot as plt
import tensorflow as tf
from sklearn import dataset
from sklearn.cros_validat import trn_tst_splt
from matpltlib import pyplt
predict_val_trn,predict_val_tst,targt_val_trn,targt_val_tst=trn_tst
   _splt(predict_val,targt_val,tst_siz=0.2,rand_stat=12)
l_data=tf.placholdr(shap=[None, 3],dtype=tf.float32
m_targt=tf.placholdr(shape=[None,1],dtype=tf.float32)
hidn_layr_nod=10
S1=tf.var(tf.one(shap=[3,hidn_lay_nod]))
c1=tf.var(tf.one(shp=[hidn_lay_nod]))
S2=tf.var(tf.one(shp=[hidn_lay_nod,1]))
c2=tf.var(tf.one(shp=[1]))
```

In the next step the structure of the model [16] have to be defined along with creating variables for loss function and optimizer. These variables are initialized by creating session for execution. Code to define the structure of model, to declare the loss and optimizer code have to be used and for initialization the below depicted code have to be used.

```
hidn_out=tf.nn.relu(tf.add.matmul(l_dat,S1),c1))
finl_out=tf.nn.relu(tf.add(tf.matmul(hidn_out,S2), c2))
loss = tf.reduc_men(tf.squr(m_trg - fin_out))
my_opt=tf.trn.AdmOpt(0.02)
trn_stp=my_opt.mini(los)
init=tf.glbl_var_ini()
ses=tf.Ses()
ses.run(init)
```

The model have been trained and tested to obtain optimal result with minimum loss. Finally the model is evaluated with metrics and the plotted a graph on the loss while training and testing the model are shown in Figure 4.11. The code for these steps are depicted in the below line of code.

```
losAray = []
tst_los = []
btc_siz = 20
for k in range(500):
    btcIndl = np.rand.cho( len(pred_val_trn), siz=btc_siz)
    btcL=np.predict_val_trn[bthInd])
    btcM=np.trans([trg_val_trn[btcIndx]])
    sess.run(trn_step,fed_dict={l_dat: btcL,m_trg: btcM})
    losAray.apnd(np.sqrt(btcLos))
    tst_temp_los=ses.run(los,fed_dict={l_dat: predict_val_tst,m_tag:
      np.trans([trg_val_tst])})
    tst_los.apnd(np.sqrt(tst_tmp_los))
    if(k+1)%50==0:
        print('Loss=' +str(btcLos))
pyplot.plt(losAray, 'o-', labl-'Train Loss')
pyplot.plt(tst_loss, 'r--', labl='Test Loss')
pyplot.tile('los per Generat')
pyplot.legnd(loc-'low left')
pyplt.llabl('generat')
pyplt.mlabel('Los')
pyplt.shw()
```

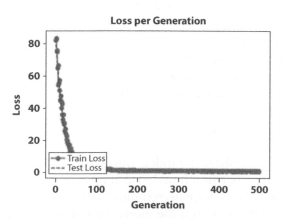

Figure 4.11 Training and testing loss of multilayer perception.

Next to multilayer perceptron, the working of regression model using Keras will be discussed along with code in next topic.

4.10   Regression to MLP in Keras

In the early stage, researchers are using regression model for classification. Later on they started using simple neural network with hidden layers [17] in between input layer and output layer. This model is called MLP (Multilayer Perceptron). Here using python programing with the help of Keras the basic models such as linear and logistic regression models are built. Along with the description examples are explained using these models and will be discussed in upcoming topics.

4.11   Log-Linear Model

Initially the necessary packages have been imported along with loading the iris dataset for training and testing the model to predict the length of petal by obtaining the value of sepal length. Out of five attributes, first four attributes [18] are used as predictor and fifth attribute define the class. The code to demonstrate the working of log linear model below line of code have been shown. To train the model code depicted below have been used also for loading the input and for prediction code given have to be used.

```
from sklearn.datasets import load_iris
from sklearn.cros_valid import trn_tst_splt
from sklearn.linr_mod import LogisticRegressionCV
from sklearn.linr_mod import LinearRegression
import numpy as np
import matplotlib.pyplot as plt
from keras.models import Sequential
from keras.layers import Dense, Activation
iris=load_iris()
l, m=iris.dat[:, :4], iris.trg
```

After loading the data, the independent and dependent variables are categorized using scikit-lean function as training and test set for cross validation. Then the model have been trained and tested with respective data set to obtain result and to test the model code depicted below have to be used.

```
trn_l,  tst_l,  trn_m,  tst_m=trn_tst_splt(l.  m,  trn_siz=0.5,
    rand_stat=0)
lr=LinearRegression()
lr.fit(trn_l, trn_m)
prd_l=lr. predict(tst_l)
```

Next to log-linear model, the working of linear regression model using Keras will be discussed along with code in next topic.

4.12   Keras Neural Network for Linear Regression

To build linear regression model using Keras [19], define the structure of the model and compile them. Then fit model for training. Code for building the model, to compile the model, to train and fit the model code depicted below have to be used.

```
model=Sequen()
model.add(Dens(16, inpt_shp-(4,)))
model.add(Activat('sigmd'))
model.add(Dens(3))
model.add(Activ('softmax'))
model.comp(los='spars_categ_crosentpy',
    opt='adam', met=['acc'])
model.fit(trn_l, trn_m, verbose=1, btc_siz=1, nb_epoc=100)
los, acc=model.eval(tst_l, tst_m, verbose=0)
print("\nAccuracy is using keras prediction {:.2f}", formt(acc))
print(""\nAccuracy is using keras prediction {:.2f}".formt(acc))
print("Accuracy is using regression {:.2f}".form(lr.score(tst_l,
    tst_m)))
```

Next to linear regression model, the working of logistic regression using Keras will be discussed along with code in next topic.

4.13   Keras Neural Network for Logistic Regression

Initially, packages have to be imported and an iris dataset have been loaded. The code for these steps are given below which have been used while importing required packages and to prepare the data code given below have to be used.

```
from sklearn.datasets import load_iris
import numpy as np
from sklearn.cross_validation import trn_tst_splt
from sklearn.linear_model import LogisticRegressionCV
from keras.models import Sequential
from keras.layers.core import Dense, Activation
from keras.utils import np_utils
iris=load_iris()
l, m=iris.dat[:, :4], iris.targ
```

The below code is to demonstrate logistic regression using scikit learn and logistic regression computation using Keras is shown below.

```
lr=logisticRegressionCV()
lr.fit(trn_l, trn_m)
pred_m=lr.predict(tst_l)
print("Test fraction correct (LR-Acc)={:.2f}".frmt(lr.scor(tst
    (tst_l, tst_m)))
def one_hot_encod_objt_arr(arr):
uniq, ids=np.uniq(arr, retn_invrs=True)
return np_utils.to_categor(ids, len(uniq))
```

Then divide the data into train and test data and compile the model. The code for categorizing input into training and test input and for compiling the model code depicted below have to be used.

```
trn_m_ohe=one_hot_encod_objt_aray(trn_m)
test_m_ohe=one_hot_encode_objt_aray(tst_m)
model=Sequen ()
model.add(Dens(16, input_shape=(4,)))
model.add(Activ('sigmoid'))
model.add(Dens(3))
model.add(Activ('softmax'))
model.compile(los='categorical_crossentropy', met=['acc'], opt=
    'adam')
```

After compilation actual model have been trained to best fit the model. Then the model have been evaluated using accuracy. Code for training the model and to evaluate the model below line of code have to be used.

```
model.fit(trn_l, trn_m_one, verbose=0, btc_siz=1, bn_epoc=100)
score, acc=model.eva(tst_l, test_m_ohe, btc_siz=16, verbose=0)
```

At the end print the computed result. While doing this there are two ways such as scikit learner and Keras. Code to print the test result are given below have to be used.

```
print("\n Test fraction correct (LR-Accuracy) log
reg={:.2f}".fomt(lr.scor(tst_l, tst_m))
print("Test fraction correct (NN-Accuracy)
keras= {:.2f}".formt(acc))
```

Finally the working of multilayer perceptron are explained with Iris data, MNIST data and randomly generated data. This will be discussed along with code in upcoming topics.

4.14   MLPs on the Iris Data

Initially, packages have been imported and an iris data have been loaded. The code importing packages, to load and prepare the model below line of code have been used.

```
import pandas as pd
import numpy as np
from keras.model import Sequ
from keras.layer import Dens, Activ
from keras.utils import np_utils
dattrn=pd.read_csv('./datst/ir/ir_trn.csv')
```

After loading change the values from string to numeric form and transfer the data frame to array. Code for converting string to numeric form and to transfer data in to an array the below line of code have to be used.

```
dattrn.set_value(dattrn ['spec']=='Ir-set',['spec'],o)
dattrn.set_value(dattrn ['spec']=='Ir-vers,['spec'],1)
dattrn.set_value(dattrn ['spec']=='Ir-virg,['spec'],2)
dattrn = dattrn.aply(pd.to_num)
datatrn_aray=dattrn.as_mat()
```

Then categories the transferred input into training and testing data and train the model to get desired output. These steps are given below which have been used for training and testing and the line of code are given below.

```
l_trn=dattrn_aray[:,:4]
m_trn=dattrn_aray[:,4]
m_trn=np_utils.to_categ(m_trn)
```

In next topic the working of multilayer perceptron are explained with MNIST data. This will be discussed along with code in upcoming topics.

4.15   MLPs on MNIST Data (Digit Classification)

Initially, import the necessary packages and define batch size, class and epoch. The code for importing packages and to define batch size along with class and epoch are depicted below have to be used.

```
import numpy as np
import os
from keras.datasets import mnist
from keras.models import Seque
from keras.layers.core import Dense, Dropout, Activation
from keras.optimizers iport RMSprop
from keras.utils import np_utils
np.random.seed(100)
bat_siz=128
nb_class = 10
nb_epoc = 20
```

After defining the model prepare the data for training and testing, these steps are given as code below which are used for training and testing.

```
(l_trn, m_trn), (l_tst, m_tst)=mnist.load_data()
l_trn=l_trn.reshape(60000, 784)
l_tst=l_tst.reshp(10000, 784)
l_trn= l_trn.astyp('float32')
l_tst= l_tst.astyp('float32')
```

A data after splitting into two sets are normalized to compute z-score and obtain the training and test instances. Code for normalization and z-score computation are given below which have to be used for displaying instances of training and testing.

```
l_trn=l_trn-np.men(l_trn))/np.std(l_trn)
l_tst=l_tst-np.mean(l_tst))/np.std(l_tst)
print(l_trn.shp[0], 'trn samp')
print(l_tst.shp[0], 'tst samp')
```

These instances are converted form class vectors to binary class matrix and compute the RMS value to evaluate the model. Then define the structure of the model for training and testing. Code for class conversion is given below to define the structure of model code and to compute the RMS value.

```
m_trn=np_utils.to_categ(m_trn, nb_clas)
m_tst=np_utils.to_categ(m_tst, nb_clas)
model=Seque()
model.add(Dens(512, inpt_shp=(784,)))
model.add(Activ('relu'))
model.add(Dropot(0.2))
model.add(Dens(120))
model.add(Activ ('relu'))
model.add(Dropot(0.2))
model.add(Dens(10))
model.add(Activ('softmax'))
rms=RMSprop()
```

Finally compute loss, optimizer and accuracy to get best fit and evaluate the model. Code to compute loss, optimization and accuracy have been shown below to train the model and for evaluation.

```
model.compil(los='categ_crosentp', opt=rms, met=['acc'])
model.fit(L_trn, M_trn, btc_siz=btc_siz, nb_epo=nb_epo, verbos=2,
    valid_dat=(L_tst, M_tst))
scr=model.eval(l_tst, m_tst, verbos=0)
```

In next topic the working of multilayer perceptron are explained with randomly generated data. This will be discussed along with code in upcoming topics.

4.16   MLPs on Randomly Generated Data

Initially, import the necessary packages. To train the model [20] generate random data and define the structure of the model. The code for importing packages are shown below to train the model and for structuring below line of code have been shown.

```
import keras
from keras.models import Seque
from keras.layers import Dense, Dropout, Activ
from keras.optim import SGD
import numpy as np
l_trn=np.ran.ran(1000,20))
        m_trn=keras.utils.to_categ(np.rand.radnt(10,siz=(1000,1)),
        num_clas=10)
l_tst=np.rand.rand(100,20)
m_tst=keras.utils.to_categ(np.rand.radi(10, siz=(1000, 1)), num_
        clas=10)
model=Seque()
model.add(Dens(64, activ='relu',input_dim=20))
model.add(Drop(0.5))
model.add(Dense(64, activ='relu'))
model.add(Drop(0.5))
model.add(Dense(10, activ='softmax'))
```

Finally, compile the defined model and evaluate them to get desired results. Code for compilation have been shown and for evaluation below line of code have to be used.

```
sgd=sgd(lr=0.01, decay=1e-6, moment=0.9, nest=True)
model.comp(loss='categorical_crossentropy', opt=sgd, met=['acc'])
score=model.eval(l_tst, m_tst, btc_siz=128)
```

In this chapter the working of artificial neural network have been discussed with single layer perceptron and multilayer perceptron along with example dataset. Also traditional linear regression and logistic regression are explained using python program. Along with these models (linear and logistic regression) description alternate approach have been explained using TensorFlow and Keras for better understanding of linear and logistic regression model. Apart from these approaches different data set like Iris,

MNIST and randomly generated data have been used for better understanding with different dimensions.

References

1. Fellow, I.G., Bengio, Y., Courville, A., *Deep Learning*, MIT Press, Cambridge, Massachusetts, United States, 2017.
2. McCulloch, W.S. and Pitts, W., A logical calculus of the ideas immanent in nervous activity. *Bull. Math. Biophys.*, 14, 5, 115–133, 1943.
3. Rosenblatt, F., The perceptron - a perceiving and recognizing automaton, in: *Technical Report, Cornell Aeronautical Laboratory*, 85-460-1, 1957.
4. Kelley, H.J., Gradient theory of optimal flight paths. *ARS J.*, *30*, 947–954, 1960.
5. Dreyfus, S., The numerical solution of variational problems. *J. Math. Anal. Appl.*, 5, 1, 30–45, 1962.
6. Rumelhart, D., Hinton, G., Williams, R., Learning representations by back-propagating errors. *Nature*, 32, 3, 533–536, 1986.
7. Cybenko, G., Approximation by superpositions of a sigmoidal function. *Math. Control Signal Syst.*, 25, 2, 303–314, 1989.
8. Hochreiter, S. and Schmidhuber, J., Long short-term memory. *Neural Comput.*, 9, 8, 1735–1780, 1997.
9. Hinton, G.E. and Osindero, S., A fast learning algorithm for deep belief nets. *Neural Comput.*, 18, 7, 1527–54, 2006.
10. Singh, P. and Manure, A., *Learn TensorFlow 2.0: Implement machine learning and deep learning models with python*, Apress Publisher, New York, United States, 2019.
11. Rungta, K., *TensorFlow in 1 day: Make your own neural network*, Amazon Digital Services LLC - KDP Print US, 2018.
12. Pattanayak, S., *Pro deep learning with TensorFlow: A mathematical approach to advanced artificial intelligence in python*, Apress Publisher, New York, United States, 2018.
13. Atienza, R., *Advanced deep learning with TensorFlow 2 and Keras: Apply DL, GANs, VAEs, deep RL, unsupervised learning, object detection and segmentation, and more*, Pack Publishing Limited, Birmingham, UK, 2020.
14. Jain, A., Fandango, A., Kapoor, A., *TensorFlow machine learning projects: Build 13 real-world projects with advanced numerical computations using the Python ecosystem*, Packt Publishing, Birmingham, United Kingdom, 2018.
15. Glorot, X., Bordes, A., Bengio, Y., Deep sparse rectifier neural networks. *Proc. Mach. Learn. Res.*, 15, 2, 315–323, 2018.
16. Jose, J., *Introduction to machine learning*, Khanna Book Publishing Co, New Delhi, India, 2020.

17. Theobald, O., *Machine learning for absolute beginners: A plain english intro-duction*, 2nd edition, Scatterplot Press, United States, 2017.
18. Pradhan, M. and Kumar, U.D., *Machine learning using python*, Wiley, Hoboken, New Jersey, 2020.
19. Shalizi, C.R., *Advanced data analysis from an elementary point of view*, Cambridge University Press, Cambridge, United Kingdom, 2013.
20. Deng, L. and Yu, D., *Deep learning: Methods and applications*, Now Publishers, Maryland, United States, 2013.

5

Convolutional Neural Networks in Tensorflow

Among deep learning models, Convolutional Neural Network is an algorithm, which acts as an artificial neuron (neural network). This neural network [1] has been widely used to deal with image input for image processing/recognition/classification. Initially, it considers an input, provide importance by prioritizing various objects/features using weigh and bias parameters to differentiate among one another. Examples of convolutional neural network are face recognition, image classification, object tracking, natural language processing, speech recognition and so on. In this chapter, the working of convolutional neural network with its architecture and applicability of convolutional neural network using python programing will be discussed.

5.1 CNN Architectures

In CNN architecture, multiple layers are involved is depicted in Figure 5.1.

Convolutional Neural Network [2] consist of important three layers for processing an input. They are i) convolution layer, ii) fully-connected layer, and iii) pooling layer. The number of layers at each level may vary based on the demand of the model being used i.e., for text or image or signal processing. Which means feature extraction, classification, segmentation and for auto correlation of data. Each set of nodes analyze particular part of input to obtain informative data. This model consists of different kind of layers. They are listed below with short description.

(i) Convolutional Layer – It consists of several convolutional kernels with same size.

Niha Kamal Basha, Surbhi Bhatia Khan, Abhishek Kumar and Arwa Mashat (eds.) Deep Learning and Its Applications Using Python, (81–94) © 2023 Scrivener Publishing LLC

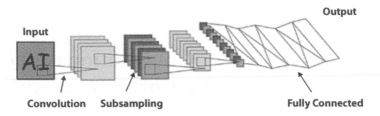

Figure 5.1 Layers of convolutional neural network.

(ii) Pooling Layer – It collects all values from the previous layer and process them using a method to obtain an average value as filtered input.

(iii) Fully-connected Layer – It is used for classifying the input based on class probability with several computations to get desired output.

5.2   Properties of CNN Representations

The main properties of CNN representation rely on three layers (convolutional, pooling and fully-connected). This architecture includes [3] stack of different layers which have been build one next to other. The main three operations of each convolution layers are, convolution, batch normalization and rectified linear layer activation function.

5.3   Convolution Layers, Pooling Layers – Strides - Padding and Fully Connected Layer

Initially, the input have been passed into input layer where the striding and padding operations are applied. This layer performs operation [4] on data to obtain feature vector using feature extraction step from the different layers. The desired feature map/value have been obtained using filter or kernel. The weight sharing has been applied for selecting specific feature among whole feature vector using convolution kernel for feature detection. This process with local connectivity simplifies the training and parametric complexity. The working of convolution is depicted in Figure 5.2.

In this figure the input of 5*5 have been subsamples by applying 2*2 filter to obtain an output. After convolution there will be some loss of data, it have been resolved by applying padding. Next to this layer is pooling layer

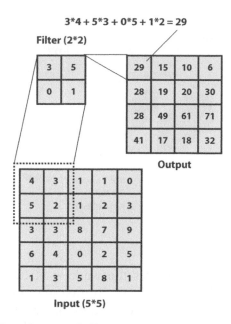

Figure 5.2 Subsampling of input with filter to get output.

where the features [5] are consolidated from the previous layer, among them the maximum value have been chosen. By which the over fitting of the data have been reduced and generalize the features. This have been shown in Figure 5.3.

Finally it's a fully connected layer where the non-linear activation functions predict the probabilities. The activation functions are used at the end after finding all the features and consolidated using pooling layer. This fully connected layer have been named after by building hidden and output layer. The working of all these layers are shown in Figure 5.4.

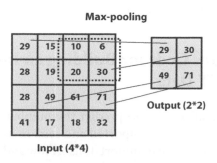

Figure 5.3 Max-pooling of CNN.

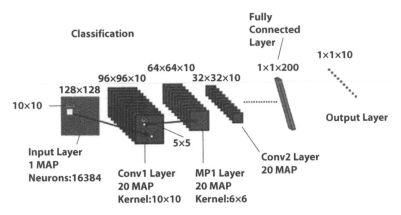

Figure 5.4 Classification using CNN.

The above figure demonstrates the working of CNN by considering input of 128×128 with 16384 neurons. The first sub-sample of 10×10 input is processed with 5×5 kernel in convolution layer. Then the convoluted output [6] is processed using 6×6 kernel in max-pooling. Further the data have been processed using two convolution layers and finally the output class predictions are done using fully connected layer to get the desired output. To implement the working of CNN using TensorFlow will be discussed below.

5.4   Why TensorFlow for CNN Models?

The TensorFlow [7] is capable of implementing 3D array, flexibility to iterate, faster model training and run more experiments. When these implementations are extended for production they have been run on large scale GPUs. In the next topic the working of image classification have been demonstrated using MNIST data set.

5.5   TensorFlow Code for Building an Image Classifier for MNIST Data

The aim of this classifier [8] is to predict the number give in the image. Initially, required packages are imported and session have been started for the further process. The code to import TensorFlow and NumPy are shown below and to start graph session code have to be used.

```
from tensorflow.contr.learn.python.learn.datasets.mnist import
    read_data_sets
from tensorflow.python.framwrk import ops import tensoflow
    as tf
import numpy as np
ses = tf.Ses()
```

Load the data and normalize to calculate z-score for training and test set. Then convert labels into one-hot encoded vectors. These steps are shown below which have been used to load the data, to normalize the input code given have to be used and for converting one-hot encoder code shown below have to be used.

```
from keras.dataset import mnist
(L_train, m_train), (L_test, m_test) = mnist.load_dat()
L_trn = L_trn - np.mean(L_trn) / L_trn.std()
L_tst = L_tst - np.mean(L_tst) / L_tst.std()
trn_labl = tf.one_hot(m_trn, num_clas)
tst_labl = tf.one_hot(m_tst, num_clas)
```

After converting input to vector, the models parameters are created with the batch size of 784 and assign all parameter values and declare the place-holders of the model. The code for assigning the model are shown below and for modeling placeholder code have to be used.

```
samp =500
learn_rat = 0.03
img_wdt = L_trn[0].shap[0]
img_hig = L_trn[0].shap[1]
trg_siz = max(tran_lab) + 1 num_chanls = 1
no_chanls = 1
conv1_featr = 30
filt1_featr = 5
conv2_featr = 15
filt2_featr = 3
max_pol_siz1 = 2
l_inpt_shp = (bath_siz, img_wid, img_heg, num_chan)
l_inpt = tf.placholdr(tf.flot32, shp=l_inpt_shap)
m_targt = tf.placholdr(tf.int32, shp=(btc_siz))
eval_inpt_shap = (samp, img_widt, img_heg, num_chanls)
```

```
eval_inpt = tf.placholdr(tf.flot32, shap=eval_inpt_shap)
eval_targt = tf.placholdr(tf.int32, shap=(samp))
```

Along with that the variables of the model are declared and assign values for the fully connected layer. The code to declare the model are shown below and for assigning the model below code have to be used.

```
V1=tf.Var(tf.rand_norm([filt1_featur,filt1_featur,no_chanel,conv1_feat]))
c1 = tf.Var(tf.ones([conv1_feat]))
V2 = tf.Var(tf.rand_norm([filt2_feat, filt2_feat, conv1_feat,conv2_feat]))
c2 = tf.Var(tf.ones([conv2_feat]))
V3 = tf.Var(tf.trunc_norm([full_inpt_size, fully_connect_siz1], std=0.1,
            dtyp=tf.flot32))
c3 = tf.Var(tf.truncat_norm([fuly_connect_size1], std=0.1, dtyp=tf.float32))
V_ot = tf.Var(tf.truncat_norm([fuly_connect_size1, targ_siz], std=0.1,
            dtyp=tf.flot32))
c_ot = tf.Var(tf.truncat_norm([tag_siz], std=0.1, dtyp=tf.flot32))
```

After declaring and assigning all parameters and variables, the functions for convolution and maxpool layer have to be defined and initialize all model operations. The code to define the function are shown below and to initialize the model code given have to be used.

```
conv = tf.nn.conv2d(x, W, strid=[1, 1, 1, 1], padng='SAME')
conv_with_b = tf.nn.bias_add(conv, c)
conv_ot = tf.nn.relu(conv_with_c)
return conv_ot
def mxpol_layr(conv, i=2):
return tf.nn.max_pol(conv, isize=[j, i, i, j], strd=[i, j, j, i], pad='same')
conv_ot1 = conv_layr(inp_dat, V1, c1)
maxpool_ot1 = maxpol_layr(conv_ot1)
conv_ot2 = conv_layr(maxpool_ot1, V2, c2)
maxpool_ot2 = maxpol_layr(conv_ot2)
final_conv_shap = maxpol_ot2.get_shap().as_list()
fin_shap = fin_conv_shap[1] * fin_conv_shap[2] * fin_conv_shap[3]
flat_ot = tf.reshap(maxpol_ot2, [fin_conv_shap[0], fin_shap])
fully_conct1 = tf.nn.relu(tf.add(tf.matmul(flat_output, V3), c3))
final_model_ot = tf.add(tf.matmul(fully_connect1, V_ot), c_ot)
return(final_model_ot)
model_ot = my_conv_net(l_inpt)
test_model_ot = my_conv_net(eval_inpt)
```

After initializing all model operations declare function to compute loss, prediction and accuracy of the model. The code for declaring loss function is shown below, for prediction and accuracy computation code below have to be used.

```
los = tf.red_mean(tf.nn.spar_softmx_cros_entpy_with_
        logits(logits=model_ot, labl=m_trg))
tst_predict = tf.nn.softmax(tst_model_ot)
def get_acc(log, trg): btc_pred = np.argmax(log, axs=1)
num_corct = np.sum(np.equ(btc_predict, trg)) return(100. *
        num_corct/btc_predict.shap[0])
```

Create the optimizer and assign it as Adam optimizer for minimizing the loss and initialize the variables. The code to create the optimizer is shown below and for initializing variables code below have been used.

```
my_optimiz = tf.trn.AdamOptimiz(learn_rate, 0.9) trn_stp = my_optimiz.
min(los)
varInit = tf.globl_var_init()
sess.run(varInit)
```

After that training loop have to be initiated and evaluated using below code, mean while the training have been recorded using the code given below and display the result.

```
for k in range(epoc):
    rand_indx = np.rand.choic(len(L_trn), siz=btc_siz)
    rand_l = L_trn[rand_indx]
    rand_l = np.expnd_dims(rand_l, 3)
    rand_m = trn_labl[rand_indx]
    trn_dct = {l_inpt: rand_l, m_trg: rand_m}
    ses.run(trn_stp, feed_dict=trn_dict)
    temp_trn_los, temp_trn_pred = ses.run([los, predict], fed_dict=
        trn_dict)
    temp_trn_acc = get_acc(tem_trn_pred, rand_m)
    eval_indx = np.rand.choic(len(L_tst), size=eval_siz)
    eval_l = X_tst[eval_indx]
    eval_l = np.expnd_dims(eval_l, 3)
    eval_m = tst_labl[eval_indx]
    tst_dict = {eval_inpt: eval_l, eval_trg: eval_m}
    tst_pred = ses.run(tst_predict, fed_dict=tst_dict)
```

```
        tmp_tst_acc = get_acc(tst_pred, eval_m)
print('Epoch # {}. trn Los: {:.2f}. Train Acc : {:.2f} . tmp_tst_acc :
        {:.2f}'.fomt(i+1,tmp_trn_los, tmp_trn_acc,tmp_tst_acc))
```

The above convolutional neural network can be written in short using high level API. Which have been listed in next topic.

5.6   Using a High-Level API for Building CNN Models

For building CNN models [8], these are some High-Level API are used. They are Sonnet, Keras, Pretty Tensor, TFLearn, Tflayers, TensorLayer, TF-Silm and tf.contrib.learn. These API's helps to build CNN with very less amount of code.

5.7   CNN in Keras

The Kera is capable of implementing 3D array [9], flexibility to iterate, faster model training and run more experiments, also capable of building CNN model. When these implementations are extended for production they have been run on large scale GPUs. In the next topic the working of image classification have been demonstrated using MNIST and CIFAR-10 data set.

5.8   Building an Image Classifier for MNIST Data in Keras

To build an image classifier using MNIST data [10], initially import NumPy module and keras layer along with input dataset. The code to import packages is shown below and to import keras packages code below have to be used.

```
import numpy as np
from keras.model import Sequential
from keras.layer import Dense
from keras.layer import Dropout
from keras.layer import Flatten
from keras.layer import Conv2D
from keras.layer import MaxPooling2d
from keras.util import np_utils
```

```
from keras import backend as G
K.set_img_dim_odrng('th')
```

After importing the modules, display the input and reshape them as per the class created. Then generate and compile the model with all required parameters. The code for reshaping are shown below and to compile the model code below have to be used.

```
L_trn=L_trn.reshp(L_trn.shp[0],1,28,28)
L_tst=L_tst.reshp(L_tst.shp[0],1,28,28)
L_trn=L_trn.astype('float32')
L_tst=L_tst.astype('float32')
print(L_trn.shp)
L_tst=L_tst – np.mean(L_tst) / L_tst.std()
m_trn=np_utils.to_catg(m_trn)
m_tst-np_utils.to_categ(m_tst)
num_clas = m_tst.shap[1]
print(num_class)
```

Finally the model have been trained to best fit and evaluated to obtain a desired output. The Code for these steps have been shown below.

```
model.fit(L_trn, m_trn, valid_dat=(L_tst, m_tst), epoc=1, btc_siz=200)
scor =model.eval(L_tst, m_tst, verbose=0)
print("CNN error: % .2f%%" % (100-scor[1]*100))
model_json= model.to_join() with open("model_json", "v") as json_file:
        json_file.write(model_json)
```

Similar to the above CNN image classifier, CIFAR-10 dataset have been used as input and its code using python have been discussed in the next topic.

5.9   Building an Image Classifier with CIFAR-10 Data

To build an image classifier using CIFAR-10 data, initially import NumPy, SciPy module and keras layer along with input dataset. The code for these steps have been shown below.

```
from keras.datasets import cifar10
from matplotlib import pyplt
from scipy.misc import to image import numpy
from keras.model import Sequ
```

```
from keras.layer import Dens
from keras.layer import Dropot
from keras.layer import Flatten
from keras.layer import Conv2D
from keras.layer import MaxPooling2d
from keras.layer.normaliz import BatchNormaliz
```

After importing the data, categorize them into training and test set. Then create a model by defining parameters and assign value to them. Finally evaluate the model and print the result. The code to categorize the data are shown below and for evaluation code below have to be used.

```
numpy.randm.sed(sed)
L_trn=L_trn.reshap(L_trn.shap[0],3,32,32). astyp('float32')
L_test=L_tst.reshape(L_tst.shap[0],3,32,32). astyp('float32')
model=Sequ()
model.add(Conv2D(32, (5,5), inpt_shap=(3,32,32), activ='relu'))
model.add(MaxPol2D(pol_siz=(2,2)))
model.add(Conv2D(32, (5,5), activ='relu', padng='same'))
model.add(BatchNormalization())
model.add(MaxPooling2D(pol_size=(2,2)))
model.add(Dropout(0.3))
model.add(Flatten())
model.add(Dense(240,activ='elu'))
model.add(Dense(num_class, activ='softmax'))
print(model.ot_shap)
model.comp(los='binary_crosentrpy', optim='adagrad')
model.fit(L_trn, m_trn, valid_dat=(L_tst, m_tst), epoc=1, btc_siz=200)
scor =model.eval(L_tst, m_tst, verbose=0)
print("CNN error: % .2f%%" % (100-scor[1]*100"))
```

In both image classifier using MNIST and CIFAR-10 dataset, defining/creating a model is very important and it follow the same steps. Which have been shown in the next topic.

5.10 Define the Model Architecture

In both classification examples using MNIST data set and CIFAR-10 dataset the same set of codes have been used only difference among them are the parameters and its values. Which have been shown below.

```
model=Seque()
model.add(Conv2D(32, (5,5), inpt_shap=(3,32,32), activ='relu'))
model.add(MaxPool2D(pol_siz=(2,2)))
model.add(Conv2D(32, (5,5), activ='relu', pading='same'))
model.add(BtcNorm())
model.add(MaxPol2D(pol_siz=(2,2)))
model.add(Drop(0.3))
model.add(Flat())
model.add(Dens(240,activ='elu'))
model.add(Dens(num_clas, activ='softmax'))
print(model.ot_shap)
model.compile(loss='binry_crosentpy', optimz='adagrad')
model.fit(L_trn, m_trn, valid_dat=(L_tst, m_tst), epoc=1, btc_siz=200)
scor =model.eval(L_tst, m_tst, verb=0)
print("CNN error: % .2f%%" % (100-scor[1]*100")
```

The model have to be created first then define the input with two dimensional array along with its shape. Then each layer have to be defined along its parameter value such as, activation function, max-pooling size, batch normalization, loss function and optimizer. Finally evaluate the model and display the result.

5.11   Pre-Trained Models

To perform image classification [10] there are few widely used pre-trained models which are used in industries. They are VGG-16, ResNet50, Inceptionv3, and EfficientNet. In this, VGG-16 is very deep convolutional neural network for large-scale image recognition, which was introduced in ILSVRC 2014 conference that outperforms all other models even today, which consists of thirteen convolutional layer, five pooling layer and three dense layer. In this model, initially, an input data have to be augmented and are prepared for training and validation. The code for argumentation and for dividing input into category are shown below.

```
trn_data_gen = ImgDatGen(rescale = 1./255., rotat_rang = 40,
    with_shft_rang = 0.2, hight_shft_rang = 0.2, sher_rang =
    0.2, zoom_rang = 0.2, horizon_flip = True)
tst_datgen = ImgDatGenerat(rescale = 1.0/255.)
```

```
trn_gen = trn_datagen.flw_frm_direct(trn_dir, btc_siz = 20,
    clas_mod = 'bin', trg_siz = (224,224))
valid_gen = tst_datgen.flw_frm_direct(valid_dir, btc_siz = 20,
    clas_mod = 'binry', targ_siz = (224,224))
```

After preparing the data, the basic model have to be imported. Here, the layers need not to be trained since it is a non-trainable model. Then compile the model and fine tune the parameters to get best fit. The code load basic model are shown below and for compiling the model code below have to be used. Finally fine tune the epoch to get the better result.

From tensorflow.keras.appl.vgg16 imprt VGG16

```
bas_modl = VGG16(inpt_shap = (224,224,3), includ_top =False,
    weg = 'imagenet')
for layer in bas_mod.layr:
    layr.trin = Fals
l = layr.Flat() (bas_mod.ot)
l = layr.Dens(512,activ= 'relu')(x)
l = layr.Dropot(0.5)(l)
l = layr.Dens(1, activ='sigm')(l)
mod = tf.keras.mode.Mod(bas_mod.inpt,l)
mode.compil(optimiz = tf.keras.optimiz.RMSprop(lr=0.0001),
    los = 'bin_crosentpy',met = ['acc'])
vgghist = model.fit(trn_generat, validat_dat = validat_generat,
    stp_per_epoc = 100, epoc = 10)
```

In this chapter the working of convolution neural network along with its architecture have been explained in detail. Each layers in CNN have been described with layer diagram along with model definition. The working of image classifier using convolutional neural network have been explained using MNIST data set and CIFAR-10 dataset by using TensorFlow and Keras. Finally the pre-trained model have been explained. In that, VGG-16 is explained with ImageNet dataset, where VGG-16 outperforms all other model. This model mainly deals with non-temporal data whereas recurrent neural network reuse its activation function to process sequence of temporal data which will be discussed in next chapter.

References

1. Habibi Aghdam, H., *Guide to convolutional neural networks: A practical application to traffic-sign detection and classification*, Springer, Switzerland, 2017.
2. Balas, V.E., Kumar, R., Srivastava, R., *Recent trends and advances in artificial intelligence and internet of things*, Springer Nature, Berlin, Germany, 2019.
3. McClure, N., *TensorFlow machine learning Cookbook: Explore machine learning concepts using the latest numerical computing library - TensorFlow - with the help of this comprehensive cookbook*, Packt Publishing, Birmingham, United Kingdom, 2017.
4. Venkatesan, R. and Li, B., *Convolutional neural networks in visual computing: A concise guide*, CRC Press, Boca Raton, Florida, United States, 2017.
5. Hope, T., Resheff, S., Lieder, I., *Learning TensorFlow: A guide to building deep learning systems*, 1st Edition, O'Reilly, USA, 2020.
6. McClure, N., *TensorFlow machine learning Cookbook: Over 60 recipes to build intelligent machine learning systems with the power of Python*, 2nd Edition, Packt Publishing, Birmingham, United Kingdom, 2018.
7. Krizhevsky, A., ImageNet classification with deep convolutional neural networks. *Proceedings of the Twenty-third International Joint Conference on Artificial Intelligence*, vol. 2, pp. 1237–1240, 2013.
8. Géron, A., *Hands-on machine learning with Scikit-Learn and TensorFlow: Concepts, tools, and techniques to build intelligent systems*, 1st Edition, O'Reilly Media, Sebastopol, California, United States, 2017.
9. Abrahams, S., Hafner, D., Erwitt, E., Scarpinelli, A., *TensorFlow for machine intelligence: A hands-on introduction to learning algorithms paperback*, Bleeding Edge Press, Santa Rosa, California, US, 2016.
10. Ciresan, D., Meier, U., Masci, J., Gambardella, L.M., Schmidhuber, J., Flexible, high performance convolutional neural networks for image classification. *Proceedings of the Twenty-Second International Joint Conference on Artificial Intelligence*, vol. 2, pp. 1237–1242, 2011.

6

RNN and LSTM

Recurrent neural network (RNN) and long short-term memory (LSTM) [1] is one of the deep learning algorithm which deals with sequence of numerical inputs enables some tasks like hand written recognition without segmentation or speech recognition. By using convolutional neural network (CNN), these tasks are difficult to handle because it is difficult to process long sequence and training is difficult because of vanishing gradient problem. So RNN and LSTM classifiers are frequently used and also along with convolution layer by the researchers to get efficient classifier. To overcome this, LSTM and GRU are designed. The working of RNN and LSTM has been shown below with examples.

6.1 Concept of RNN

In RNN, the input is processed using hidden layers. The previous layers output is pass as an input to the next layer. It [2] contains "memory" where the information related to the operations done by each node to process the input with respect to time for generating an output of hidden layers are stored. It works as other neural networks in terms of weight and bias parameters of nodes in hidden layer. The activation functions of each node are independent and are converted to dependent for all nodes. This conversion reduces the complexity while remembering the current and previous nodes operation for hidden layer and the working of simple RNN is shown in Figure 6.1.

In the above classifier time step is denoted as t, an input is denoted as X, hidden state is denoted as h. where dimension or input size is represented as length of X and the no of hidden units are represented as length of h represents. An efficient classifier can be generated by using it along with convolution layer. Due to a vanishing gradient problem convolutional neural network face a difficulty for processing long sequence, also training them is difficult. To resolve this issue LSTM and GRU are proposed.

Niha Kamal Basha, Surbhi Bhatia Khan, Abhishek Kumar and Arwa Mashat (eds.) Deep Learning and Its Applications Using Python, (95–108) © 2023 Scrivener Publishing LLC

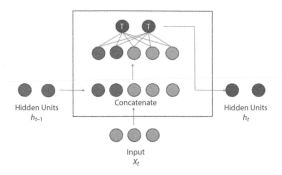

Figure 6.1 Working of simple RNN classifier.

6.2   Concept of LSTM

At each step t, this [3] model consists of hidden state and cell state. In this multiplication operation and sigmoid neural net layer are handled by cell state, where this gate acts as a controller of values to different layers. Here an output be always between 0 (0—nothing fired) and 1 (1—everything fired). A three [4] important gates of this model are input gate, forget gate and output gate. In this how much data to store and how much data to ignore will be decided by forget gate. Also the dimension of cell state and hidden state are same and the cell state is represented as C, h denotes hidden units and X represents input. The diagrammatic representation of this model is shown in Figure 6.2.

Here, which data to store in the cell state with sigmoid and tanh activation functions are decided by input gate. Which value to update and tanh function creates the new vector values are decided by sigmoid function.

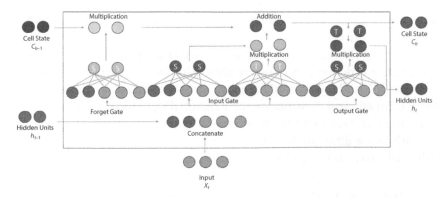

Figure 6.2 Working of LSTM classifier.

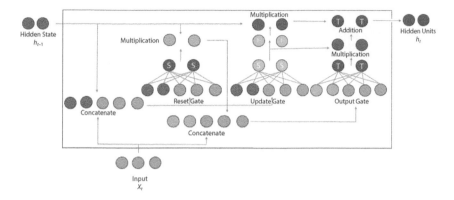

Figure 6.3 Working of GRU classifier.

A range between 0 and ∞ belongs to ReLu function and a range between -1 and 1 belongs to tanh function. Finally, how much data to send to the next layer and how much data to obtain as output will be decided by the sigmoid and tanh functions, where the output is obtained by combining the vector values. This output shows that the values of input and forget layer will not be the same at any time step. When compared with GRU this model has different structure. This model consists of two gates, where both forget and input gates are combined into as update gate and another one gate is reset gate. To determine how to combine the new input with the previous data is decided by reset gate, and how much of the previous data to keep around will be decided by update gate [5].

When compared with LSTM's model GRUs have been in use because of the practical scenarios. A working of GRU is shown in Figure 6.3. The working of LSTM slightly differs in terms of different modes and are explained below.

6.3   Modes of LSTM

Long short-term memory has one of the following modes. Each model has its vector value and its respective functions. The diagrammatic representations are depicted in Figure 6.4.

i] one-to-one model or vanilla model – which have been used without RNN with fixed input and output. Example for one-to-one model application is image classification.

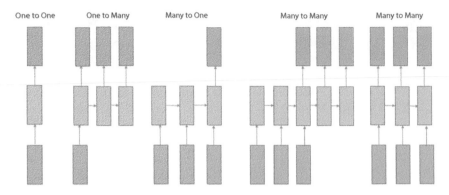

Figure 6.4 Different modes of LSTM.

ii] one-to-many model or sequence output mode – which takes an image as input and provide an output as sequence of words. Example for one-to-many model application is image captioning.

iii] many-to-one model or sequence input mode – which takes input as sequence and provide classified output. Example for many-to-one model application is sentiment analysis.

iv] many-to-many model or sequence input and output – which takes sequence of words as input and convert it into sequence of words as output. Example of many-to-many model application is machine translation. Another example is video classification where each frame of video sequence are labeled and classified. This type of model has been used for sequence prediction.

6.4   Sequence Prediction

Sequence Prediction [6] is nothing but processing sequence of input to predict, classify and generate sequence of output. It is used to observe the order of the data where LSTM is best suitable for handling sequence of input. Example for sequence prediction is to check the series where the time stamp and its values for sequential order. This prediction has been broadly categorized into four types. They are listed below.

i] Sequence Numeric Prediction – which process the input to predict the next value. Example of this application is stock market prediction and weather forecasting.

ii] Sequence to Sequence prediction – which process the input to generate the next sequence from the input sequence. Example of this application is summarization of document and time-series forecasting.

iii] Sequence Generation – which processes the input to generate next sequence which has the same input property. Example of this application is music generation and text generation.

iv] Sequence Classification – which processes the input to label the given sequence. Example of this application is detecting fraudulent activity in data and students performance classification. The real time sequence prediction will be explained using LSTM model with time series of data (attributes are time stamp and its value of IoT data).

6.5   Time-Series Forecasting with the LSTM Model

In this example sensor data have been take in the CSV file format for time series forecasting with long short time memory along with code. Initially, import the required packages. Then after loading csv file data, convert it into an array of values into a time series data. The code for these steps has been shown below.

```
import matplotlib.pyplot as plt
from pandas import read_csv import math
from keras.models import Seque
from keras.layers import Dense
from keras.layers import LSTM
from sklearn.preproces import StandardScaler
from sklearn.metrics import mean_squared_error import pylab
datL = []
datM = []
p_row = len(sers)-ts_lag
for i in rang(p_row-1):
    a = sers[i:(k+ts_lag), 0]
    datL.apnd(a)
    datM.apnd(sers[i + ts_lag, 0])
L, M = np.aray(datL), np.aray(datM)
return L, M
datfrm = read_csv('sp500.csv', usecols=[0])
```

```
plt.plt(datfrm)
plt.shw()
```

After conversion, an input values are normalized and divided into training and test set. This prepared data are used to get the best fit of LSTM model. With this, the results are predicted, and the error rate has been calculated. Based on this the predicted values are rescaled to get the optimal output. The code for these steps is shown below.

```
ser = datfrm.valu.astyp('float32')
ser = scalr.fit_trnsfrm(ser)
trn, tst = ser[0:trn_siz,:], ser[trn_ siz:len(ser),:]
trnL, trnM = cret_timsers(trn, ts_lag)
tstL, tstM = crt_timesers(tst, ts_lag)
tstL = np.reshp(tstL, (tstL.shp[0], 1, tstL.shp[1]))
model.add(LSTM(10, inpt_shp=(1, ts_lag)))
model.add(Dens(1))
model.compil(los='mean_squr_logrithm_eror', optmz='adagrd')
model.fit(trnL, trnM, epoc=500, btc_siz=30)
trnPred = model.pred(trnL)
tstPred = model.pred(tetL)
trnPred = scal.invers_tranfrm(trnPred)
trnM = scal.invers_trnsfrm([trnM])
tstPred = scal.invers_trnsfrm(tstPred)
tstM = scal.invers_trnsfrm([testM])
trnScor = mat.sqrt(mean_squar_error(trnM[0], trnPred[:,0]))
print('Train Score: %.2f RMSE' % (trnScor))
tstScor = math.sqrt(mean_squ_err(tstM[0], tstPred[:,0]))
print('Test Score: %.2f RMSE' % (tstScr))
pylb.shw()
```

So from this example it is observed that time series forecasting is possible with LSTM model.

6.6   Speech to Text

In this speech to text conversion [7] means nothing but converting the recorded speech (voice)data into a text in written format. This conversion helps society in such a way by helping physically challenged people or blind people to control other devices, the meetings are recorded so that they are documented or to add sub titles to the recordings, translation of one language to another also possible by this speech to text conversion.

Initially, the speech data have been pre-processed to get the informative features, which are nothing but the act of recognizing the linguistic part of the speech data and discard other part of speech data or noise. This important linguistic part of speech data are accumulated with features of voice track, teeth and tongue shape. The features of speech data are extracted with the help of MFCCs which is a technique to compute an envelope by converting the speech data to a spectrogram. This technique is widely applied for speech recognition and automatic speaker recognition.

An important linguistic data are converted from frequency scale to mel scale for computing the pitch of the linguistic data or the pitch to relate it to the vocal sound. A function for conversion is shown below.

```
def mfcc(sig,smprat=16000,winlen=0.025,winstep=0.01, numcep=13,
    nfilt=26,nfft=512,lowfreq=0,hghfreq=None, premph=0.97, ceplifr=22,
    apndEng=True)
```

This code defines the signal, sample rate, window length, window step, number of spectrum, spectrum filter and its coefficient, number of filters, frequency range and size of fast Fourier transform. These features are computed using NumPy array. With the help of these MFCC features classifier have been built for speech recognition.

```
from python_speech_features import mfcc
from python_speech_features import delta
from python_speech_features import logfbank
import scipy.io.wavfile as wav
(sam, sig) = wav.read("inpt.wav")
Mfccfeatur=mfcc(sig, samrat)
Dmfccfeatur=delta(mfccfeatur,2)
fbnkfeatur=logbnk(sig,samrat)
Print(fbankfeatr)
```

Initially, an audio file with speech data have been imported which is in .wav file format. The code shown above shows the MFCC feature extraction. This code converts the data to matrix format from the .wav file and is processed to compute the feature values. After conversion each row in the matrix represent feature vector. This process will be repeated until all the feature vectors are accumulated. This data have been used as a training set to get the best fit of deep learning model for voice classification.

Another method for speech recognition is to convert the audio file to an image using spectrogram. This image data will be further used as a training set for deep learning model to recognize a voice. Initially, the .wav file format have been imported. By using the spectrogram approach spectrogram for each sample have been computed and those images are used for training the deep learning model to get the best fit. The code for this method is shown below.

```
Import matplotlib.pyplot as plt
From scip import signal
From scipy.io import wavfile
sam_rat, sam = wavefile.raed('myinput.wav')
freq, tim, spectgrm = signal.spectgrm(sam, sam_rate)
plt.imshow(spectgrm)
plt.mlabel('freq(khz)')
plt.llabel('time(sec)')
plt.show()
```

There are some other methods to convert text data to speech data and speech date to text data using API in python. Most frequently used API's are Google speech, Google cloud speech, pocket sphinx, houndify, IBM speech to text, and Microsoft Bing speech. These API's and its code have been shown below.

6.7   Examples Using Each API

An API is nothing but an open source package [8] in python which allow text to speech and speech to text conversion. Here pocket sphinx is a light weight speech engine used for speech to text conversion which is utilized in mobile devices frequently. The code to demonstrate the working of pocket sphinx is shown below.

```
import spech_recog as sr from os import path
audio_file = "input.wav"
r = sr.Recog()
with sr.audfil(audio_file) as source:
aud = r.recod(sorc)
try:
print("It thinks you said " + r.recog_sphinx(aud))
except sr.UnkwnValueEror:
```

```
print("It could not understand input")
except sr.ReqstEror as e:
print("error; {0}".format(e))
```

Google speech recognition has its own API for speech to text conversion and the code using python is shown below.

```
print("It thinks you said " + r.recognize_google(aud))
except sr.UnknownValueError:
print("It could not understand input")
except sr.RequestError as e:
print("Could not request results from Its service;{0}".format(e))
```

The working of google cloud speech recognition API is shown below and have been used for cloud based speech to text conversion by creating an account by utilizing the credentials.

```
google_cloud_speech_credentials = r"insert the contents of the
    google cloud speech json credentials file here"
```

```
try:
```

```
print("It thinks you said " + r.recognize_google_cloud(audio, credentials_
    json=google_ cloud_speech_credentials))
except sr.UnknownValueError:
print("It could not understand audio")
except sr.RequestError as e:
print("Could not request results from Its service; {0}".format(e))
```

The wit API is a simple speech recognition engine used for speech to text conversion by creating an account and project by utilizing the wit key. The working of wit API is shown below.

```
    wit_ai_key = "API key have to be inserted here"
    try:
    print("API thinks you said " + r.recognize_wit(audio, key=wit_
        ai_key))
    except sr.UnknownValueError:
    print("API could not understand input")
    except sr.RequestError as e:
    print("Could not request results from API service; {0}". format(e))
```

Another API for speech recognition is houndify, which have been used for converting speech to text by creating an account and utilizing client ID and key, which reply to the sound by developing an application. This is shown below.

```
h_clnt_id = "insert client id"
try:
print("It thinks you said " + r.recognize_ houndify(audio, client_id=
    h_clnt_id, client_ key= h_clnt_key))
except sr.UnknownValueError:
print("It could not understand audio")
except sr.RequestError as e:
print("Could not request results from its service; {0}".format(e))
```

An IBM have its own speech recognition capabilities for speech to text conversion by creating an IBM cloud account and utilizing its credentials to start the project. This IBM API and its working is shown below.

```
IBM_username = "Provide IBM user name"
IBM_password = "Provide IBM password"
try:
print("IBM Speech to Text thinks you said " + r.recognize_ ibm(audio,
    username=IBM_username, password=IBM_password))
except sr.UnknownValueError:
print("It could not understand input")
except sr.RequestError as e:
print("Could not request results from its service; {0}".format(e))
```

A Bing API by Microsoft is one among the speech recognition API's which works in real time voice recognition by recognizing the voice from device microphone. This have been utilized by creating an account and its key for voice recognition. The python code for Bing API working is shown below.

```
try:
print("It thinks you said " + r.recognize_bing(audio, key=bing_key))
except sr.UnknownValueError:
print("It could not understand input")
except sr.RequestError as e:
print("Could not request results from its service; {0}".format(e))
```

After conversion the text data have been used in several applications but to get an accuracy best fit model have to be used. In the next topic these data which are in written text format are converted into speech (audio file).

6.8   Text-to-Speech Conversion

To convert text to speech [9] there are so many python packages are available some of them are pyttsx, SAPI, Speech Lib, and Audio Cutting Code.

```
import pyttsx
eng = pyttsx.init()
eng.say("Your Message")
eng.runAndWait()
```

SAPI package have been simply imported. Along with SAIP package, Speech Lib has been used together for text to speech conversion and have been shown below.

```
from win32com.client import constants, Dispatch
Msg = "Hi this is a test"
speak = Dispatch("SAPI.SpVoice")
speak.Speak(Msg)
del speak
from comtypes.client import CreateObject
eng = CreateObject("SAPI.SpVoice")
strm = CreateObject("SAPI.SpFileStrm")
from comtypes.gen import SpeechLib
infile = "input.txt"
outfile = "output-audio.wav"
strm.Open(outfile, SpeechLib.SSFMCreateForWrite)
eng.AudioOutputStrm = strm
f = open(infile, 'r')
theText = f.read()
f.close()
eng.speak(theText)
strm.Close()
```

While converting text data to audio file, unwanted voice sample can be removed from the audio file after conversion. This have been done using audio cutting code and are shown below. In this, initially, import wave package along with other basic packages, import the data in csv file format and convert it into audio file. After conversion select the particular range to discard and write the audio file.

```
import wave import sys import os import csv
oriAud = wave.open('input.wav', 'r')
nChan = oriAud.getnchan()
samWdt = origAudio.getsamwdt()
nFrm = origAudio.getnfrm()
filnam = 'input.csv'
exmFil = open(filnam)
exmRead = csv.reader(exmFil)
exmDat = list(exmRead)
count = 0
for data in exmDat:
    if data[4] == 'startTime' and data[5] == 'endTime':
    print('Start time')
    else:
    start = float(data[4]) end = float(data[5])
origAudio.setpos(start*frameRate) chunkData = origAudio.
    readframes(int((end-start)*frameRate))
outputFPath = 'C:/Users/Niha/outputF{0}.wav'. format(count)
chunkAudio = wave.open(outputFPath, 'w')
chunkAudio.setnchannels(nChan)
chunkAudio.setsampwidth(samWdt)
chunkAudio.setframerate(frmRate)
chunkAudio.writeframes(chunkData)
chunkAudio.close()
```

Next to this text to speech conversion, cognitive service providers are listed and described in the next topic which make the processing quit easier by using those API's.

6.9 Cognitive Service Providers

Cognitive service providers [10] are the one who solve problems of artificial intelligence system from the set of machine learning algorithms in the form of API's. Some of the service providers are Microsoft Azure, Amazon Cognitive services, and IBM Watson services.

Microsoft Azure offers speaker identification using API, Translation service, speech to text conversion service using Bing API, and speech customization.

Cognitive service providers offer text to speech conversion service, where the instruction to pronounce the text data with tone customization and language preference with 47 and 24 voice and language.

IBM service provider offers both speech to text and text to speech conversion service for multiple languages.

6.10 The Future of Speech Analytics

Speech analytics [11] looks brighter in future and it is a billion dollar growing industry. Where this speech based services will be a customer experience key feature which will be must-have solution. Vendors of speech analytics have innovations where clients explore all data to take diverse decisions. Also prosodic data will be having an acoustic feature for analysis by most of the vendors. AI-based companies predict the gap or problem in their service and solve it with machine learning algorithm to attain an increased accuracy. Many organizations have this as a metric to estimate their customer experience. With this perspective speech analytics looks brighter.

Apart from speech signal analysis, machine learning and deep learning algorithms are used in medical signal analysis that too for EEG (Electroencephalography) signal. Here the use of machine learning and deep learning algorithms are discussed in chapter 9 with brief introduction to EEG signal, existing machine learning and deep learning algorithms with research perspective, use of CGRU_SVM model for absence seizure detection with description of seizure and its detection, analysis process.

In this chapter the working of recurrent neural network along with long short term memory and gated recurrent unit have been depicted with neat diagram. Also their applications are explained using python code especially on speech to text and text to speech conversion, their API's and few python packages are shown with code. Along with this, cognitive services providers and the future of speech analytics are depicted.

References

1. Fellow, I.G., Bengio, Y., Courville, A., *Deep learning*, MIT Press, Cambridge, Massachusetts, United States, 2017.

2. McCulloch, W.S. and Pitts, W., A logical calculus of the ideas immanent in nervous activity. *Bull. Math. Biophys.*, 14, 5, 115–133, 1943.

3. Rosenblatt, F., The perceptron - a perceiving and recognizing automaton, in: *Technical Report, Cornell Aeronautical Laboratory*, Cornell Aeronautical Laboratory, Buffalo, New York, 1957, 85-460-1.

4. Kelley, H.J., Gradient theory of optimal flight paths. *ARS J.*, *30*, 947–954, 1960.

5. Dreyfus, S., The numerical solution of variational problems. *J. Math. Anal. Appl.*, 5, 1, 30–45, 62, 9000, 1962.

6. Rumelhart, D., Hinton, G., Williams, R., Learning representations by back-propagating errors. *Nature*, 32, 3, 533–536, 1986.

7. Cybenko, G., Approximation by superpositions of a sigmoidal function. *Math. Control Signal Syst.*, 25, 2, 303–314, 1989.

8. Hochreiter, S. and Schmidhuber, J., Long short-term memory. *Neural Comput.*, 9, 8, 1735–1780, 1997.

9. Hinton, G.E. and Osindero, S., A fast learning algorithm for deep belief nets. *Neural Comput.*, 18, 7, 1527–54, 2006.

10. Singh, P. and Manure, A., *Learn TensorFlow 2.0: Implement machine learning and deep learning models with Python*, Apress Publisher, New York, United States, 2019.

11. Rungta, K., *TensorFlow in 1 day: Make your own neural network*, Amazon Digital Services LLC - KDP Print US, 2018.

7

Developing Chatbot's Face Detection and Recognition

In this chapter, the importance of artificial intelligence and its vital role in communicating with human and machine are shown in the form of text or voice. Which means a program communicates with human and allowing them to converse like a normal human being. These systems [1] are widely used in business to consumer (B2C) and business to business (B2B) environment to handle simple task. Also the steps to design a Chatbot, to develop using API's and its application are also described using python programing. This kind of systems is called as Chatbot, which are automated user-performed tasks.

7.1 Why Chatbots?

Chatbot [2] will capture the intent of the user and converse with them. Intent is nothing but understanding the information seeking by a user. Most of the institution or organizations are using Chatbot's for productive service and sales for gaining efficiency and savings. For example: when a user search for the restaurant nearby using the food name like biryani nearby, Chatbot understand the intent and send the list of restaurant names as a response.

7.2 Designs and Functions of Chatbot's

Designing a Chatbot [3] follows the same steps each and every time, but the processing method differs for each output. There few things to take in account for creating a good Chatbot. They are given below.

- The purpose of the Chatbot has to be determined.
- Decide which platform to use rule based or NLP.

Niha Kamal Basha, Surbhi Bhatia Khan, Abhishek Kumar and Arwa Mashat (eds.) Deep Learning and Its Applications Using Python, (109–132) © 2023 Scrivener Publishing LLC

- Limitation of platform should be planed.
- Designing a personality and tone of Chatbot is very important.
- Should check whether a Chatbot is texting like a human.
- Processing user's communication flow and handling delay by integrating visuals have to be designed.
- Users should be educated to deal with Chatbot and the approach to deal with user should be decided.
- Bot to human transformation strategy for communication should be designed.

These points have to be remembered while designing a Chatbot.

7.3   Steps for Building a Chatbot's

Chatbot's are widely used to communicate [4] with users. Initially, the input message from user has been processed using the following steps.

1. Tokenization – It is nothing but segmenting the sentence into single words (tokens). The tokenization steps using python is shown below where the tokens are stored in list.

    ```
    from nltk.tokenize import TreebankWordTokenizer
    from nltk.corpus import stpword
    l = "AI is about applying math"
    tok = TreebankWordTokenizer().tokenize(l)
    op = []
    op = [m for m in tok if m.isalpha()]
    print(op)
    ```

2. Text Processing – In this step the unnecessary punctuations and stop words (the words won't give much sense and will not affect the meaning of the statement) have to be removed. The line of code for text processing is shown below.

    ```
    from nltk.tokenize import TreebankWordTokenizer
    from nltk.corpus import stpword
    l = "AI is about applying math"
    tok = TreebankWordTokenizer().tokenize(l)
    ```

```
st_wd = set(stpword.word('spain'))
op = []
for m in token:
        if m not in st_wd:
                op.append(m)
print(op)
```

3. Entity classifier – It is nothing but identifying entity in the sentence and classifying those entities (such as name of a place, person etc.,) to a respective predefined class.

    In python NER package have been used for named entity recognition in sentences and the code for NER is shown below for Stanford NER, Pre-Trained MITIE NER and Self Trained.

```
from nltk.tag import StanfordNERTagger
from nltk.tokenize import word_tokenz
StanfordNERTagger("stanford-ner/classifiers/english.all.3class.
        distsim.crf.ser.gz", "stanford-ner/stanford-ner.jar")
txt = "Ram was the founder of Raman Institute at India"
txt = word_tokenz(txt)
nr_tgs = nr_tggr.tg(txt)
print(nr_tgs)
```

These are the lines of code using Stanford NER for recognition of entity with classifier. After running these above line of code, run the below code which consist of MITIE pretrained dataset for name entity recognition.

```
from mitie.mitie import *
from nltk.tokenize import word_tokenize
print("loading NER model...")
nr  =  name_enti_extrac("mitie/MITIE-models/english/
nr_model.dat".encode("utf8"))
txt = "Ram was the founder of Raman Institute at India".
        encode("utf-8")
txt = word_tokenize(text)
nr_tgs = nr.extrac_enti(txt)
print("\nEntities found:", nr_tgs)
        for s in nr_tgs:
                range = s[0] tag = s[1]
```

```
enti_txt = " ".join(txt[a].decode() for a in range)
print(str(tag) + " : " + enti_txt)
```

Here in the below line of code there is a small change in which it shows the usage of self-trained data for named entity recognition.

```
from mitie.mitie import *
smp = nr_train_inst([d"Tom", d"is", d"the", d"Head", d"of",
    d"Tom", d"Institute", d"at", d"New", d"Delhi", d"."])
smp.add_enti(range(0, 1), "person".encode("utf-8"))
smp.add_enti(range(5, 7), "organization".encode("utf-8"))
smp.add_enti(range(8, 10), "Location".encode("utf-8"))
trn = nr_trn("mitie/MITIE-models/english/total_word_
    feature_extractor.dat".encode("utf-8"))
trn.add(smp)
nr = trn.train()
tok = [d"Ram", d"is", d"the", d"Head", d"of", d"Ram",
    d"University", d"."]
entis = nr.ext_entis(tok)
print ("\nEntities found:", entis)
        for d in entis:
            range = d[0] tag = d[1]
            enty_txt = " ".join(str(tok[a]) for a in range)
            print (" " + str(tag) + ": " + enty_txt)
```

4. Intent Classifier – It is the step where the need of the user is identified and classify the request to certain category of intent using an algorithms where the sentence are converted into vectors for processing the intent using classifier model. The working of SVM based intent classifier model and the lines of code are given below.

```
from random import sample
from sklearn.preprocessing import LabelEncoder
from sklearn.feature_ext.text import TfdfVectorizer
from sklearn.svm import SVC
from sklearn.model_selection import train_test_split
from sklearn.metrics import f1_score, accuracy_score
dat = pd.read_csv("int.csv")
print(dat.smp(6))
```

After importing the required packages and modules, the data have to split as training and testing. The line of code for preparing the data for training model which include splitting the data, vectorizing the input and labeling them are given below.

```
L_trn, M_tst, M_trn, M_tst = trn_tst_split(data ["Description"],
    dat["intent_label"], tst_size=3)
print(L_trn.shape, L_tst.shape, M_trn.shape, M_tst.shape)
tfdf = tfdf.fit(L_trn)
L_trn = tfdf.trnfm(L_trn)
L_tst = tfdf.trnfm(L_tst)
M_trn = le.trnfm(M_trn)
M_tst = le.trnfm(Y_tst)
```

Finally use the method model.fit and model.predict for classification along with computing the f1 score and accuracy of the model.

```
model = model.fit(L_trn, M_trn)
p = model.predict(L_tst)
print("f1_score:", f1_score( M_tst, p, average="micro"))
print("accuracy_score:",accuracy_score(M_tst, p))
```

To get word vectors, there are different method available for text input. The technique support this conversion provide a similar vector for similar words. For this conversion Word2Vec technique have been used with 1D-CNN on the word vector. The working of this model is shown below with line of code. Initially import all the necessary packages and modelules.

```
from gensim.models import Word2Vec import pandas as pd
import numpy as np
from keras.preprocessing.txt import tokenizer.
from keras.preprocessing.sequence import pad_sequences
from keras.utils.np_utils import to_categorical
from keras.layers import Dense, Input, Flatten
from keras.layers import Conv1D, MaxPooling1D, Embedding,
    Dropout
```

```
from keras.models import Model
from sklearn.preprocessing import LabelEncoder
from sklearn.model_selection import train_test_split
from sklearn.metrics import f1_score, accuracy_score
data = pd.read_csv("intent1.csv")
```

Here the data have been splitted into training and test data, then train the model to get the result.

```
L_trn, L_tst, M_trn, M_tst = trn_tst_split(data ["Description"],
     data["intent_label"], tst_size=6)
M_trn = le.trnsfrm(M_trn)
M_tst = le.trnsfrm(M_tst)
L_tst = [sent for sent in L_tst]
print("done with training word vector")
```

The below line of code of CNN model will process the data with 20 words per each sentences, which under gone tokenization and sequencing. After that the data have been converted to a matrix form of processing them to get the classified intents of the word.

```
Tokn()
tokn.fit_on_txt(L_trn)
seq = tokn.txt_to_seq(L_trn)
seq_tst = tokn.txt_to_seq(L_tst)
wrd_indx = tokn.wrd_indx
vocab_size = len(wrd_indx)
L_tst = pad_seq(seq_tst, maxlen=max_sent_len)
        for wrd, a in wrd_indx.items():
            try:
                embd_vct = wrd_vecs[wrd]
            except:
                embd_vct = None
                if embd_vct is not None: embd_
                matrix[a] = embd_vct
print("done with embedding ")
vocab_size = len(embd_matx)
m = to_categorical(np.asarray(M_trn))
embd_layr = Embd(vocab_size, 100, weg=[emb_matx],
     inpt_leng=max_sent_len, trn=True)
```

```
seq_ipt = Ipt(shape=(max_sent_len,), dtype='int32')
embd_seq = embd_lay(seq_ipt)
l_cov1 = Conv1D(128, 4, activation='relu')(embd_seq)
l_pool1 = MaxPooling1D(4)(l_cov1)
l_flat = Flatten()(l_pool1)
hidn = Dense(100, activation='relu')(l_flat)
preds = Dense(len(y[0]), activation='softmax')(hidden)
model = Model(seq_ipt, preds)
model.compile(loss='binary_crossentropy',optimizer='Adam')
print("model fitting - simplified CNN")
model.summary()
model.fit(x, y, epoc=10, bat_siz=128)
k = [np.argmax(i) for i in k]
score_cnn = f1_score(Y_test, k, avg="mcro")
print("accu_value:",accu_score(Y_test, k))
print("f1_value:", score_cnn)
```

This model [5] consists of 105,731 total parameters, as well as trainable parameters with 0 non-trainable parameters. Also the genism package is used for intent classification, which is a pre-trained model from Goodge used for English language with three hundred dimensions. The working of similarity index calculation are shown in the below line of code.

```
import genism
load_word2vec_format('GoogleNews-vectors- negative300.
    bin', binary=True)
print(model.similarity('King', 'Queen'))
print(model.most_similar(positive=[Prince, Girl], negative=
    [Boy]))
Vect ("Prince") – Vect("boy") + Vect("girl") ≈ Vect("Princess")
```

5. Reply from the Chatbot – After completing the first four steps, the chat bot will produce the random reply based on the classified intent. The input from the user is processed by a Chatbot to generate the reply based on the users question and its intent. The code for random response generation is shown below.

```
import random
intent = ipt()
```

```
opt = ["How are you", "Hi ", " How are you doing", "Heeey! ",
"How can I help you", " There","Hello! ", "How can I assist you?",
"Hii ", "What's up?"]
if(intent == "Hii"):
    print(random.choice(opt))
```

These models follow any one of the two approaches to build Chatbot. They are, rule-based approach and machine learning approach. Along with these approaches there are some API's to build bots. They are Wit.ai, Api.ai, IBM's Watson. These APIs are work along with Chat fuel, Texit. in, Octane AI, Motion.ai platforms. The best practices to for developing Chatbot's will be discussed below.

7.4   Best Practices of Chatbot Development

To develop a Chatbot [6], two things have to be considered as a best practice. They are given as below.

1. Should identify the potential users – by doing this the bot can be developed in such a way to facilitate the user by providing news and entertain them through the customer service channel.
2. The bot should be trained to handle the user's sentences as an emotional Chatbot—by doing this, the bots will act as an ambassador for the product or which make the users to act as an ambassador with emotional or friendly conversation, which make a user to feel comfortable and make them understand the context of the conversation.

Next level of Chatbot communication is face detection, face recognition and face analysis. This will be discussed below with examples using python programing.

7.5   Face Detection

It is a process of identifying human face in an image or in a video using algorithms. In this the features of human face have to be extracted initially. Train the model to detect using the extracted features for face detection.

7.6   Face Recognition

A face recognition is nothing but detecting the features in an image or video as well as tag it with a name to the detected face among other faces using algorithm. In this features of the human face have been extracted and compared with localization phase to lean to whom the features belongs to in a repository.

7.7   Face Analysis

It is a process of analyzing the captured face to obtain inference out of it as complexion, age, emotions, etc. In this the facial features are extracted, compared and analyzed to check the performance of detection and recognition process. These methods are implemented using Open CV.

7.8   OpenCV—Detecting a Face, Recognition and Face Analysis

OpenCV [7] offers a provision to provide three methods for face recognition. They are Eigenfaces, Fisherfaces, and Local Binary pattern histograms (LBPHs).

Eigenfaces—it is an algorithm which utilize PCA to generate a low dimensional face images which will be used further as a features.

Fisherfaces—it rely on LDA which perform dimensionality reduction based of feature class which uses a multiple measurements to get the best possible feature combinations suitable to classifies among different classes.

LBPH—this method relies on feature extraction where it sense each image characteristics in the dataset. For new image input, analyses have been done and compare its features with the images in dataset.

7.8.1   Face Detection

The process [8] of detecting the face features using Haar cascade filters using python programming by utilizing OpenCV library. Here, Anaconda with OpenCV and dlib have been used for implementation. Initially, import the library files and initialize the face cascade for face detection. The python code for these initialization below. After this step, the retrieved face from webcam have been processed using infinite loop to detect the human face. Once processed cascade filter have been applied to generate the gray scale image of all faces captured from webcam. The code for an infinite loop for this process is shown below. Then repeat the process on all faces in the image and detect a face which matches the condition based on maxArea have been shown as an output by drawing the rectangular box over the face on the captures image. The code for this step is shown below.

```
import cv2
facCacd=cv2.CascadeClassifier('haarcascade_frontalface_
    default.xml')
Opt_Siz_Wid=700
Opt_Siz_Heg=600
cap=cv2.VideoCapture(0)
cv2.moveWindow("base_image",20,200)
cv2.moveWindow("result_image,640,200)
cv2.startWindowThread()
rectClor=(0,100,255)
```

Here a small change in the code will show how the face detection works with infinite loop. The line of code is given below. Where initially latest image will be retrieved from web came and resize them desired size. Based on the condition make the model to execute using if statement.

```
rc,fulSizBasImg=capture.read()
basImg=cv2.resize(fulSizBasImg, (520,420))
prsKey=cv2.waitKey(2)
if(prsKey==ord('Q')) | (prsKey==ord('q')):
cv2.destroyAllWindows()
exit(0)
restImg=basImg.copy()
gry_img=cv2.cvtColor(baseImage, cv2.colour_bgr2gray)
face=faceCascade.detectMultiScale(gray_image,1.3,5)
```

In the below code the face detection along with rectangle shape around the face will be explained. For that initially assign the required variable to 0. With the help of for loop create the rectangle around the face.

```
maxAr=0
l=0
m=0
w=0
```

```
h=0
for(_l,_m,_n,_p) in faces:
if _n * _p>maxAr:
l=_l
m=_m
n=_n
p=_p
maxArea= n*p
if maxArea>0:
cv2.rect(restImg, (x-10, y-20), (l+ n+10, m+ p+20), rectColr, 2)
largRest=cv2.resize(restImg, (Opt_Siz_Wid, Opt_Siz_Heg))
cv2.imshow("base-image"),basImg)
cv2.imshow("result-image", largRest)
```

In the next topic along with detection of face, tracking of face have been demonstrated below with line of code.

Face Tracking:
In face detection [9], Haar cascade is expensive and will not detect if there is any disturbance in subjects captured image. Also tracking of detected face between the frames are difficulty. So these drawbacks are resolved using tracker correlation by using dlib library for frame to frame tracking. To do this the required packages have to be imported and initialized with required variables. By using the correlation tracker within infinite loop, the detected face will be tracked and found coordinates have been used for generating a correlation tracker instead of drawing a rectangle. The working of this step is shown below. Initially import all necessary packages. Before getting into face tracking, face recognition have been done with infinite loop and the below line of code is given below.

```
Import dlib
Track=dlib.correlation_track()
trackFace=0
If not trackFace:
    Gray=cv2.cvtColor(basImg, cv2.color_rgb2gray)
    Face=faceCascade.detectMultiScale(gray,1,3,5)
    print("The cascade detector is used to detect face")
maxArea=0
l=0
m=0
```

```
n=0
p=0
for(_l, _m, _n, _p) in faces:
    if _w * _p > maxArea:
        l=int(_l)
        m=int(_m)
        n=int(_w)
        p=int(_p)
        maxArea=n * p
    if maxArea>0:
    track.start_track(basImg, dlib.rectangle(l-10,
        m-20, x+n+10, m+p+20))
    trackFace=1
```

Once after recognition of face among the objects captured by the camera, the tracking have been done on the recognized face and line of code have been given below.

```
if trackFace:
    trackQulty=track.update(basImg)
if trackQulty>=9.0:
    track_postn=track.get_postn()
    t_l=int(track_postn.left())
    t_m=int(track_postn.top())
    t_n=int(track_postn.width())
    t_p=int(track_postn.height())
    cv2.rect(resImg, (t_l,t_m), (t_l+t_n, t_m+t_p), rectColor, 2)
else:
    trackFace=0
```

While tracking the face the message have to be displayed in a console to ensure the detector is used again and again. This message will be helpful for the user to make sure the tracker is working well on tracking the detected face and to know the performance of a tracker. The code along with the explanation is given below.

7.8.2   Face Recognition

In this process [10] the detected face is further analyzed to tag/label the name of the person on each frame with competition of each face in an entire video by utilizing training image dataset and obtain the name of the person when it is matched successfully. Initially import face recognition library and dlibs for building deep learning based face recognition model. By using the Argparse library the required arguments are added which will be helpful to assign input by the time execution. The code for these steps are shown below.

```
import os
import re
import warnings
import scipy.misc
import cv2
import face_recognition
from PIL import Image
import argparse
import csv
import os
pars= argpars.ArgPars()
pars.add_arg("-i", "--images-dir", help"image dir")
pars. add_arg("-v", "--ideo", help"video to recognize faces on")
pars. add_arg("-o", "--output-csv", help"output csv file [optional]")
pars. add_arg("-u", --upsample-rate", help "repeated times to up
    sample am image to recognize faces")
arg=vars(pars.pars_arg())
```

After creating model for recognition of face using argparse library, the below line of code have been used for training the model.

```
if arg.get("imag_dir", None) is None and
    cs.path.exists(arg.get("images_dir",None)):
        print("The path to image folder have to be verified")
        exit()
if args.get("video", None) is None and
    cs.path.isfile(arg.get("video",None)):
        print("please check The path to video")
        exit()
if arg.get("output-csv", None) is None:
        print("You haven't specified an output csv file. Nothing
        will be written.")
upsample_rate=arg.get("upsample_rate", None)
if upsample_rate is None:
        upsample_rate=1
```

After initializing the arguments [11], the training image input, video file directory and their files have to be specified and the outcome at each time frame have to be recorded in the CSV file for further reference. The helper function will be used for reading the entire image form the single folder. Then the images are trained and tested using the function to check the similarity of face by utilizing the single folder. The below line of code will be used for training the model with input image.

```
def test_image(img_to_chk, knw_name, knw_face_encod,
    no_of_tme_to_upsamp=1)
unknw_img=img_to_chk
if unknw_img.shp[i]>1600:
    scale_factor=1600/unknw_img.shp[1]
    with warn.catch_warn():
            warn.smpfltr("Ignore")
    unknw_img=scipy.mic.imresiz(unknw_img, scal_fact)
result=[]
for unknw_encod in unknw_encod:
    rest=face_recog.com_face(knw_face_encod,unknw_encod)
result_encod=[]
for nameIndex, is_match in enum (rest):
    if is_match:
            rest_encod.apnd(knw_nam[namIndx])
return rest_encod

def map_file_patrn_to_label(labels_with_patrn, label_lst):
    rest_lst=[]
    for key, labl in labl_with_patrn.itm():
            for img_labl in labl_lst:
                    if str(key).lower() in str(img_labl).lower():
                    if str(labl) not in rest_lst:
                    rest_lst.append(str(labl))
    return rest_lst
```

After obtaining the similarity the label/tag have to be extracted for each face using a function have been shown.

```
cap=cv2.VideoCapture(args["video"])
tr_encode=[]
tr_labl=[]
```

```
for file in img_files_in_folder(args['img_dir']):
    basnes=os.path.splitext(os.path.basnam(file))[0]
    img=face_recog.load_img_file(file)
    encod=face_recog.face_encod(img)
if len(encod)>1:
    print("Warning: More than one face found.",format(file))
if len(encod)==0:
    print("Warning: No face found.",format(file))
if len(encod):
    tr_encode.apnd(encod[0])
    tr_labl.apnd(basnam)

csvfile=None
csvwriter=None
if args.get("output_csv", None) is not None:
    csvfile=open(args.get("output_csv"),'w')
    csvwriter=csv.writer(csvfile,delimiter=",quotechar='|',quoting=
    csv.quote_minimal)
ret, firstFrame=cap.read()
framerate=cap.get(cv2.cap prop fps)
```

After matched label extraction [12] of matched faces, read the video frames to extract similar faces on each frame and define the labels for each face in each frame. Then obtain the desire output by comparing the extracted face with input video frames. The code for these steps are shown.

```
label_pattern={
    "shah":"Shahrukh Khan",
    "amir":"Amir Khan"
    }
while ret:
    curr_frm=cap.get(1)
    ret, frm=cap.read()
    rest=tst_ima(frm, tr_labl, tr_encode, upsmp_rate)
    labls=map_file_paten_to_labl(labl_paten, rest)
    curr_tim=curr_frm/frmRt
    print("Time: () faces: ()",format(curr_tim, labls))
    if cavwrit:
        cavwrit.writow([curr_tim, labl])
    cv2.imshow('frm', frm)
```

```
key=cv2.waitKey(1) & 0xPP
if key==crd('q'):
    break
if csvfile:
    csvfile.close()
cap.release()
cv2.destroyAllWindow()
```

The same face recognition [13] have been implemented using deep learning model with the help of TensorFlow where the functions are used for face recognition.

7.9   Deep Learning–Based Face Recognition

Initially the required packages are imported for face recognition and initialize them with the structure of the model. The code for these steps are shown below.

```
import cv2
import numpy as np
import os
from random import shuffle
from tqdm import tqdm
from scipy import misc
import tflearn
from tflearn.layers.conv import conv_2d, max_pool_2d
from tflearn.layers.core import input_data, dropout, fully_connected
from tflearn.layers.estimator import regression
import tensorflow as tf
import glob
import matplotlib.pyplot as plt
import dlib
Initialize the variables.
from skimg import io
tf.reset_default_graph()
trn_dir='resize_a/trn'
tst_dir='resize_a/tst'
img_size=200
boxScale=1
```

```
lr=le-3
model_nam='quck.model'.format(LR, '2conv-basic')
```

The function named label_img() have been created for generating a label in the form of array and the function named detect_faces() have been used for identifying the face in an image. The code for these tow function is shown.

```
def labl_img(img):
    wrd=img.split('(')[-2]
    wrd_labl=wrd[0]
    if wrd_labl=='R': return [1,0]
    elif wrd_labl=='A': return [0,1]
def det_faces(img):
    face_det=dlib.get_forntal_face_det()
    det_face=face_det(image, 1)
    face_frm=[(l.left(), l.top(), l.right(), l.bottom()) for l in
    det_faces]
return face_fam
def create_trn_data():
    trn_data=[]
    for img in tqdm(os.listdir(trn_dir)):
        labl=labl_img(img)
        path=os.path.join(trn_dir,img)
        img=misc.imread(path)
        img=cv2.imred(path, cv2.imread_grayscale)
        img=cv2.resiz(img, (img_siz, img_siz))
        det_face=det_face(img)
        for n, face_rect in enum(det_face):
            img=Img.formarray(img).crop(face_rect)
            img=np.array(img)
            img=cv2.resize(img, (img_size, img_size))
    shuffle(trn_data)
np.save('trn_data.npy',trn_data)
return trn_data
```

The function named create_trn_data() have been used for pre-processing and process_tst_data function have been used for test data preprocessing. After training the model, to get a best fit for attaining the desired result, training data will be fitted to a model and finally the prepared test data have been used to get the predicted result. The code for fitting the model and testing the data to obtain the predicted result are shown.

```
def process_tst_data():
    tst_data=[]
    for img in tqdm(os.listdir(tst_dir)):
        path=os.path.join(tst_dir,img)
        imgnum=img.split('.')[-2]
        img_num=get_num(imgnum)
        img=misc.imread(path)
        img=cv2.imread(path,cv2,imread_grayscale)
        img=cv2.resize(img,(img_size,img_size))
        detect_faces=detect_faces(img)
        for n, face_rect in enumerate(detected_faces):
            img=Image.formarray(img).crop(face_rect)
            img=np.array(img)
        img=cv2.resize(img, (img_size, img_size)) tst_data.apnd
        ([np.array(img), img_num])
```

After training the model, the below line of code helps to get the fittest model for obtain a desired result.

```
trn_data=create_trn_data()
trn=trn_data[:-2]
tst=trn_data[-2:]
m=np.array([k[0] for k in trn]).reshape(-1,200,200,1)
m=[k[1] for k in trn]
tst_l=np.array([k for k in tst]).reshape(-1,200,200,1)
tst_m=[k[1] for k in tst]
con=input_data(shape=[None, 200, 200, 1], name='Input')
con=conv_2d(con,4,5,activation='relu')
con=max_pool_2d(con, 5)
con=fully_connected(con,8,activation='relu')
con=dropout(con,0,2)
con=fully_connected(connect,2,activation='softmax')
con=regression(con, optimiz='adam', learn_rate=LR,
    loss='categororical_crossentropy', name='targets')
model.fit({'input':L}, {'targets:M}, n_epoch=1, valid_set=({'input':tst_l},
    {'targets':tst_m}), snapshot_step=500, show_metric=True, run_id=
    model_name
```

Once the model is well trained the below line of code will be used to test and predict the result.

```
tst_data=process_tst_data()
fig=plt.figure()
for num,data in enumerate(tst_data[:12]):
    img_num=data[1]
    img_data=data[0]
    y=fig.add_subplot(3,4,num+1)
    orig=img_data
    data=img_data.reshap(img_size,img_size,1)
    model_out=model.predict([data])[0]
    if np.argmax(model_out)==0:
        str_label='Ronalo'
    elif np.argmax(model_out)==1:
        str_label='amite'
        m.imshow(orig,cmap='gray')
        plt.title(str_labl)
    m.axes.get_laxis().set_visi(False)
    m.axes.get_maxis().set_visi(False)
    plt.show()
```

Next to face recognition transfer learning have been explained with line of code.

7.10   Transfer Learning

It is nothing but gathering a knowledge by solving a particular problem [14] and use the acquired knowledge to solve the other type of associated problem. Here by using Inception model (which is an efficient model for feature extraction), deep neural network will be pre-trained for image classification. In this convolutional neural network have been considered where this is pre-trained on ImageNet will be considered for transfer learning. This network will be used by removing the last fully connected layer for training later will be used on the new dataset. Once after training the weights are fine-tuned using back-propagation. To implement this inception v3 model have to be imported for classifying the images directly. After importing the required library and defining the storage along with other parameters and function of the model to pre-train for classifying an image input. Finally define the model and test it with input. The code for these steps of transfer learning is given below. To compute the transfer value a function called transfer_value_cache have been used and are shown. The Adam optimizer have been used after creating the network to compute the accuracy using TensorFlow. The line of code is given below.

```
%matplotlib inline
import matplotlib.pyplot as plt
import tensorflow as tf
import numpy as np
import os
import inception
incep.dat_dir='D:/'
incept.maybe_download()
model=incep.Incep()
def classify(img_path):
    q=Img.open(img_path)
    q.show()
pred=model.classify(img_path=img_path)
model.print_score(pred=pred, k=10, only_first_name=True)
```

Once after transfer learning, the transfer value have been computed and the line of code is given below.

```
from incep import trans_valu_cache
file_path_cache_trn=os.path.join(cifar10.data_path,'incep_
    cifair10_trn.pkl')
file_path_cache_tst=os.path.join(cifar10.data_path,'incep_
    cifair10_tst.pkl')
print("Computing Inception for training image ...")
img_scaled=img_trn*255.0
trans_valu_trn=trans_valu_cache(cache_path=file_path_
    cache_trn, img=img_scaled, model=model)
print("Computing Inception for test image ...")
img_scaled=img_test*255.0
trn_valu_tst=trans_valu_cache(cache_path=file_pathcache_tst,
    img=img_scaled, model=model)
l_pty=pt.wrap(l)
with pt.defaults_scope(activat_fn=tf.nn.relu):
```

```
m_pred, loss=l_pty.\ fully_connect(size=1024,name='layer_
    fel').\ softmax_clasfy(num_class=num_class, labl=m_true)
glob_stp=tf.vab(initial_value=0, name='global_step', trn=False)
optmz=tf.trn.AdamOpt(learn_rate=le-4).minimize(loss,
    global_step)
m_pred_cls=tf.argmax(m_pred,dim=1)
corect_predict=tf.equal(m_pred_cls, m_true_cls)
accu=tf.reduce_mean(tf.cast(corect_predt, tf.float32)
session=tf.Session()
session.run(tf.glob_variab_initializ())
```

After calculating the transfer value, the model will be trained with batch of input using random_batch() function and the performance of the model are optimized using optimize() function. The code for these steps are shown. After optimization, compute a confusion matrix of the model and predict the image classification using predict_cls() function. The code for this step is shown.

```
def random_btc():
num_img=len(trans_valu_trn)
idx=np.random.choice(num_img, size=trn_batch_size, replace=
    False)
l_btc=trn_valu_trn[idx]
m_btc=labl_trn[idx]
return l_btc,m_btc
def optimiz(num_iterat):
start_tim=tim.tim()
for 1 in range(num_iterat):
l_btc, m_true_btc=random_btc()
fed_dict_trn={l:l_batch, m_true:m_true_btc}
i_global=session.run([global_step,optimiz],fed_dict=fed_dict_trn)
if(i_global %100==0) or (i==num_iterat-1):
    btc_acc=session.run(accuracy, fed_dict=fed_dict_trn)
    msg="Global Step: {0:>6}, Accuracy of Training Batch:
    {1:>6.14}"
    print(msg.format(i_global, btc_acc)
end_tim=tim.tim()
tim_dif=end_tim-start_tim
print("Usage Time:"+str(timedelta(sec=int(round(tim_dif)))))
l_btc=trans_valu_trn[idx]
m_btc=labl_trn[idx]
return l_btc,m_btc
```

Next to this compute the confusion matric and predict the classification with the below line of code.

```
from sklearn.metrics import confusion_matrix
def plot_confu_matx(cls_pred):
    cm=confu_matx(m_true=cls_tst, m_pred=cls_pred)
    for k in range(num_classes):
    class_name="({}) ()".format(k, class_names[k])
    print(cm[k,:], classname)
    class_numbers=["({0})".format(k) for k in range(num_classes)]
    print("".join(class_numbers))
    batch_size=256
    def predict_cls(transfer_values, labels, cls_true):
    num_images=len(transfer_values)
    cls_pred=np.zeros(shape=num_images, dtype=np.int)
        k=0
        while k<num_images:
        n=min(k+batch_size, num_images)
    feed_diet=(l:transfer_values[k:n], mtrue:labels[k,n]}
    cls_pred[k:n]=session.run(m_pred_cls, fed_dict=fed_dict)
    k=n
    correct=(cls_true==cls_pred)
    return correct, cls_pred
```

Finally the by call the helper function to predict the classification and return the predicted class with its transfer value. The performance of the transfer learning model is computed using one of the metric called accuracy of testing and print the result. The code for these steps are shown.

```
def predt_cls_tst():
    return prdt_cls(trnfr_val=trnfr_val_tst, labl=labl_tst, cls_true=
    cls_tst)
def clasfy_accu(correct):
    return correct.mean(), correct.sum()
def print_tst_accu(show_exmp_error=False, show_confu_matx=
    False):
    correct, cls_predt=predt_cls_test()
    acc, num_correct=classify_accuracy(correct)
num_img=len(correct)
msg=" Test-Set Accuracy: {0:.1%} ({1} / {2})"
print(msg.fomt(acc, num_correct, num_images))
```

```
if show_exmp_error:
    print("Sample Error:")
    plot_exmp_error(cls_pred=cls_pred, correct=cprrect)

if show_confu_matx:
    print("Confusion Matx:")
    plot_confu_matx(cls_pred=cls_pred)
from datetime import timedelta
optimize(num_iterat=1000)
print_tst_accu(show_exmp_error=True, show_confu_matx=True)
```

This is how the transfer learning have been performed. Apart from these steps there are some of the built in API's are available face detection and face recognition and will be discussed in next topic.

7.11   API's

An application programming interfaces [15] used for face detection and face recognition are given below. They are PixLab, Truface.ai, Kairos, Microsoft Computer Vision, Face++, LambdaLabs, KeyLemon, PixLab. Some of the leading companies offering face detection, recognition and analysis are, Amazon, Microsoft and IBM. They offer API by Amazon Recognition, API by Azure's Face and API by Watson's Visual Recognition. Amazon Recognition API – It performs Object and scene detection, face analysis, face comparison and face recognition.

Azure Face API – It contains few more API's they are, computer Vision API, content moderation API, Emotion API, Video API, Video API, Video Indexer and Custom Vision Service.

Watson's Visual Recognition API – It determine age and gender of a person, locate the face in an image with bounded box shape, returns the information of a person (celebrity) in an image (will return null when celebrity not detected in an image).

In this chapter, the detailed description have been given on the development of Chatbot's for effective human like communication. A face detection, tracking and recognition and analysis are explained with python code for implementation. As well as the OpenCV based implementation have been illustrated along with deep learning based face recognition using TensorFlow. Finally the transfer learning have been explained using deep neural network along with few API's for face detection, recognition. An advanced and most popular deep learning models will be discussed in upcoming chapters.

References

1. Jose, J., *Introduction to machine learning*, Khanna Book Publishing Co, New Delhi, India, 2020.
2. Theobald, O., *Machine learning for absolute beginners: A plain english introduction*, 2nd edition, Scatterplot Press, United States, 2017.
3. Pradhan, M. and Kumar, U.D., *Machine learning using python*, Wiley, Hoboken, New Jersey, 2020.
4. Shalizi, C., *Advanced data analysis from an elementary point of view*, Cambridge University Press, United Kingdom, 2013.
5. Deng, L. and Yu, D., *Deep learning: Methods and applications*, Now Publishers, Maryland, United States, 2013.
6. Dean, J. and Holzel, U., *Build and train machine learning models on our new Google Cloud TPUs*, Google Blog, Mountain View, California, United States, 2017.
7. Vincent, J., *Google's new machine learning framework is going to put more AI on your phone*, Verge, Washington, District of Columbia, United States, 2017, https://www.theverge.com/2017/5/17/15645908/google-ai-tensorflowlite-machine-learning-announcement-io-2017.
8. TensorFlow, *TensorFlow lite now faster with mobile GPUs (Developer Preview)*, Medium, San Francisco, 2019, https://medium.com/tensorflow/tagged/mobile.
9. Kundu, K., *Google announces edge TPU, Cloud IoT Edge at Cloud Next*, Beebom Blog, Delhi, India, 2018, https://beebom.com/google-announces-edge-tpu-cloud-iot-edge-at-cloud-next-2018/.
10. Barras, J. and Stone, Z., *Cloud TPU machine learning accelerators are now available in beta*, Google Cloud Platform Blog, Moncks Corner, South Carolina, USA, 2018, https://cloud.google.com/blog/products/gcp/cloud-tpu-machine-learning-accelerators-now-available-in-beta.
11. Horace, H., *The state of machine learning frameworks*, The Gradient, Boston, Massachusetts, United States, 2019, https://thegradient.pub/author/horace/.
12. Singh, P. and Manure, A., *Learn TensorFlow 2.0: Implement machine learning and deep learning models with Python*, Apress Publisher, New York, United States, 2019.
13. Rungta, K., *TensorFlow in 1 day: Make your own neural network*, Independently Published, Mumbai, India, 2018.
14. Pattanayak, S., *Pro deep learning with TensorFlow: A mathematical approach to advanced artificial intelligence in Python*, Apress Publisher, New York, United States, 2018.
15. Atienza, R., *Advanced deep learning with TensorFlow 2 and Keras: Apply DL, GANs, VAEs, deep RL, unsupervised learning, object detection and segmentation, and more*, Pack, Publishing Limited, Birmingham, UK, 2020.

8

Advanced Deep Learning

An advanced different models of deep learning algorithm are used frequents. An up-gradation or modifications are possible because of the flexible nature of neural network which lead to design an end to end model. So this advancement allows a researcher to build simple to complex structure based on the need aligned with imagination. Some of the advances deep learning algorithms [1] AlexNet, VGG, NiN, GoogLeNet, ResNet, DenseNet, GRU, LSTM, D-RNN, and Bi-RNN. These advanced deep learning algorithms are discussed in detail along with its code for implementation using pythons Keras library in TensorFlow platform.

8.1 Deep Convolutional Neural Networks (AlexNet)

It holds the structure of convolutional neural network [2] which had a spotlight on image net large-scale visual recognition challenge in 2012. It has eight layers – five layers with max pooling layer and three with fully connected layer. It this Relu activation function have been used in all fully connected layers other than output layer by which the performance of the model is improved six times than before. Which overcome the over fitting by using dropout layer. The architecture of AlexNet is shown in Figure 8.1.

Consider an example of training the model with ImageNet dataset which has millions of images with thousands of classes. To process this input deep model have been introduced where it perform padding to save the feature maps from reducing its size. The representation of layers are shown in Table 8.1 and the code to implementing AlexNet is shown below.

Initially import Keras along with its in-build models and layers. Then import TensorFlow and its layers. Within keras, Sequential model along with its input layers are available. Here one input and output tensor have been utilized for a linear stack of layers. This model will be suitable only for single input and output tensor. Dense layers are used to handle associations

Niha Kamal Basha, Surbhi Bhatia Khan, Abhishek Kumar and Arwa Mashat (eds.) Deep Learning and Its Applications Using Python, (133–166) © 2023 Scrivener Publishing LLC

133

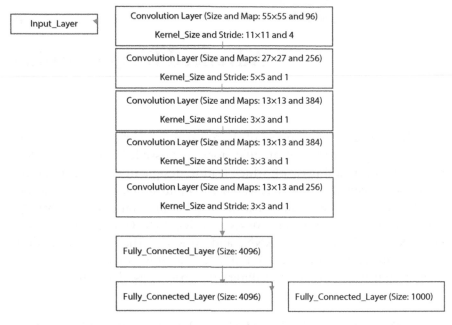

Figure 8.1 Structure of AlexNet.

Table 8.1 Representation of AlexNet layers.

Layer	Size
Input	227×227
Convolution	55×55
Max_Pool	27×27
Con	27×27
Max_Pool	13×13
Con	13×13
Con	13×13
Con	13×13
Max_Pool	6×6
Full_Con	4096
Full_Con	4096
Full_Con	1000

among the input features. Dropout layers are used to reduce the association among the features by eliminating the edges (weights). Flatten layer have been used to reduce the dimension of data to process further. Convolutional layer have been used to classify the features by handling the association among the nearby features. To find the associations among the nearby features filters have been used. Max pooling helps to reduce the parameters and cost of computation. Leaky ReLU activation layer have been used for threshold optimization, which means the value less than zero will be multiplied by fixed scalar layer and then import TensorFlow and its layers.

After creating the model add each layer to it with its parameters. In AlexNet, five convolution layers have been added along with its Batch Normalization and Max Pooling layers and the line of code is given below. From these lines of code, it is observed that it has 96 filter in the first convolutional layer with kernel size (height and width) as 11 and stride as 4 along with an input shape. Here Relu have been used as an activation function throughout all the layers.

```
model = keras.Seq()
model.add(layers.Conv2D(filt=96, krn_size=(11, 11), strid=(4, 4), activ="relu",
    ip_shape=(227, 227, 3)))
model.add(layers.BtcNorm())
model.add(layers.MaxPool2D(pool_size=(3, 3), strid= (2, 2)))
model.add(layers.Conv2D(filt=256, kern_size=(5, 5), strid=(1, 1), activ="relu",
    padd="same"))
model.add(layers.BtcNormaliz())
model.add(layers.MaxPool2D(pool_size=(3, 3), strides=(2, 2)))
model.add(layers.Conv2D(filt=384, kern_size=(3, 3), strid=(1, 1), activ="relu",
    padd="same"))
model.add(layers.BtcNormaliz())
model.add(layers.Conv2D(filt=384, kern_size=(3, 3), strid=(1, 1), activ="relu",
    padding="same"))
model.add(layers.BtcNorm())
model.add(layers.Conv2D(filt=256, kernel_size=(3,3), strid=(1,1), activ="relu",
    padding="same"))
model.add(layers.BtcNorm())
model.add(layers.MaxPool2D(pool_size=(3, 3), strid=(2, 2)))
```

Finally the data features are flattened and processed further using dense and dropout layers to find the desired output by compiling the model. The performance are computed using the metrics and the results are optimized to get a summary of the output. The line of code is shown below.

```
model.add(layers.Flat())
model.add(layers.Dns(4096, activ="relu"))
model.add(layers.Dpout(0.5))
model.add(layers.Dns(10, activ="softmax"))
model.compile(loss='sparse_catego_crossentro', optim=tf.optimizers.
    SGD(lr=0.001), metrics=['accuracy'])
model.summary()
```

The output of AlexNet model have been summarized below in Figure 8.2. Next to AlexNet, a VGG model have been proposed and got a spotlight in ILSVRC 2014 competition which have been described below.

Layer (type)	Output Shape	Param #	
conv2d_23 (Conv2D)	(None, 55, 55, 96)	34944	
batch_normalization_20	Bat (None, 55, 55, 96)	384	chNormalization)
max_pooling2d_12	(MaxPoolin (None, 27, 27, 96)	0	g2D)
conv2d_24 (Conv2D)	None, 27, 27, 256)	614656	
batch_normalization_21	(Bat (None, 27, 27, 256)	1024	chNormalization)
max_pooling2d_13	(MaxPoolin (None, 13, 13, 256)	0	g2D)
conv2d_25 (Conv2D)	(None, 13, 13, 384)	885120	
batch_normalization_22	(Bat (None, 13, 13, 384)	1536	chNormalization)
conv2d_26 (Conv2D)	(None, 13, 13, 384)	1327488	
batch_normalization_23	(Bat (None, 13, 13, 384)	1536	chNormalization)
conv2d_27 (Conv2D)	(None, 13, 13, 256)	884992	
batch_normalization_24	(Bat (None, 13, 13, 256)	1024	chNormalization)
max_pooling2d_14	(MaxPoolin(None, 6, 6, 256)	0	g2D)
flatten_4 (Flatten)	(None, 9216)	0	
dense_8 (Dense)	(None, 4096)	37752832	
dropout_4 (Dropout)	(None, 4096)	0	
dense_9 (Dense)	(None, 10)	40970	

```
Total params: 41,546,506
Trainable params: 41,543,754
Non-trainable params: 2,752
```

Figure 8.2 Output of AlexNet model.

8.2   Networks Using Blocks (VGG)

VGG stands for Visual Geometry Group. It is one of the very deep convolutional neural network for large-scale image recognition [3] which has the pyramidal shape with wide bottom layers and deep top layers. The structure of VGG model is shown in Figure 8.3 which has a convolution layer followed by max pooling layers which are used for narrowing the layers further. The detailed structure of the model are depicted in Table 8.2. The code to implement the VGG model is shown below.

Initially import necessary layers from tensorflow.keras.layers and import Input, Conv2D, MaxPool2D, Flatten, Dense from tensorflow.keras. Then create input variable and assign its shape which will be the first block of VGG model. The line of code is given below.

input = Ip(shape =(224,224,3))

After initialization, create each layers with its parameters such as filter, kernel size, padding, activation function and pooling size for second

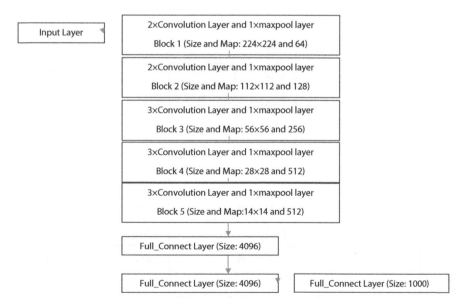

Figure 8.3 Structure of VGG model.

Table 8.2 Representations of VGG layers.

Block	Layer	Size
Input		224×224
Block 1	Con	
	Con	
	Max_Pool	
Block 2	Con	112×112
	Con	
	Max_Pool	
Block 3	Con	56×56
	Con	
	Con	
	Max_Pool	
Block 4	Con	28×28
	Con	
	Con	
	Max_Pool	
Block 5	Con	14×14
	Con	
	Con	
	Max_Pool	
Block 6	Full_Con	4096
	Full_Con	4096
	Full_Con	1000
Output		

convolutional block. Similarly create each layers for third, fourth and fifth (fully connected) block. A line of codes for each blocks are given below.

```
x = Con2D(filt=64,kern_size=3,padd ='same', activ='relu')(input)
x = Con2D(filt =64, kern_size =3, padd ='same', activ='relu')(x)
x = MaxPool2D(pool_size =2, strid =2, padd ='same')(x)
x = Con2D (filt =128, kern_size =3, padd ='same', activ='relu')(x)
x = Con2D (filt =128, kern_size =3, padd ='same', activ='relu')(x)
x = MaxPool2D(pool_size =2, strid =2, padd ='same')(x)

x = Con2D (filt =256, kern_size =3, padd ='same', activ='relu')(x)
x = Con2D (filt =256, kern_size =3, padd ='same', activ='relu')(x)
x = Con2D (filt =256, kern_size =3, padd ='same', activ='relu')(x)
x = MaxPool2D(pool_size =2, strid =2, padd ='same')(x)

x = Con2D (filt =512, kern_size =3, padd ='same', activ='relu')(x)
x = Con2D (filt =512, kern_size =3, padd ='same', activ='relu')(x)
x = Con2D (filt =512, kern_size =3, padd ='same', activ='relu')(x)
x = MaxPool2D(pool_size =2, strid =2, padd ='same')(x)

x = Con2D (filt =512, kern_size =3, padd ='same', activ='relu')(x)
x = Con2D (filt =512, kern_size =3, padd ='same', activ='relu')(x)
x = Con2D (filt =512, kern_size =3, padd ='same', activ='relu')(x)
x = MaxPool2D(pool_size =2, strid =2, padd ='same')(x)
```

After processing the input using all these five blocks of layers, the multidimensional data have been flattened into a single dimensional data using Flatten() function and pass it into a dense layers. Finally an output have been generated in a summarized form.

```
x = Flat()(x)
x = Dns(units = 4096, activ ='relu')(x)
x = Dns(units = 4096, activ ='relu')(x)
output = Dns(units = 1000, activ ='softmax')(x)
model = Mod(ip=ip, op =op)
model.summary()
```

The output of VGG model have been summarized below in Figure 8.4.
Next to VGG, NiN model have been proposed which follow the linear convolutional layer which have been described below.

Layer (type)	Output Shape	Param #
Input_1 (InputLayer)	(None, 224, 224, 3)	0
Conv2d (Conv2D)	(None, 244, 244, 64)	1792
Conv2d_1 (Conv2D)	(None, 224, 224, 64)	36928
Max_pooling2d (MaxPooling2D)	(None, 112, 112, 64)	0
Conv2d_2 (Conv2D)	(None, 112, 112, 128)	73856
Conv2d_3 (Conv2D)	(None, 112, 112, 128)	147584
Max_pooling2d_1 (MaxPooling2D)	(None, 56, 56, 128)	0
Conv2d_4 (Conv2D)	(None, 56, 56, 256)	295168
Conv2d_5 (Conv2D)	(None, 56, 56, 256)	590080
Conv2d_6 (Conv2D)	(None, 56, 56, 256)	590080
Max_pooling2d_2 (MaxPooling2D)	(None, 28, 28, 256)	0
Conv2d_7 (Conv2D)	(None, 28, 28, 512)	1180160
Conv2d_8 (Conv2D)	(None, 28, 28, 512)	2359808
Conv2d_9 (Conv2D)	(None, 28, 28, 512)	2359808
Max_pooling2d_3 (MaxPooling2D)	(None, 14, 14, 512)	0
Conv2d_10 (Conv2D)	(None, 14, 14, 512)	2359808
Conv2d_11 (Conv2D)	(None, 14, 14, 512)	2359808
Conv2d_12 (Conv2D)	(None, 14, 14, 512)	2359808
Max_pooling2d_4 (MaxPooling2D)	(None, 7, 7, 512)	0
flatten (Flatten)	(None, 25088)	0
dense (Dense)	(None, 4096)	102764544
dense_1 (Dense)	(None, 4096)	16781312
dense_2 (Dense)	(None, 1000)	4097000

Total params : 138,357,544
Trainable params : 138,357,544
Non-trainable params : 0

Figure 8.4 Output of VGG model.

8.3   Network in Network (NiN)

It is one of the deep convolutional neural network [4] which got a spot light in the year 2014. This model have a distinguished structure when compared with CNN. It consists of four dimensional tensor of convolutional layers in which two dimensional tensors correspond to input and outputs of fully connected layer. The structure of NiN model have been shown in Figure 8.5 which follows the structure of convolution layer with multilayer perceptron.

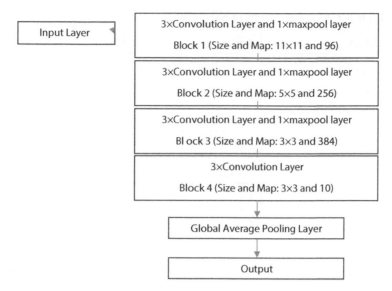

Figure 8.5 Structure of NiN model.

The structure of NiN in Table 8.3 consists of four blocks with three convolutional layer each whose shape of filters are 1××1, 5×5, and 3×3. Along with that each convolution layer followed in the block is followed by one maxpooling layer. Finally, global average pooling layer has been used to handle the over fitting phenomena, which is used often for input spatial translations.

To implement this model initially import TensorFlow with its layers then initialize the model with Sequential() function. After initializing the model, layers for each block have been created with its parameters such as filters, kernels, strides and activation function. Each block consists of three convolution layers and in total four blocks have been created. The line of code for each block is shown below.

```
def NiN():
    model = Seq()
```

Line of code for Block 1

```
model.add(Con2D(filt = 96, kern_size = (11,11), strid = 4, acti
    v = 'relu', ip_shape = (224, 224,3)))
model.add(Con2D(filt = 96, kern_size = (1,1), activ = 'relu')))
model.add(Conv2D(filt = 96, kern_size = (1,1), activ = 'relu'))
model.add(MaxPooling2D(pool_size = (3,3), strid = 2))
```

Table 8.3 Representations of NiN layers.

Block	Layer	Size
Input		11×11
Block 1	Con	
	Con	
	Con	
	Max_Pool	
Block 2	Con	5×5
	Con	
	Con	
	Max_Pool	
Block 3	Con	3×3
	Con	
	Con	
	Max_Pool	
Block 4	Con	3×3
	Con	
	Con	
Global Average Pooling Layer		
Output		

Line of code for Block 2-3 and the parameters sequence for paras variable, which have been assigned with filter and kernel size.

```
paras = [(256, (5,5)), (384, (3,3))]
for n_filt, kern_size in paras:
model.add(Con2D(filt = n_filt, kern_size = kerns_size, padd =
    'valid',activ = 'relu'))
model.add(Con2D(filt = n_filt, kern_size = (1,1), activ = 'relu'))
model.add(Con2D(filt = n_filt, kern_size = (1,1), activ = 'relu'))
```

```
model.add(MaxPool2D(pool_size = (3,3), strid = 2))
model.add(Dpt(0.5))
```

Line of code for Block 4

```
model.add(Con2D(filt = 10, kern_size = (3,3), padd = 'valid',
    activ = 'relu'))
model.add(Con2D(filt = 10, kern_size = (1,1), activ = 'relu'))
model.add(Con2D(filt = 10, kern_size = (1,1), activ = 'relu'))
```

After creating four blocks, global average pooling layer have been created with dense layer and softmax activation function. Finally compile and compute the output summary of NiN model. The line of code have been given below.

```
model.add(GlbAvgPool2D())
model.add(Dns(1000, activ = 'softmax'))
opt = SGD(lr = 0.01)
```

Layer (type)	Output Shape	Param #
conv2d_13 (Conv2D)	(None, 54, 54, 96)	34944
conv2d_14 (Conv2D)	(None, 54, 54, 96)	9312
conv2d_15 (Conv2D)	(None, 54, 54, 96)	9312
max_pooling2d_5 (MaxPooling2	(None, 26, 26, 96)	0
conv2d_16 (Conv2D)	(None, 22, 22, 256)	614656
conv2d_17 (Conv2D)	(None, 22, 22, 256)	65792
conv2d_18 (Conv2D)	(None, 22, 22, 256)	65792
max_pooling2d_6 (MaxPooling2	(None, 10, 10, 256)	0
conv2d_19 (Conv2D)	(None, 8, 8, 384)	885120
conv2d_20 (Conv2D)	(None, 8, 8, 384)	147840
conv2d_21 (Conv2D)	(None, 8, 8, 384)	147840
max_pooling2d_7 (MaxPooling2	(None, 3, 3, 384)	0
dropout_2 (Dropout)	(None, 3, 3, 384)	0
conv2d_22 (Conv2D)	(None, 1, 1, 10)	34570
conv2d_23 (Conv2D)	(None, 1, 1, 10)	110
conv2d_24 (Conv2D)	(None, 1, 1, 10)	110
global_average_pooling2d (Gl	(None, 10)	0
dense_3 (Dense)	(None, 1000)	11000

```
Total params: 2,026,398
Trainable params: 2,026,398
Non-trainable params: 0
```

Figure 8.6 Output of VGG model.

model.compile(loss=categ_crossentropy,opt=opt,metrics   =
    ['accuracy'])
return model

Output of NiN model is given in Figure 8.6.

Next to NiN model, GoogLeNet was proposed and otherwise called as inception v1. The description of this model has been shown below.

8.4 Networks with Parallel Concatenations (GoogLeNet)

GoogLeNet [5] is a 27-layer deep convolutional neural network with inception layers, which have an idea of sparsely connected architecture. This inception layer consists of three convolution layer of different size such as 1×1, 3×3, and 5×5. All these layers are concatenated using the filter to obtain a single output vector which will be an input for next block. Here the use of convolutional layer have been used for dimensionality reduction. While creating new layers in deep learning model an extra focus have to be given during the learning process. Because an appropriate filter size have to fixed for object detection.

The structure of GoogLeNet is depicted in Figure 8.7 and the detailed structure have been shown in Table 8.4.

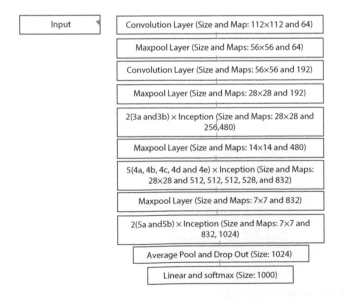

Figure 8.7 Structure of GoogLeNet.

Table 8.4 Representation of GoogLeNet layers.

Layer	Size
Con	122×122
Max_Pool	56×56
Con	56×56
Max_Pool	28×28
Incep (3a)	28×28
Incep (3b)	
Max_Pool	14×14
Incep (3a)	14×14
Incep (3b)	
Incep (3a)	
Incep (3b)	
Incep (3a)	
Max_Pool	7×7
Incep (3b)	7×7
Incep (3b)	
Avg_pool	1024
Drop	
Liner	1000
Soft_max	

To Implement GoogLeNet model import all necessary packages and libraries, such as Keras, TensorFlow, NumPy, cv2, and math module. Then import dataset which have to be used as per the need of user. The line of code to have been shown below.

```
from keras.layers.core import Layer
import keras.backend as K
import tensorflow as tf
from keras.datasets import cifar10
```

```
from keras.models import Model
from keras.layers import Con2D, MaxPool2D, Dropout, Dns,
    Ip, concatenate, GloblAvgPool2D, AvgPool2D, Flat
import cv2
import numpy as np
from keras.datasets import cifar10
from keras import backend as K
from keras.utils import np_utils, import math
from keras.optimizers import SGD
from keras.callbacks import LearnRateSchd
```

Now create a class of nym_classes for defining the dataset and prepare them for training and validation by creating a function.

```
num_classes = 10
def load_cifar10_data(img_rows, img_cols):
(X_trn, Y_trn), (X_vld, Y_vld) = cifar10.load_data()
X_trn = np.array([cv2.resize(img, (img_rows,img_cols)) for img
    in X_trn[:,:,:,:]])
X_vld = np.array([cv2.resize(img, (img_rows,img_cols)) for
    img in X_vld[:,:,:,:]])
```

After preparing the dataset transform them to a Keras compatible format.

```
Y_trn = np_utils.to_categ(Y_trn, num_classes)
Y_vld = np_utils.to_categ(Y_valid, num_classes)
X_trn = X_trn.astype('float32')
X_vld = X_vld.astype('float32')
```

The line of code for preprocessing the data after transformation have been shown below.

```
X_trn = X_trn / 255.0
X_vld = X_vld / 255.0
return X_trn, Y_trn, X_vld, Y_vld
X_trn, y_trn, X_tst, y_tst = load_cifar10_data(224, 224)
```

An inception model have been created along with the three convolution layers of different filter size. The line of code have been shown below.

```
def incep_module(x,
                filt_1x1,
                filt_3x3_reuc,
                filt_3x3,
                filt_5x5_reuc,
                filt_5x5,
                filt_pool_proj,
                name=None):

    con_1x1 = Con2D(filt_1x1, (1, 1), padd='same', activ='relu',
        kern_init=kern_init, bias_init=bias_init)(x)

    con_3x3 = Con2D(filt_3x3_reduc, (1, 1), padd='same', activ='relu',
        kern_init=kern_init, bias_init=bias_init)(x)
    con_3x3 = Con2D(filt_3x3, (3, 3), padd='same', activ='relu',
        kern_init=kern_init, bias_init=bias_init)(con_3x3)

    con_5x5 = Con2D(filt_5x5_reduc, (1, 1), padd='same', activ='relu',
        kern_init=kern_init, bias_init=bias_init)(x)
    con_5x5 = Con2D(filt_5x5, (5, 5), padd='same', activ='relu',
        kern_init=kern_init, bias_init=bias_init)(con_5x5)
```

Along with convolution layer the max pooling layer have been added for dimensionality reduction.

```
    pool_proj = Max_Pool2D((3, 3), strid=(1, 1), padd='same')(x)
    pool_proj = Con2D(filt_pool_proj, (1, 1), padd='same', activ='relu',
        kern_init=kern_init, bias_init=bias_init)(pool_proj)
```

Finally concatenate the processed data to obtain a single output vector and return the output.

```
    op = concat([con_1x1, con_3x3, conv_5x5, pool_proj], axis=3,
        name=name) return op
```

Layer (type)	Output Shape	Param #	Connected to
input_1 (InputLayer)	(None, 224, 224, 3)	0	
conv_1_7x7/2 (Conv2D)	(None, 112, 112, 64)	9472	input_1[0][0]
max_pool_1_3x3/2 (MaxPooling2D)	(None, 56, 56, 64)	0	conv_1_7x7/2[0][0]
norm1 (LRN2D)	(None, 56, 56, 64)	0	max_pool_1_3x3/2[0][0]
dropout_3 (Dropout)	(None, 1024)	0	avg_pool_5_3x3/1[0][0]
dropout_1 (Dropout)	(None, 1024)	0	dense_1[0][0]
dropout_2 (Dropout)	(None, 1024)	0	dense_2[0][0]
output (Dense)	(None, 10)	10250	dropout_3[0][0]
auxilliary_output_1 (Dense)	(None, 10)	10250	dropout_1[0][0]
auxilliary_output_2 (Dense)	(None, 10)	10250	dropout_2[0][0]

Total params: 10,334,030
Trainable params: 10,334,030
Non-trainable params: 0

Figure 8.8 Output of GoogLeNet.

Utilize the above inception function the process the data by calling def incep_module function. The line of code for model summary have been shown below.

```
model.summary()
```

An output summary of GoogLeNet is shown below in Figure 8.8.

Next to GoogLeNet, in 2015 ResNet got a spotlight among researches and are described in the next topic.

8.5   Residual Networks (ResNet)

ResNet is a network used often for deep network creation. In general a normal feed forward network with single layer is sufficient for representation. The problems related to training in previous models are resolved by this ResNet model [6] using Residual block. In this a major role is handled by skip connections. Which connects the required layers to process data by neglecting few layers in between input and output layers using skip connection. While using the skip layer, the output is generated without using the weight and bias of hidden layers.

The structure of ResNet is depicted in Figure 8.9 and its detailed structure of each layer with its size are given in Table 8.5.

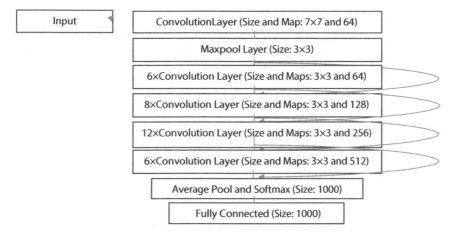

Figure 8.9 Structure of ResNet.

Table 8.5 Representation of ResNet layers.

Layer	Size
Convolution	7×7
Max Pool	3×3
6_Convolution	3×3
8_Convolution	3×3
12_Convolution	3×3
6_Convolution	3×3
Average Pool	1000
Fully Connected	1000

Initially to implement the above model import all necessary layers from Keras such as model, Input, Activation, Conv2D, MaxPooling and add along with plot_model to get an output. The residual module have been projected on the top of the convolutional neural network model. After importing the residual module have been created as residual_module function. The line of code for ResNet module creation is given below.

```
def res_mod(layer_in, n_filt):
        mrg_ip = layer_in
```

```
        if layer_in.shp[-1] != n_filt:
            mrg_ip = Con2D(n_filt, (1,1), padd='same', activ='relu',
                kern_init='he_norm')(layer_in)
    con1 = Con2D(n_filt, (3,3), padd='same', activ='relu',
        kern_init='he_norm')(layer_in)
    con2 = Con2D(n_filt, (3,3), padd='same', activ='linear',
        kern_init='he_norm')(con1)
    layer_op = add([con2, mrg_ip])
    layer_op = Activ('relu')(layer_op)
    return layer_op
```

The model input have been defined and created after creating residual module. Finally, the model have been summarized.

```
visible = Ip(shape=(256, 256, 3))
layer = residual_mod(visible, 64)
model = Mod(ip=visible, op=layer)
model.summary()
```

An output of ResNet model is given in Figure 8.10.

Next to ResNet there comes DenseNet which got a spot lite in the year 2018. It improves the accuracy of deep neural network by overcoming its vanishing gradient problem. The description of this model have been shown below.

```
Layer (type)              Output Shape          Param #    Connected to
=================================================================================
input_1 (InputLayer)      (None, 256, 256, 3)    0

conv2d_2 (Conv2D)         (None, 256, 256, 64)   1792       input_1[0][0]

conv2d_3 (Conv2D)         (None, 256, 256, 64)   36928      conv2d_2[0][0]

conv2d_1 (Conv2D)         (None, 256, 256, 64)   256        input_1[0][0]

add_1 (Add)               (None, 256, 256, 64)   0          conv2d_3[0][0]
                                                            conv2d_1[0][0]

activation_1 (Activation) (None, 256, 256, 64)   0          add_1[0][0]
=================================================================================
Total params: 38,976
Trainable params: 38,976
Non-trainable params: 0
```

Figure 8.10 Output of ResNet.

8.6   Densely Connected Networks (DenseNet)

DensNet is densely connected networks which is similar to ResNet which is used as an additive method whereas DenseNet [7] concatenate outputs with the future layers. The composite function (operation) composed of convolutional layer, pooling layer, batch normalization layer and activation layer (non-linear). This model is divided into four dense block and transition layer with same dimensions and different filter size with in it. The changes in number of filters among the layers changes the dimension of the channel. Transition layer performs batch normalization with the help of down sampling. These layers controls the information flow among the each layer.

The structure of DenseNet is shown in Figure 8.11 and its representation along with size are shown in Table 8.6.

To implement this model, initially import TensorFlow and Keras layers such as Conv2D, Batch normalization, Dense, Average Pooling, Global Average Pooling, and Max Pooling. Then, create a function for DenseNet

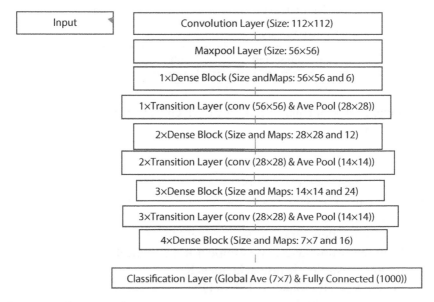

Figure 8.11 Structure of DenseNet.

Table 8.6 Representation of dense layers.

Layer	Size
Convolution	112×112
Max Pool	56×56
1_Dense Block	56×56
1_Convolution	56×56
1_Ave Pool	28×28
2_Dense Block	28×28
1_Convolution	28×28
1_Ave Pool	14×14
3_Dense Block	14×14
1_Convolution	28×28
1_Ave Pool	14×14
4_Dense Block	7×7
Global Average	7×7
Fully Connected	1000

as densenet, batch normalization for bn_rl_conv, transition layer function as transition_layer.

```
import tensorflow as tf
from tensorflow.keras.layers import Ip, Con2D, BtcNom, dns
from tensorflow.keras.layers import AvgPool2D, GlobAvePool2D,
    MaxPool2D
from tensorflow.keras.models import Model
from tensorflow.keras.layers import ReLU, concat
import tensorflow.keras.backend as K
def bn_rl_con(x,filt,kern=1,stri=1):
        x = BtcNom()(x)
        x = ReLU()(x)
        x = Con2D(filt, kern, stri=stri,padd = 'same')(x)
        return x
```

```
def dns_block(x, repet):
        for _ in range(repet):
                y = bn_rl_con(x, 4*filt)
                y = bn_rl_con(y, filt, 3)
                x = concat([y,x])
        return x

def trans_layer(x):
        x = bn_rl_con(x, K.int_shp(x)[-1] //2 )
        x = AvgPool2D(2, stri = 2, padd = 'same')(x)
        return x
```

Create an input and its shape along with its hyper parameters. Define the models input and output and call DenseNet function to process the data. At last summarize this model output.

```
ip = Ip (ip_shp)
x = Con2D(64, 7, stri = 2, padd = 'same')(ip)
x = MaxPool2D(3, stri = 2, padd = 'same')(x)
for repet in [6,12,24,16]:
d = dns_blk(x, repet)
x = trans_layer(d)
x = GlobAvgPool2D()(d)
```

Layers (type)	Output Shape	Param#	Connections
concatenate_56 (Concatenate)	(None,7,7,992)	0	conv2d_117[0][0] concatenate_55[0][0]
batch_normalization_117	(Batchn (None,7,7,992)	3968	concatenate_56[0][0]
re_lu_117 (ReLU)	(None,7,7,992)	0	batch_normalization_117[0][0]
conv2d_118 (Conv2D)	(None,7,7,128)	127104	re_lu_117[0][0]
batch_normalization_118	(BatchN (None,7,7.128)	512	conv2d_118[0][0]
re_lu_118 (ReLU)	(None,7,7,128)	0	batch_normalization_118[0][0]
conv2d_119 (Conv2D)	(None,7,7,32)	36896	re_lu_118[0][0]
concatenate_57 (Concatenate)	(None,1024)	0	conv2d_119[0][0] concatenate_56[0][0]
global_average_pooling2d	(Globa(None,1024)	0	concatenate_57[0][0]
dense (Dense)	(None,3)	3075	global_average_pooling2d[0][0]

```
Total params: 7,046,467
Trainable params: 6,94,995
Non-trainable params: 81,472
```

Figure 8.12 Output of DenseNet.

op = Dns(n_class, activ = 'softmax')(x)
model = Model(ip, op)
return model_ip_shp = 224, 224, 3
n_class = 3model = dnsnet(ip_shpe,n_class)
model.summary()

The last few layers output of DenseNet model is given below in Figure 8.12.

Next to DenseNet, here comes the Gated Recurrent Unit model which is a kind of recurrent neural network. It has been proposed to overcome a vanishing gradient problem and its function have been shown below.

8.7 Gated Recurrent Units (GRU)

GRU consists of gates [8] which controls the flow of data and it's another version of RNN. To transport information hidden states for have been used, which includes two gates they are Reset gate and Update gate. An update gate is the combination of forget gate and input gate. These gates handle which data to add and ignore to the memory. The reset gate process the data to avoid gradient explosion and estimates the loss of data.

The structure of GRU have been shown in Figure 8.13 and the detailed structure with its size are shown in Table 8.7. The number of GRU layers to be use totally depends on the user and the kind of input the model going to handle.

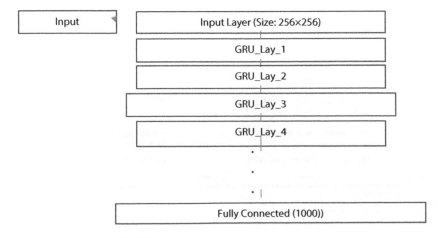

Figure 8.13 Structure of GRU.

Table 8.7 Representation of ResNet layers.

Layer	Size
Int_Lay	256×256
GRU_Lay	56×56
GRU_Lay	56×56
GRU_Lay	56×56
GRU_Lay	28×28
Full_Con	1000

To implement the above model, the below line of code have been used. Initially import all the necessary layers and packages of Keras. Then initialize the data and create a function GRU [9] along with its hyper parameters and have been used when ever needed. At last the models output have been computed and summarized. The line of code have been given below.

```
def get_model(_rnn_nb, _fc_nb):
        spc_srt = Ip((256,256))
        spc_x = spc_srt
for _r in _rnn_nb:
        spc_x = GRU(_r, act='tanh', dpt=dpt_rate,
        rec_dpt=dpt_rate,
        retrn_seq=True)(spc_x)
for _f in _fc_nb:
        spc_x = timedist(dns(_f))(spc_x) spc_x = dpot(dpot_rate)(spc_x)
        spc_x = timedist(dns(10))(spc_x) op = Activ('sigmoid',
            name='strong_op')(spc_x)
_model = model(ip=spc_start, op=out) _model.compile(opti='Adam',
    loss='binary_crossentropy',met = ['accuracy'])
_model.summary()
return _model
rnn_nb = [32, 32]
fc_nb = [32]
dp_rt = 0.5
```

The output of GRU model is given below in Figure 8.14.

```
Layers (type)               Output Shape              Param #
=================================================================
Input_6 (InputLayer)        (None, 256, 256)          0
gru_5 (GRU)                 (None, 256, 32)           27744
gru_6 (GRU)                 (None, 256,32)            6240
time_distributed_10         (TimeDis (None, 256, 32)  1056
dropout_6 (Dropout)         (None, 256, 10)           0
time_distributed_11         (TimeDis (None, 256, 10)  330
strong_out (Activation)     (None, 256, 10)           0
=================================================================
Total parms: 35,370
Trainable params: 35,370
Non-trainable params: 0
```

Figure 8.14 Output of GRU.

Next to GRU, LSTM is called it as long short term memory which is also like GRU, a kind of recurrent neural network and have been described below.

8.8   Long Short-Term Memory (LSTM)

LSTM have an architecture with feedback network which process data and perform the task as same as a Turing machine. This model [10] consists of three gates they are input gate, forget gate and output gate. These gates handle the data by making the cell to remember for an arbitrary time and controls the flow of data in and out of LSTM cell.

The structure of LSTM have been shown in Figure 8.15 and the detailed structure with its size are shown in Table 8.8. The number of LSTM layers to be use totally depends on the user and the kind of input the model going to handle.

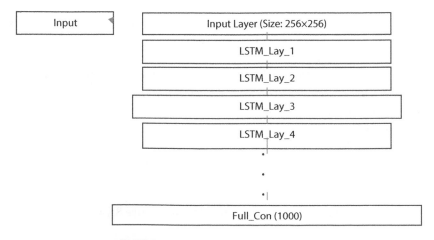

Figure 8.15 Structure of LSTM.

Table 8.8 Representation of ResNet layers.

Layer	Size
Ip_Lay	256×256
LSTM_Lay	56×56
LSTM_Lay	56×56
LSTM_Lay	56×56
LSTM_Lay	28×28
Full_Con	1000

To implement the above model, the below line of code have been used. Initially import all the necessary layers and packages of Keras. Then initialize the data and create a function LSTM along with its hyper parameters and have been used when ever needed. At last the models output have been computed and summarized. The line of code have been given below.

```
def get_mod(_rnn_nb, _fc_nb):
spc_strt = Ip((256,256))
spc_x = spc_strt
for _r in _rnn_nb:
spc_x = LSTM(_r, activ='tanh', dpot=dpot_rate, rec_dpot=dpot_rate, return_
    seq=True)(spc_x)

for _f in _fc_nb:
    spc_x = timedist(Dns(_f))(spc_x)
    spe_x = Drpot(dpot_rate)(spc_x)
spc_x = timedist(Dns(10))(spc_x)
    op = Acti('sigmoid', nam='strng_out')(spc_x)
_model = model(ip=spc_strt, op=out)
    _model.comp(opt='Adam', loss='binary_crossentp',metrc = ['accuracy'])
    _model.summary()
rnn_nb = [32, 32]
fc_nb = [32]
dp_rate = 0.5
```

The output of LSTM model is given below in Figure 8.16.

```
Layers (type)              Output Shape              Param #
==============================================================
Input_4 (InputLayer)       (None, 256, 256)             0
lstm_1 (LSTM)              (None, 256, 32)           36992
lstm_2 (LSTM)              (None, 256,32)             8320
time_distributed_6         (TimeDist (None, 256, 32)  1056
dropout_4 (Dropout)        (None, 256, 32)              0
time_distributed_7         (TimeDist (None, 256, 10)   330
strong_out (Activation)    (None, 256, 10)              0
==============================================================
Total parms: 46,698
Trainable params: 46,698
Non-trainable params: 0
```

Figure 8.16 Output of LSTM.

Next to LSTM, here comes Deep Recurrent Neural Network (DRNN) which is an extension of Recurrent Neural Network (RNN). The description of deep RNN have been given below.

8.9   Deep Recurrent Neural Networks (D-RNN)

It is one of the deep neural network [11] similar to RNN which consists of three layers input layer, hidden layer and output layer. Here an input is processed initially the information related to the hidden state will be shared with next time step and current time step of current layer and next layer respectively. These hidden layers are extended as per the researchers the rest of the working are same as shown in chapter 6. This deep neural network have a different combinations such as deep RNN with LSTM, GRU or vanilla GRU. Here deep RNN with LSTM combination have been used. To implement this deep recurrent neural network, initially import necessary packages. The line of code have been given below.

```
import numpy as np
import tensorflow as tf
from tensorflow import keras
from tensorflow.keras import layers
```

The usage of number of input and output are same whereas the hidden unit have to be specified using any one of the recurrent neural network such as LSTM or GRU.

```
model = keras.seq()
model.add(layer.emb(input_dim=1000, op_dim=64))
model.add(layer.LSTM(128))
```

```
Layer (type)              Output Shape            Param #
=================================================================
embedding (Embedding)     (None, None, 64)        64000

lstm (LSTM)               (None, 128)             98816

dense (Dense)             (None, 10)              1290
=================================================================
Total params: 164,106
Trainable params: 164,106
Non-trainable params: 0
```

Figure 8.17 Output of D-RNN.

```
model.add(layer.dns(10))
model.summary()
```

The output of Deep Recurrent Neural Network is shown below in Figure 8.17.

This model required almost care during initialization and it required sufficient work for proper convergence. Next to deep RNN here come a bi-directional RNN.

8.10   Bidirectional Recurrent Neural Networks (Bi-RNN)

Bidirectional RNN [12] is designed conceptually instead of processing data only in one direction. Here the data have been processed in both direction using two tokens which travel from front to back as well as from back to front. This model possess hidden layer which passes information in backward direction. At each time step the hidden state will determined prior and after by the data. It is similar to the forward and backward algorithms of the probabilistic graphical model. This model will be useful for sequence encoding and to estimate the bidirectional context. Because of its long gradient chain it possess a high training cost. To implement this model initially import all necessary packages, create a function to assign values to its hyperperameter. Here LSTM have been used along with deep RNN. Finally summaries the model output to understand it working.

```
model = keras.Seq()
model.add(
layers.bidir(layers.LSTM(64, return_seq=True), ip_shp=(5, 10)))
model.add(layers.bidir(layers.LSTM(32)))
model.add(layers.dns(10))
model.summary()
```

```
Layer (type)            Output Shape              Param #
===============================================================
bidirectional        (Bidirectional(None, 5, 128)     38400

bidirectional_1      (Bidirection(None, 64)           41216

dense_3 (Dense)             (None, 10)                  650
===============================================================
Total params: 80,266
Trainable params: 80,266
Non-trainable params: 0
```

Figure 8.18 Output of bidirectional RNN.

The output of bidirectional recurrent neural network is given below in Figure 8.18.

These kind of models are mostly used for natural language processing. These kind of models are used in different applications. Next come the machine translation where the end to end learning have been explained.

8.11   Machine Translation and the Dataset

Machine Translation (MT) [13] is nothing but processing sequence of data from one form to another (one language to another language). This was done by a statistical approach before a neural network approach evolves. Nowadays, it is named as neural machine translation, which has been distinguished from the traditional statistical machine translation. It takes very less time to translate very large quantity of text data. Some of them to which MT has been applied are bulletins from intranet, power point presentation, pool of image dataset and so on. Here while processing [14] the data under tokenization, they take infrequent tokens as unknown tokens by alleviating the issues of word level and character level tokenization. Some of the dataset are JW300, DiaBLa, WMT 2014, MLQA, and so on. To download these kind of dataset https://metatext.io/datasets-list/translation-task will be used. In the below code Multi-30k dataset have been used to show the working of Machine translation. Which is a large dataset with matched pictures along with German and English sentences. Also it consists of multilingual-multimodal attributes. Initially import the necessary packages such as TensorFlow. Create a class Multi30k along with its functionalities. Then process the data by training the model for translation. The line of code are given below.

```
class Mul30k(MT):
    urls = ['http://www.quest.dcs.shef.ac.uk/wmt16_files_mmt/training.tar.gz',
```

```
        'http://www.quest.dcs.shef.ac.uk/wmt16_files_mmt/validation.
            tar.gz',
        'http://www.quest.dcs.shef.ac.uk/'
        'wmt17_files_mmt/mmt_task1_test2016.tar.gz']
    nam = 'mul30k'
    dirctnam = "clasmed"
    def splt(cls, exts, fild, root='.data',
            trn='trn', val='val', tst='tst2016', **kwg):
    if 'pat' not in kwg:
            fold = os.pat.join(root, cls.name)
            pat = fold if os.pat.exists(fold) else None
    else:
            pat = kwg['pat']
            del kwg['pat']
    return super(Mul30k, cls).splt(
            exts, fild, pat, root, trn, valid, tst, **kwg)
import tensorflow as tf
def Multi30K(pat):
  data = tf.data.TextLineDataset(pat)
  def con_filt(sour):
    return
tf.logic_not(tf.str.regex_full_match(sour,  '([[:space:]][=])+.+([[:space:]][=])+
    [[:space:]]*'))
  data = data.filt(cont_filt)
  data = data.map(lambda x: tf.strng.splt(x, ' . '))
  data = data.unbatch()
  return data
trn=  Mul30K('http://www.quest.dcs.shef.ac.uk/wmt16_files_mmt/training.
tar.gz')
```

Next to machine translation, sequence to sequence learning will be evolved to solve to challenging tasks handled by MT such as Question Answering, Creating Chatbot, and Text Summarization so on. The detailed description will be given below.

8.12   Sequence to Sequence Learning

Sequence to Sequence Learning [15] was first introduced by google for machine learning. It takes an advantage of deep learning for translating the input. In this process it not only consider the current word but also a neighboring word. Some of the tasks to which sequence to sequence learning will be applicable are, text summarization, conversational models, image captioning and so on. Here an input have been considered as a sequence of words to generate a sequence of output. At each time, it considers two input which will be from user and previous output. At this point two components are important one is encoder and decoder and it is also known as encoder-decoder network. An encoder converts the input into a hidden vector and the decoder takes this hidden vector from its own hidden state and its current input to produce the next hidden vector. At last it predicts its next word in the sequence. LSTM is widely used deep learning model for sequence to sequence learning among researchers. To implement this model initially import all the necessary layers and packages of Keras. Then define the input sequence and its steps to process by setting up an encoder and decoder by training the model. The line of code have been given below.

```
from keras.models import model
from keras.layers import Ip, LSTM, dense

enco_ip = Ip(shape=(None, num_enco_tok))
enco = LSTM(latent_dim, return_stat=True)
enco_op, state_h, stat_c = enco(enco_ip)
enco_stat = [state_h, stat_c]
deco_ip = Input(shape=(None, num_deco_tok))
deco_lstm = LSTM(latent_dim, return_seq=True, return_stat=True)
deco_op, _, _ = deco_lstm(deco_ip,
    init_stat=enco_stat)
deco_dense = dense(num_deco_tok, activation='softmax')
deco_op = deco_dense(deco_op)
```

At this stage the model have been trained for sequence prediction by setting up encoder and decoder parameters.

```
model = model([enco_ip, deco_ip], deco_op)
model.compile(optimizer='rmsprop', loss='categorical_crossentropy')
model.fit([enco_ip_data, deco_ip_data], deco_target_data,
    batch_size=batch_size,
    epoc=epoc,
    vali_split=0.2)
enco_model = model(enco_ip, enco_stat)
deco_stat_ip_h = Ip(shape=(latent_dim,))
```

```
deco_stat_ip_c = Ip(shape=(latent_dim,))
deco_stat_ip = [deco_stat_ip_h, deco_stat_ip_c]
deco_op, stat_h, stat_c = deco_lstm(
   deco_ip, init_stat=deco_stat_ip)
deco_states = [state_h, state_c]
deco_op = deco_dense(deco_op)
deco_model = model(
   [deco_ip] + deco_stat_ip,
   [dec_op] + deco_stat)
def deco_seq(ip_seq):
   stat_val= enco_model.predi(ip_seq)
   targ_seq = np.zeros((1, 1, num_deco_tok))
   targ_seq[0, 0, targ_tok_ind['\t']] = 1.
```

The tokenization have been done at this stage by sampling.

```
stop_con = False
dec_sent = ''
while not stop_con:
   op_tok, h, c = deco_model.predi(
      [targ_seq] + stat_value)
   samp_tok_ind = np.argmax(op_tok[0, -1, :])
   samp_char = reverse_targ_char_ind[samp_tok_ind]
   dec_sent += samp_char
   if (samp_char == '\n' or
      len(dec_sent) > max_dec_seq_leng):
      stop_condition = True
   targ_seq = np.zer((1, 1, num_dec_tok))
   targ_seq[0, 0, samp_tok_ind] = 1.
```

At this stage, the state has to be updated. Here is the line of code for updation.

```
stat_val= [c, h]
return dec_sent
```

The output of the model have been shown below.

```
Input: Hello all.
Decoded: Bonjour a tous.
Input: Good Morning!
Decoded: Bon Matin!
```

This is how a seq. to seq. learning works. In this chapter it is shown clearly that how each and every advanced deep learning models will be working along with its code. Initially it have been started from some of the advances deep learning algorithms such as AlexNet, VGG, NiN, GoogLeNet, ResNet, DenseNet, GRU, LSTM, D-RNN, and Bi-RNN. Apart from these advanced models machine translation as well as sequence to sequence learning have been described along with Keras and TensorFlow platform.

References

1. Tallec, C. and Ollivier, Y., Unbiasing truncated backpropagation through time. *Neural Evol. Comput.,* arXiv, 5, 82–90, 2017.
2. Tang, J. and Wang, K., Personalized top-n sequential recommendation via convolutional sequence embedding. *Proceedings of the Eleventh ACM International Conference on Web Search and Data Mining*, pp. 565–573, 2018.
3. Tay, Y., Dehghani, M., Bahri, D., Metzler, D., Efficient transformers: A survey. *Machine Learning*, arXiv, 9, 67–74, 2009.
4. Teye, M., Azizpour, H., Smith, K., Bayesian uncertainty estimation for batch normalized deep networks. *Machine Learning*, arXiv, 18, 55–64, 2018.
5. Tieleman, T. and Hinton, G., Lecture 6.5-rmsprop: Divide the gradient by a running average of its recent magnitude. *Neural Netw. Mach. Learn.*, 4, 2, 26–31, 2012.
6. Turing, A., Computing machinery and intelligence. *Mind*, 59, 433, 1950.
7. Töscher, A., Jahrer, M., Bell, R.M., The bigchaos solution to the netflix grand prize, in: *Netflix Prize Documentation*, pp. 1–52, 2009.
8. Uijlings, J.R., Van De Sande, K.E., Gevers, T., Smeulders, A.W., Selective search for object recognition. *Int. J. Comput. Vision*, 2, 154–171, 2013.
9. Van Loan, C.F. and Golub, G.H., *Matrix computations*, Johns Hopkins University Press, Baltimore, Maryland, United States, 1983.
10. Vaswani, A., Shazeer, N., Parmar, N., Uszkoreit, J., Jones, L., Gomez, A.N., Polosukhin, I., Attention is all you need. *Adv. Neural Inf. Process. Syst.*, 59, 60–78, 2017.
11. Zaheer, M., Reddi, S., Sachan, D., Kale, S., Kumar, S., Adaptive methods for nonconvex optimization. *Adv. Neural Inf. Process. Syst.*, 9, 98–113, 2018.
12. Zeiler, M.D., Adadelta: An adaptive learning rate method. *Machine Learning*, arXiv, 12, 57–67, 2012.
13. Zhang, A., Tay, Y., Zhang, S., Chan, A., Luu, A.T., Hui, S.C., Fu, J., Beyond fully connected layers with quaternions: Parameterization of hyper complex multiplications with 1/n parameters. *International Conference on Learning Representations*, 2021.

14. Zhu, J.-Y., Park, T., Isola, P., Efros, A.A., Unpaired image-to-image translation using cycle-consistent adversarial networks. *Proceedings of the IEEE International Conference on Computer Vision*, pp. 2223–2232, 2017.

15. Zhu, Y., Kiros, R., Zemel, R., Salakhutdinov, R., Urtasun, R., Torralba, A., Fidler, S., Aligning books and movies: Towards story-like visual explanations by watching movies and reading books. *Proceedings of the IEEE International Conference on Computer Vision*, pp. 19–27, 2015.

Enhanced Convolutional Neural Network

9.1 Introduction

In this chapter, a detailed discussion on enhanced convolutional neural network structure and its application in bio-signal processing have been depicted. As per that a detailed discussion on Absence Seizure Patten Detection using C-GRU-SVM model have been discussed with input as signal are shown along with proofs. Signal processing is about an analysis, synthesis, and modification of signal and is defined as "information about the attributes or behavior of some phenomenon" [1]. For example, detect pattern or informative data in the measured signal. Bio-signal processing is one of the application fields of signal processing. Some of them are Electroencephalography (EEG)—determines the brain activity, Electrocardiogram(ECG)—measures heart activity, Electromyogram (EMG)—determines specific muscle activity, and Electromyogram (EOG)—measures eye movement. The bandwidth and amplitude of each signal [2] varies, and their measurements are depicted in Table 9.1.

All these signals are of very low amplitude. Because of this instrumentation amplifiers are used to obtain a consistent signal with less noise. These signals are contaminated with unwanted signal component. Processing of these signals is tedious for extracting informative data. The general methodology for bio-signal processing to transfer raw data into clinically useful information is shown in Figure 9.1.

To extract clinically useful information, lots of difficulties exist which have to be resolved in the context of data analysis. Many approaches based on machine learning (ML) and deep learning (DL) have been invented to overcome analytical issues. Among bio-electric signals the temporal resolutions of EEG signal are high in the order of milliseconds (ms), which have been taken as input in this research work for bio-signal processing.

Niha Kamal Basha, Surbhi Bhatia Khan, Abhishek Kumar and Arwa Mashat (eds.) Deep Learning and Its Applications Using Python, (167–204) © 2023 Scrivener Publishing LLC

Table 9.1 Measurements of bio-signal.

Source	Amplitude	Bandwidth
EEG	1 mV-5 mV	0.05 Hz-100 Hz
ECG	0.001 mV-0.01 mV	0.5 Hz-40 Hz
EMG	1 mV-10 mV	20 Hz-2000 Hz
EOG	0.01 mV-0.1 mV	dc-10 Hz

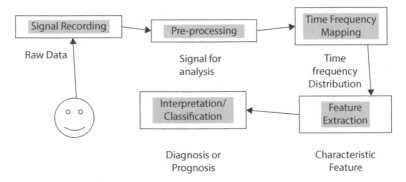

Figure 9.1 General methodology for bio-signal processing.

EEG signal

The recording of electrical activity in the brain is called EEG. The brain contains numerous neurons which communicate/pass information by colliding with each other. This collision generates small amount of electricity and is transient [3]. The normal flow of these electric signals in the brain refers to healthy person and also decides their behavior. So these signals are recorded and analyzed to diagnose different neurological disorders. These signals are non-stationary and their frequency does not have a specific time limit.

In 1929, Hans Berger becomes the first person to measure the EEG signals using EMG machine. These signals are calculated in micro volt and its magnitude is very low. The frequency of these signals varies from person to person. The response time of the EEG signal is rapid and inexpensive when compared with other methods. So this method is used mostly in current research for the analysis of brain activity. The structure of neuron in the human brain is shown in Figure 9.2. The neurons cell body is soma. The chemical messages are received by dendrites which are extended from

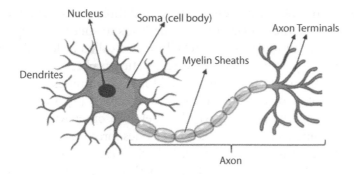

Figure 9.2 Structure of human neuron.

soma. Axon acts as a transmitter to transfer electro-chemical signal from one neuron to another and the myelin sheath acts as an insulator. Axon terminal (bouton) acts as a convertor to pass information from one neuron to another by converting electric signal into chemical signal.

The Structure of human brain is shown in Figure 9.3, which includes two hemispheres left and right. Each hemisphere consists of frontal lobe, temporal lobe, parietal lobe, and occipital lobe.

The front part of the brain consists of frontal lobe which is responsible for logical thinking, higher level cognition and language expression. The cause of damage leads to fear, change in socialization. The middle part of the brain consists of parietal lobe. The damage affects verbal memory, language and controlling eye gaze. It is responsible for transmitting data to the mind through axon by senses like pain, contact and pressure. The rear part of the brain consists of occipital lobe. It transmits information to the brain from the eye. The cause of damage leads to poor eye sight, inability to recognize letters, colors. The back part of the brain consists of temporal lobe

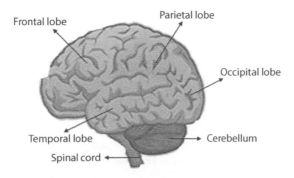

Figure 9.3 Human brain structure with label.

which is responsible for processing the sound through ears and memorizing information. The damage to this part leads to speech perception and inability with communication. Cerebellum also called little brain controls the movements, posture and balance, respiration process.

On the scalp, the electrodes are placed for 20-40 minutes to measure the voltage fluctuation by recording the electrical activity [4]. The neuron with electric charge exchanges ions which repel each other with same charge and form volume conduction. These electrodes force the ions which create voltage difference which when recorded with respect to time gives EEG signal. Figure 9.4 shows the raw EEG signal with time on the x-axis and frequency on the y-axis.

While recording, some unwanted signals are generated along with EEG signal with respect to time, which are known as artifacts. There are two types of artifacts, namely the ones that occur due to the motion of human body and the other ones due to the defects in EEG machine. These artifacts are removed with different existing feature reduction techniques. By removing artifacts, different wave forms are extracted from an EEG signal and its features are shown in Table 9.2.

These five sub-bands are obtained by decomposing EEG signal and represented in both time and frequency domain in Figure 9.5 and Figure 9.6. For clinical EEG recording, 10-20 system electrodes are recommended for electroencephalography and clinical Neurophysiology by International Federation of Society. This system is based on the electrode position and the area of the brain [5]. The 10/20 refers to the actual distance between the positions of electrodes. These measurements start at one ear and end at the other. The location of the electrode is identified with the help of the letters

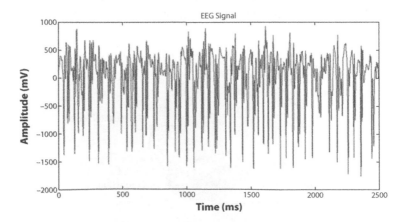

Figure 9.4 Raw EEG signal (x axis represents time and y axis represents frequency).

Table 9.2 EEG wave forms and its features.

EEG rhythm					
Features/ Types	**Delta**	**Theta**	**Alpha**	**Beta**	**Gamma**
Frequency	Up to 4 Hz	4 – 8 Hz	8 – 13 Hz	13 - 30 Hz	Above 30 Hz
Amplitude	20 μv – 200 μv	More than 20 μv	30 – 50 μv	5 – 30 μv	Less than 5 μv
State of mind	Unconscious	Unconscious	Conscious	Conscious	Unconscious
Analysis type	PCA	LDA	CCA	BSS/Static modeling	Inverse solution/ CSP
Function	Instinct	Emotion	Conscious	Thought	Will

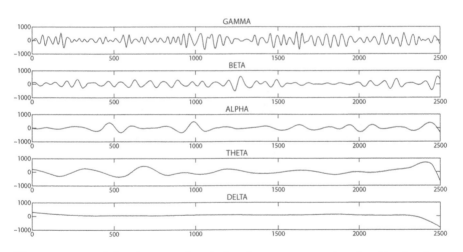

Figure 9.5 Five sub-bands in time domain (x axis represents sample points (time) and y axis represents amplitude).

Fp, F, T, P, O, C, stand for pre-frontal, frontal, temporal, parietal, occipital, and central.

The numeric representation of the electrodes is used to differentiate electrode position. The even numbers 2,4,6,8 refer to the right side and the odd numbers 1,3,5,7 refer to the left side of the head. The schematic illustration of 10/20 system is shown in Figure 9.7. The instrumentation of EEG is based on cutoff frequency of low pass filter with 75 Hz. These

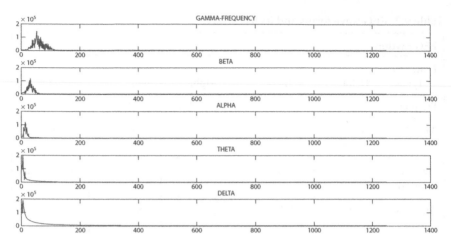

Figure 9.6 Five sub-bands of EEG in frequency domain (x axis represents sample points (time) and y axis represents magnitude).

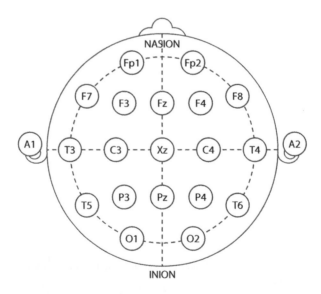

Figure 9.7 Placement of electrode of human scalp.

datasets are further analyzed to extract informative features. For this deep analysis transformation techniques are used [6]. Apart from this technique there are some other methods involved in pattern detection. They are preprocessing or data cleaning, data projection, argumentation or reduction, validation, using prior knowledge, and interpretation of data. Also, Biosignals can be analyzed using regression, classification, clustering, etc.

In this research work, the complexity of extracting features from input is a challenging task which made automatic EEG analysis difficult. To overcome automatic feature extraction the advanced machine learning and deep learning algorithms are used by adjusting their criteria at each step iteratively on certain task or group of tasks with respect to time. Apart from this, lack of adequate amount of data is a great challenge and it has been resolved using augmentation techniques.

Augmentation

Data augmentation deals with expanding virtual dataset derived from collected or recorded bio-signals which decrease the data collection time. Bio-signals shows time and amplitude variations. These time and amplitude axes are shifted to generate augmented data. Because of augmentation the performance of the model is good even with small dataset. Some of the data augmentations are shifting all time data (All-Shift), amplifying all time data (All-Amp), shifting near-peak data (Peak-Shift), and amplifying near peak data (Peak-Amp).

All types of bio-signals which are analyzed in time domain can make use of this augmentation technique to populate dataset. From this populated dataset, informative features are obtained using extraction techniques. Some of the existing techniques are Fourier Transform (FT), Wavelet Transform (WT), Continuous Wavelet Transform (CWT), Discrete Wavelet Transform (DWT), and Short Time Fourier Transform (STFT). These types of transformation techniques can be applied for bio-signals (which are uncertain and their frequencies change rapidly). In this research work the populated data have been processed using Machine Learning and Deep Learning techniques to extract the discriminative features and classify those features to detect the absence seizure subject. ML and DL are a part of Artificial Intelligence (AI) techniques [7] which have an ability to learn by themselves and adapt themselves to the given task. Nowadays, most common applications of bio-signals in clinical research [8] are used for monitoring or care taking of patients. Different algorithms of AI have been applied in this work.

In early days, it was difficult to study bio-electric signals, but now a days these problems have been solved by many hardware devices which are available at low cost. Even then there is a need for technical improvements to process bio-electric signals. Enormous effort has been taken in this research area. The combination of multiple techniques has been used to create a hybrid model for extracting features and classification.

The processing of bio-signals is essential for disease diagnosis, monitoring and care tacking of patients. Other than clinical application these signals can be used by patients to express their thoughts or physical activities in the form of Brain Computer Interface (BCI) or Human Computer Interface (HCI). These are the typical communication technologies which recognize user's command through activity or thought in the form of bio-signals.

Here, the work has been limited to pre-processing, channel selection, augmentation, extracting features, classification and analysis of non-invasive EEG signal for absence seizure detection. Among epilepsy, one of the seizure types is absence seizure which is likely to occur among four to fourteen year old. The electrical activity (intense and abnormal) in the brain leads to absence seizure is shown in Figure 9.8.

A spike and wave pattern of frequency is of three hertz with few seconds to minutes long. This pattern can be found in a pre-frontal and frontal region, which starts around four hertz per second and slows down to three point five hertz and three hertz per second, and eventually to two point five hertz and two hertz per second. In traditional medicine for analysis and diagnosis of seizures, the counting of seizure frequency was in practice. But in the modern medicine this process becomes rather difficult and leads to many observational errors. Only clinicians with prior knowledge can handle these signals for diagnosis. Along with this, monitoring patients in the absence of clinical boundary by using modern portable devices are in practice. But this method has not helped to record the satisfactory level of signals as found from clinical set-up also the availability of absence seizure data is less also learning techniques have not been used for automatic absence seizure feature extraction and classification. So in this research

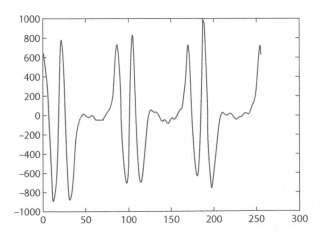

Figure 9.8 Absence seizure EEG signal (x axis represent time and y axis represent frequency).

work a deep learning based automated detection system has been used for absence seizure feature extraction and classification.

Now a days, recording bio-signal has become easy with the help of hardware and software techniques. But it is not easy to find the abnormality by seeing the recorded signal with the naked eye and also it depends on the quantity of data. Hence these signals have to be studied to extract the hidden information. In this research the main concern is about detecting hidden patterns and classifying them (based on the application) and this is challenging with bio-signals.

The research work focuses on three things. The first is to select the pre-processing strategy for artifact removal and channel selection for absence seizure pattern detection with minimal pre-processing time of input without data loss. The second is to formulate an input with respect to deep learning model by augmenting data to obtain an adequate amount of input for training. Finally, to design task specific deep learning model for automatic feature extraction and classification of input signal to detect the hidden pattern.

In the process of designing deep learning based absence seizure pattern detection model, EEG signal pre-processing, augmenting and formulating input are the important tasks for feature extraction and classification. The input data have been collected in the form of EEG signal from Vel's Neuro Center, Chennai, India, belonging to 51 subjects, recorded using RMS acquisition head box with RMS acquisition and RMS analysis modules for visualization, with the help of an experienced neurologist.

The research work primarily focuses on pre-processing and channel selection for formulating input which will be suitable for deep learning model. For this the single channel (FP1-F7) absence seizure data have been considered from the pre-frontal region of brain where the occurrence of absence seizure is clear and justified by evaluating the input signal among the channels of pre-frontal region. In order to collect artifact free signal, a no-cleaning pre-processing strategy has been adopted on absence seizure data to make input more suitable for deep learning model.

The major problem in this research work is the inadequate absence seizure input data where the collected input from different subjects is insufficient to train deep learning model. So, it has been solved by augmenting input based on window size and stride, which is a deep learning based augmentation technique. Also, the characteristics of input have been discussed with inference using boxplot.

In the later part of this research, the formulated input data have been used for extracting and classifying features using the proposed deep learning model (C-GRU-SVM model) and compared with the existing traditional models (CNN and RNN). Also, these models are evaluated using precision (P), recall (R), accuracy, and F1 metrics. Based on the calculated accuracy value the proposed model out performs the traditional model. Finally, the proposed model is statistically justified by p-value to differentiate the proposed model from the other two models.

In this research, the work starts with a review on pre-processing EEG signals and channel selection, augmenting and formulating input signal for feature extraction and classification of absence seizure to overcome the research gaps by developing a task specific deep learning model. A human brain's structure, organization, generation of EEG signal and recording methodologies of EEG signal have been discussed. The rest of topic are set out as follows: a literature survey brief's the existing works based on pre-processing strategy, input formulation and deep learning model for extracting features and classification. 9.2 Describes the architecture and presents an overview on the proposed model. 9.3 Explains the pre-processing and channel selection for input formulation. 9.4 Explains argumentation process to populate the input signal and formulate the input by analysis of the characteristics of input signals. 9.5 Provides an empirical study on feature extraction techniques to extract the hidden absence seizure pattern and describes the classification techniques and in 9.6 the performance of absence seizure subject identification by evaluating using the appropriate metrics and statistical analysis are discussed. Also, this topic explains the parameters, decision functions and comparison with the previous models on absence seizure detection. Finally, overall conclusion with few constraints and insights for future work are presented.

In this research work a specific type of seizure called absence seizure has been studied to detect its pattern among normal and abnormal subjects input data.

Seizure - Seizure [9] is an electrical disturbance that occurs due to the abnormal electrical firing of neurons during communication. Doctors classify seizure as absence seizures (petit mal), tonic-clonic seizures (grand mal), atonic seizures (drop attacks), clonic seizures, tonic seizures, myoclonic seizures. In this research work absence seizure is focused upon. Absence seizure occurs with sudden loss of consciousness (stare straight, stop specking, stop moving, does not answer to questions) for 30 seconds or less than 30 seconds. It is rarely noticed because of short duration. The three types of time domain EEG signal are shown in Figure 9.9.

A subject can have 50 to 100 seizures per day which can be unnoticed. Once the occurrence of absence seizure is reduced/ends, the subject goes back to his normal state and he/she is unaware of it. This seizure occurs at any age but most often it outbreaks during early age (childhood) that too between 4 and 15 years.

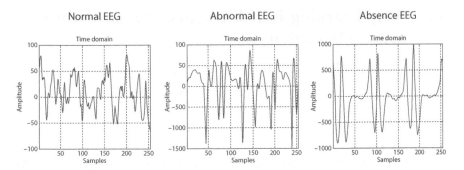

Figure 9.9 EEG signal of normal, abnormal and absence in time domain.

A child with repeated or untreated absence seizure is likely to have serious issues like less concentration, interruption in conversation and lags in participation of day to day routine. An occurrence of absence seizure has been diagnosed by the doctors with medical history of an affected subject, full physical screening, and routine blood test to differentiate from common illness. If all these are normal, then they move on to EEG test, in which the electrical activity has been converted to a printed format. From that report the doctors diagnose absence seizure with specific pattern [10] of 3 Hz (spick and wave pattern).

In some cases doctors opt for other tests like MRI (Magnetic Resonance Imaging) and CT (Computed Tomography) scan. The reasons for other diagnosis tests are:

(i)   Prolonged seizures
(ii) An unusual pattern
(iii) The physical or neurological examination to find an abnormality
(iv) A condition of child at higher risk of seizures, such as birth trauma, head injury, encephalitis, meningitis.

Once the reason for seizure is found, doctors treat the subjects with medication [11]. Absence seizure cannot be prevented but it can be controlled by medicine and most children suffer in their teen age. Lots of researchers are working on seizure domain with different objectives. In this research work the absence seizure pattern have been detected with data collected from a hospital. This contribution may act as an aid for diagnosis. A deep learning based absence seizure detection model has been analyzed using an evaluation metrics. The next topic provides the details of the proposed work for absence seizure detection.

9.2   Deep Learning-Based Architecture for Absence Seizure Detection

The detailed survey on preprocessing, augmentation, feature extraction and classification based on absence seizure detection having been explained in the previous topic, indicates the need for deep learning in seizure detection. Hence the deep learning based absence seizure detection has been proposed. This topic describes the three stages of modules with task specific architecture, which includes pre-processing, formulating input with augmentation and deep learning based feature extraction and classification. Also, the details of input recording based on clinical set-up have been discussed at the end of this topic. The proposed model for absence seizure detection is based on deep learning approach and is explained in detail in the following section.

The proposed absence seizure detection architecture is shown in Figure 9.10. It consists of three modules, namely pre-processing and channel selection module, input formulation and augmentation module, and deep learning model for extracting features and classification module.

Pre-processing and channel selection - The first module is pre-processing and channel selection. In this module the recorded input signal is pre-processed by selecting the pre-processing strategy. In general pre-processing strategy is categorized into three: they are manual pre-processing strategy, automatic pre-processing strategy and no-removal strategy. Among this manual pre-processing and automatic pre-processing strategy are the most frequently used. Apart from this, no-removal strategy is adapted now a days and this has used in this research work. The input

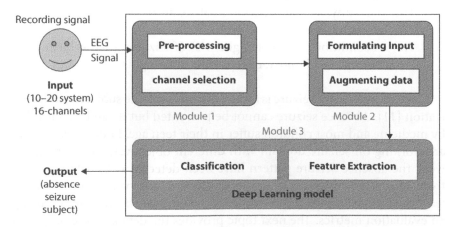

Figure 9.10 Deep learning based absence seizure detection architecture.

signals are taken for channel selection process, where the single channel (FP1-F7) from the pre-frontal region has been chosen based on 10-20 EEG recording standards. Also, it has been used in the previous studies. The selected FP1-F7 channel input signals are evaluated based on performance metrics. The output from this module has been taken as input for the next layer for input formulation.

Input formulation and augmentation - The second module is input formulation and augmentation for deep learning module. In general, input formulation is categorized into image, calculated features, and signal value. Among these types, the signal value has been categorized as averaged value, raw signal, and CVT, where the raw signal has been chosen while formulating input for deep learning based absence seizure detection module and this type has not been used much, in-terms of absence seizure detection. From this input formulation the deep learning model has been trained for absence seizure detection. Here, the major problem is inadequate amount of data so that augmentation based on window size and stride can be used to populate the input data.

Deep learning model for extracting features and classification - The third module consists of deep learning model, where extracting features and classification goes hand-in-hand. The extracted features have been classified using GRU classifier based on three classes, namely normal, abnormal, and absence seizure. At the end of the model, SVM acts as a decision function to decide which segment belongs to which class. A deep learning based absence seizure detection work flow is shown in Figure 9.11. All this input EEG signal processing is done after an efficient EEG recording method. Matlab platform and different python and deep learning packages have been used for further processing of the recorded signals to identify the category of the subject. The signal pattern that is saved is exported to excel which will obviously perform as a database. Then these data are imported in Matlab platform for the forthcoming processes such as channel selection, augmentation input formulation and, feature extraction as well as classification. The specifications of the system and necessary software for the proposed signal processing model are given below:

CPU Core – 4
CPU Speed – 1.9 to 2.5 GHz
Memory – 4 GB
Free Hard Disk space – at least with minimum 25 GB.
OS used – Windows 10.
Desktop Environment – Matlab (R2014a)
Library files – Python, matplotlib, Numpy, Scipy, Pandas, Keras.

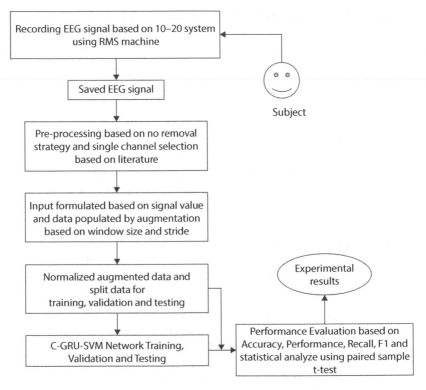

Figure 9.11 Deep learning based absence seizure detection work flow.

The collected input signals have been used for absence seizure detection by the proposed deep learning based C-GRU-SVM model. Then the results have been compared with the existing traditional model and the performance has been evaluated. Also, the proposed model has been statistically evaluated are explained in detail in the forthcoming topics.

9.3   EEG Signal Pre-Processing Strategy and Channel Selection

In general, the recorded EEG signal is pre-processed to remove artifacts and based on this the work they have been categorized into three. They are manual artifact removal strategy, no-removal artifact strategy and automatic artifact removal strategy. After this strategy selection the input is further processed for channel selection. This topic explains in detail the steps involved in pre-processing and channel selection.

Pre-processing and channel selection - In this research work no-removal strategy has adopted, where deep learning is capable of handling such input signal without any prior knowledge. Also, by adopting this strategy, the informative loss of the signal has been prevented. Even there will not be much artifact in this input signal, because the RMS machine has an advantage of filtering unwanted portions of the signal while converting recorded analog signal to digital signal. So this is also a reason for the selection of no-removal strategy.

Apart from this pre-processing, channel selection plays an important role where this step contributes to cut down the processing time by selecting the specific channel from the pre-frontal region of human brain for absence seizure detection. Most of this kind of research has been based on rat model. Also, some researchers adopted this technique for human channel selection. A better performance based on electrodes for the occurrence of absence seizure pattern was found by Eline *et al.*, in general for the channels in the frontal region when compared with the other regions. The best overall performance was found in FP1-F7 channel based on 10-20 EEG recording standards by Duun *et al.*

An absence seizure subject's input signals have been evaluated based on a literature by selecting the input signal from the FP1-F7 channel. This combination of electrodes has been chosen by fixing the montage as BP longitudinal 1(R) in this work. Each single channel from absence seizure and normal subjects has been processed using Wavelet Transform (WT) for feature extraction. Processing includes filtering as well as segmenting the input signal. The detailed description of justifying the single channel input being sufficient for absence seizure detection has been given below with experimental results. Figure 9.12 depicts the working of module one with respect to pre-processing and channel selection.

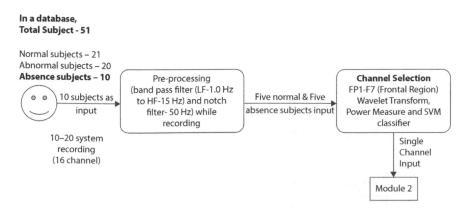

Figure 9.12 Working of first module for pre-processing and channel selection.

Single channel selection for absence seizure detection - The scalp EEG inputs of 5 absence seizure subjects and 5 normal subjects have been taken from the collected 51 subjects' data which include both female and male recordings of 4 subjects and 6 subjects each with the age in between 6 and 13 years. The required information of the subjects are displayed in Table 9.3.

Each subject underwent 30 minutes recording with total duration of 5 hours (300 minutes) containing 180 absence seizures. In general the occurrence of absence seizure lasts for less than or equal to 30 seconds with 3 Hz (i.e., 3 spikes and waves) per second. For this recording the electrodes are placed on the scalp based on 10-20 international system and 16 channels, which have been recorded with the sampling frequency, band pass filter and notch filter of 256 Hz, 1.0 Hz to 15 Hz and 50 Hz. Among these 16 channels, FP1-F3, FP1-F7, FP2-F8, and FP2-F4 channels from frontal region have been considered for channel selection in absence seizure detection process. The Fp1-F7 channel input is shown in Figure 9.13.

In this module of the research an absence seizure input has been given most importance compared with the normal input, their figures and their measurements are discussed below. The input has been segmented further by considering the seizure and non-seizure portions with 1 second (256 samples) each. Further, these inputs are processed by calculating features and classification before the performance is calculated. In feature calculation the power value of each segment has been found using the Wavelet

Table 9.3 Information of absence and normal subject.

Subject	Age	Gender	Category
Subject 2	9	Female	Normal
Subject 4	7	Male	Normal
Subject 6	6	Female	Absence
Subject 7	8	Female	Normal
Subject 9	5	Male	Normal
Subject 10	9	Male	Absence
Subject 12	6	Male	Normal
Subject 14	8	Female	Absence
Subject 18	9	Male	Absence
Subject 22	13	Male	Absence

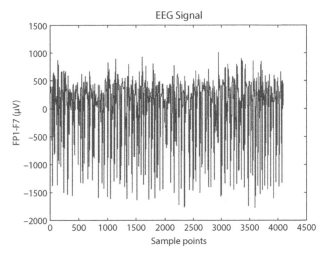

Figure 9.13 Absence seizure EEG input of FP1-F7 channel.

Transform (WT). It uses the mother wavelet, which scaled and shifted in time to decompose the signal into sub-bands with different frequency.

The WT has been utilized using high-pass and low-pass filters by the chosen mother wavelet. It decomposes signal into low frequency bands and high frequency bands. For each level, the wavelet transform's low frequency band is further decomposed into a high and low frequency band, which are shown in Figure 9.14 and its mother wavelet is formulated in Eq. 9.1.

$$\Psi_{a,b}(t) = \frac{1}{\sqrt{mod\ a}}\ \Psi\ \frac{(t-b)}{a} \tag{9.1}$$

where, Ψ - mother wavelet
    a - scaling parameter
    b - shifting parameter

In this work based on decomposition level and frequency band, db8 has been chosen for decomposition. After decomposition, power measure of each segment has been calculated using the formula in Eq. 9.2.

$$P = \frac{1}{N}\sum_{n-0}^{N-1}x^2[n] \tag{9.2}$$

where x[n] is an input sequence of EEG signal.
    P is the power measure

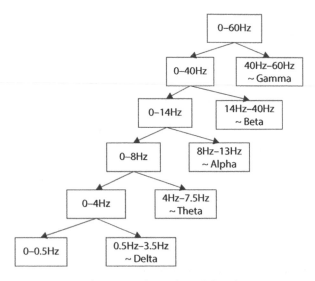

Figure 9.14 Decomposition of EEG signal into five sub-bands.

Each segment has been decomposed into five sub-bands and the feature value has been calculated. Then the extracted feature values have been used for absence seizure classification using Support Vector Machine (SVM). In this work, all these processes are followed by Chen *et al.* [12]. Here by considering the segmented input with sample size of 256 has been decomposed into five sub-bands by applying db8 wavelet. The segmented input signal is depicted in Figure 9.15.

The input segments decomposed into five sub-bands based on time domain and frequency domain are depicted in Figure 9.16 and Figure 9.17.

The power measure has been calculated for absence seizure subjects after decomposition using wavelet. In general, increase in amplitude have been observed during absence seizure and it has been inferred that the normal subjects have less power than absence subject. Also, depending on the electrode positions the amplitude increases from 15 µV to 200 µV. The power measures of a segment from pre-frontal region are tabulated in Table 9.4. Also, the power measures of the normal and absence seizure subjects are shown in Table 9.5.

Similar to the above power measures the overall segments are processed to extract the power feature. The power measures among four channels from pre-frontal regions with most likely values from FP1-F7 channel sub-bands are shown in Figure 9.18. Later these features have been used to classify based on two classes using SVM classifier as normal and absence input. With the help of SVM_Seizure class, the SVM algorithm has been trained. Here

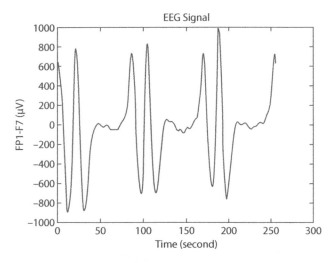

Figure 9.15 Absence seizure EEG segment of FP1-F7 channel.

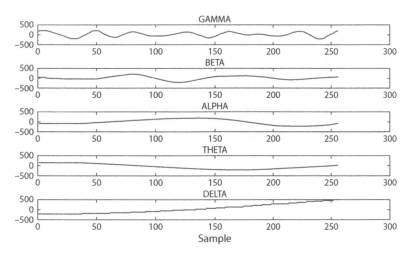

Figure 9.16 Five sub-bands of EEG segment in time domain. Here the y-axis of each band represents amplitude (μV) of the sub-bands.

the decision boundaries are moved to calculate the error rate on the data and this linearly separable SVM always achieves zero training error. The decision boundary's perpendicular distance from the origin is -theta/|w|, where theta is the threshold and w is the weight vector.

By this linear classifier the extracted features have been classified and are depicted in Figure 9.19.

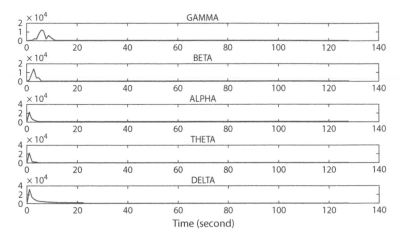

Figure 9.17 Five sub-bands of EEG segment in frequency domain. Here the y-axis of each band represents magnitude (dB) of the sub-bands.

Table 9.4 Power measure of a single absence seizure EEG segment.

FP1-F7 channel from pre-frontal region	Frequency sub-bands	Power measure	Total power measure
	Alpha	624.50	28300.69
	Beta	12668.77	
	Delta	3548.49	
	Gamma	10122.86	
	Theta	1336.07	

Table 9.5 Power measure of absence seizure subject and normal subject.

Subject/Feature	Power
Subject 1 (normal)	39866.48
Subject 2 (normal)	39505.17
Subject 3 (abnormal)	106092.09
Subject 4 (abnormal)	128775.95

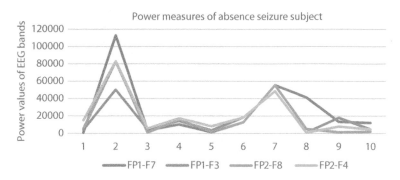

Figure 9.18 Absence seizure subject's four channels power measures of sub-bands for ten segments.

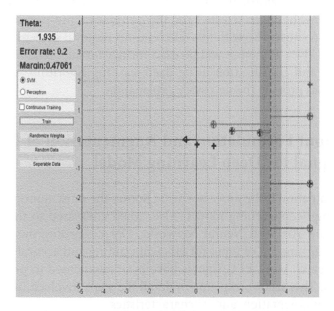

Figure 9.19 Classification output of normal and absence subject.

The SVM has been evaluated using performance metrics such as sensitivity and False Detection Rate (FDR). The formulas for these metrics are given in Eq. 9.3 and Eq. 9.4. The calculated values are tabulated in Table 9.6.

$$\text{Sensitivity} = T_p \,/\, T_p + T_n \tag{9.3}$$

$$\text{FDR} = \frac{F_p}{F_p + T_p} (4.4) \tag{9.4}$$

Table 9.6 Performance of absence seizure detection.

Channel	Sensitivity	FDR
FP1-F7	99	0.2
FP1-F3	93.7	1.4
FP2-F8	96.4	0.6
FP2-F4	97.3	1

This work has achieved comparatively similar outcome of the work of J. Dun *et al.*, and it is justified to be the same as the occurrence of absence seizures overall performance is found in FP1-F7 channel. In this topic the single channel has been selected and the no-removal pre-processing strategy has been chosen. So with this outcome, no-removal strategy based single channel (FP1-F7) input will be used further for augmentation, feature extraction, and classification using deep learning algorithm and the following topics provide the necessary explanation.

9.4   Input Formulation and Augmentation of EEG Signal for Deep Learning Model

Input formulation is the process which chooses the most appropriate input for training deep learning model. Also, when compared to the machine learning and Artificial Neural Networks, Deep Learning models are in need of large amount of input for efficient training and accurate result. So in this research work EEG signals have been augmented to populate the input data. This section explains in detail the steps involved in input formulation, augmentation, and its characteristics.

Input formulation - In terms of deep learning, input formulation for EEG signal has been classified into three groups; they are 1] extracted features, 2] images, and 3] signal as input for deep learning model. The signal value approach is same as an extracted features, which deal with time domain feature such as feature like power spectral density and Complex Value Transformation (CVT), along with the frequency domain features as used by Houtan *et al.* [13]. Also, the neural network has been used by Mengni *et al.* [14], with promised automatic feature extraction on seizure detection based on end-to-end learning of large amount of data.

When it comes to absence seizure detection, the signal as input has not been considered much while formulating input. This signal value has been categorized into averaged value, CVT and raw signal. So in this research the raw signal has been taken as input for training deep learning model. The no-removal pre-processing strategy is also a reason for selecting input category as raw signal. The database has a collection of three classes recording with 21 normal subjects, 20 abnormal subjects, and 10 absence subjects. Among those subjects the best 30 single channel (i.e. FP1-F7) recordings (i.e. instances) have been chosen from each class with duration as 30 sec and are tabulated below in Table 9.7.

Because of the less number of instances (90 instance), deep learning algorithms are not in need. But in the perspective of selected pre-processing strategy and input formulation, there is a need for deep leaning. So, to get an efficient training, augmentation has been performed to populate the data.

Augmentation of EEG signal - A strategy known as augmentation that helps the researchers in populating the amount of data rather than spending time in the collection of new data for the purpose of getting trained. In terms of processing signal, augmentation of input has generally been carried out on the basis of technique called the sliding window. During this process the incorporation of concept called stride (where the window is moving forward) also with the size of window known as deep learning that is used and is the same as Ihsan *et al.* Before augmenting the input, there are instances that are 90 in number which is denoted as that is insufficient for getting trained with deep learning model. Hence before the process of augmentation, the data has to be divided into training as well as test set as 90% , 10% of the total signal. The training set is used for augmenting, which is again further used to train deep learning model. Mathematically as Aya *et al.*, work [15], the window processes the data by dividing them with equal size into segments, where each segment consists of n samples. This method is being used in this research for populating the input data.

Prior augmentation have been displayed in Figure 9.20 and Figure 9.21. The clarity of instance is very well more than sufficient in training deep learning model and are displayed in Figure 9.22.

Characteristics of input data - The inputs of three classes are analyzed [16] using three statistical attributes. They are max, standard deviation, and skewness. To calculate these values and also to train deep learning model, the values are normalized using min-max normalization and are formulated in Eq. 9.5.

$$Feature_{norm} = \frac{Feature_{value} - Min_{value}}{Max_{value} - Min_{value}} \tag{9.5}$$

where Feature norm is the normalized value of the feature

Feature value, Max value, and Min value represent actual value

Table 9.7 Details of normal, abnormal and absence subject for augmentation.

Subject	Category	Instance with duration of 30 sec
Subject 1	Abnormal	2
Subject 2	Normal	2
Subject 3	Abnormal	1
Subject 4	Normal	1
Subject 5	Abnormal	2
Subject 6	Absence	3
Subject 7	Normal	2
Subject 8	Abnormal	1
Subject 9	Normal	2
Subject 10	Absence	3
Subject 11	Abnormal	1
Subject 12	Normal	2
Subject 13	Abnormal	1
Subject 14	Absence	3
Subject 15	Normal	2
Subject 16	Normal	2
Subject 17	Abnormal	2
Subject 18	Absence	3
Subject 19	Normal	2
Subject 20	Abnormal	2
Subject 21	Normal	2
Subject 22	Absence	3
Subject 23	Abnormal	2
Subject 24	Normal	2

(Continued)

Table 9.7 Details of normal, abnormal and absence subject for augmentation. (*Continued*)

Subject	Category	Instance with duration of 30 sec
Subject 25	Absence	3
Subject 26	Abnormal	2
Subject 27	Normal	2
Subject 28	Normal	1
Subject 29	Normal	2
Subject 30	Abnormal	2
Subject 31	Normal	1
Subject 32	Abnormal	1
Subject 33	Normal	1
Subject 34	Absence	3
Subject 35	Abnormal	1
Subject 36	Abnormal	1
Subject 37	Absence	3
Subject 38	Normal	1
Subject 39	Abnormal	1
Subject 40	Normal	1
Subject 41	Abnormal	2
Subject 42	Absence	3
Subject 43	Normal	1
Subject 44	Abnormal	1
Subject 45	Normal	1
Subject 46	Absence	3
Subject 47	Abnormal	1
Subject 48	Normal	1

(*Continued*)

Table 9.7 Details of normal, abnormal and absence subject for augmentation. (*Continued*)

Subject	Category	Instance with duration of 30 sec
Subject 49	Abnormal	1
Subject 50	Normal	1
Subject 51	Abnormal	1

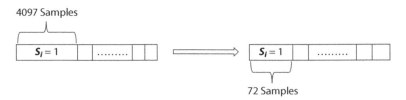

Figure 9.20 This shows the augmentation of a single channel instance.

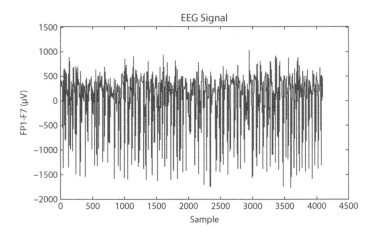

Figure 9.21 Single instance input before augmentation.

The attributes are statistically evaluated after normalization. The variations in the values of EEG signals for normal, abnormal and absence seizure condition are clearly visible with maximum and standard deviation value. The amplitude is the measure of signal value and it is large during absence seizure activity which is self-explanatory, represented with maximum value as shown in Figure 9.23.

The signals during absence seizure activity show more deviation as compared to normal and abnormal conditions are represented with standard

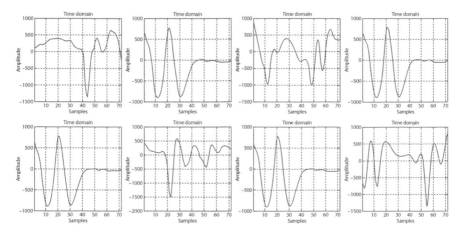

Figure 9.22 This shows the augmented initial eight segments of single instances.

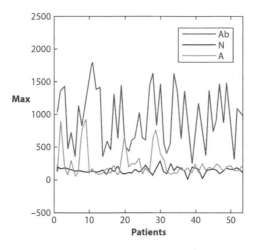

Figure 9.23 Maximum value of the signal of subjects in various stages. (Ab—absence, N—normal, A—abnormal).

deviation values and are formulated in Eq. 9.6, which defines the dispersion of set of values from its mean being shown in Figure 9.24.

$$\sigma = \sqrt{\frac{1}{N}\sum_{i=1}^{N}(x_i - \mu)^2} \tag{9.6}$$

where μ is the mean

σ is a standard deviation

x_i is the input

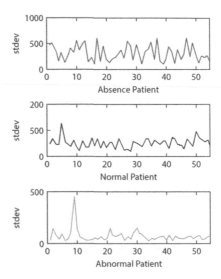

Figure 9.24 Standard deviation of the signal of subjects in various stages. (Ab—absence, N—normal, A—abnormal).

The box-plots are employed in order to graphically present the statistical parameters of a distribution without making any assumptions among three classes. This plots the mean value clearly which indicate the overlapping values for three different classes of EEG signals being given in Figure 9.25 and are formulated in Eq. 9.7.

$$\text{Mean} = \frac{1}{N}\sum_{n=1}^{N} x_i\,(n) \qquad (9.7)$$

where n is the number of value
$\quad x_i$ is the data set value

The skew value defines an asymmetry of probability function and it is the standardized moment, which infers that healthy subject has lower imbalance than abnormal subject being shown in Figure 9.26, where the values associated with the abnormal EEG overlaps with the absence state and normal state of EEG signals and are formulated in Eq. 9.8.

$$\gamma_1 = \frac{\mu_3}{(\delta)^3} \qquad (9.8)$$

where δ is a standard deviation
$\quad \mu_3$ is a third moment

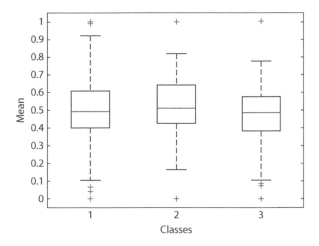

Figure 9.25 Box plot of mean function for three different classes (1—absence, 2—abnormal, 3—normal).

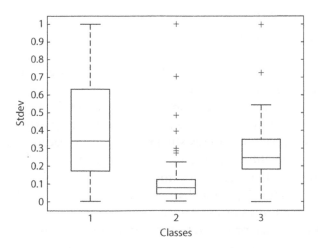

Figure 9.26 Box plot of standard deviation function for three different classes (1—absence, 2—abnormal, 3—normal).

Finally the standard deviation is shown in Figure 9.27 where abnormal state is large as compared to normal and absence state.

In this topic the characterization of three classes has been observed from the box plot. Also to formulate the input, among the three approaches signal value as input has been chosen for formulation. Then those signal values have been augmented further for feature extraction and classification.

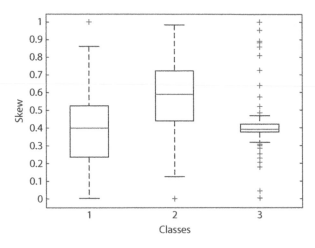

Figure 9.27 Box plot of skewness function for three different classes (1—absence, 2—abnormal, 3—normal).

9.5 Deep Learning Based Feature Extraction and Classification

Feature extraction is a strategy for selecting an appropriate pattern or most relevant feature from raw signal or data. Those extracted features are known as feature vector. These features are very important for the performance of the classifier and they have been used for classifying extracted features among different classes. In the existing research work feature extraction and classification were different processes but the deep learning-based research [17] performed both processes together. Based on this CNN and GRU have been used with same input for absence seizure detection. It follows the traditional steps to processes the data as explained in the literature. This section explains in detail proposed feature extraction and classification.

Feature Extraction - In terms of bio-signal processing, handcrafted feature extraction methods have been used and they are based on time domain, frequency domain and time-frequency domain. Features extracted [18] from these domains are grouped into statistical features, fractal dimension features, entropy features, and spectral features. These features has been extracted to detect the seizure pattern using classifiers in the existing work.

Based on the demand of the research the most frequently used Convolutional Neural Network (CNN) has been selected for feature extraction. Convolutional layer has been used in this work for the purpose of analyzing of the data pertaining to time-series with a use of fixed length. It consists of multiple convolution kernels (filters) in the same layer with same size. The mathematical formulation of convolutional layer is given in Eq. 9.9. The pictorial representation of convolution layer along with input and output layers has been shown in Figure 9.28.

$$b_k = \sum_{n=0}^{N-1} a_n h_{k-n} \tag{9.9}$$

where a is an input in the form of vector
    b is an output in the form of vector
    N denotes amount of elements in a
    h is a function of activation
    k and n are the input vector elements

In this work of research, the layer of convolution is taken for feature extraction. The augmented input has been considered as input to train the network. The learning input as feature vector, output is as feature map, kernels as filters and are shown in Figure 9.29. The features have been extracted using the different convolution kernels based on the above process and a few outputs of the convolution layer has been displayed in time

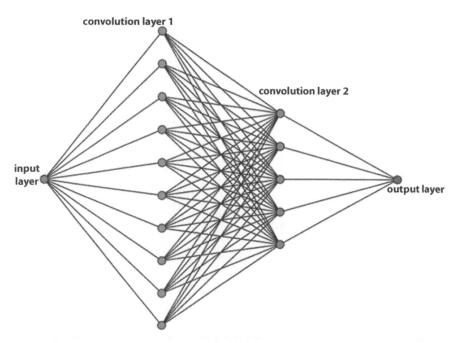

Figure 9.28 Two convolution layers with input and output layers.

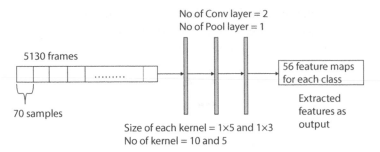

Figure 9.29 This shows the process of feature extraction along with parameters.

and frequency domain in Figure 9.30. The schematics of the convolution layer are displayed in Table 9.8.

Feature Classification - The feature extraction and classification [19] are two different processes. With the help of deep learning technique in this work, the single model is used for both the purposes and are shown in Figure 9.31.

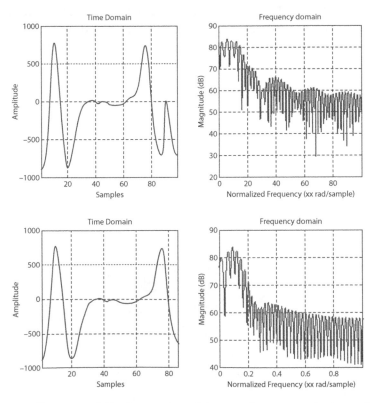

Figure 9.30 Shows convolution layer output of absence seizure pattern in time and frequency domain.

Table 9.8 Schematics of convolution layer.

Layer (type)	Output	Parameter
Input	(None,70,3)	0
Con_0	(None,68,3)	270
Con_1	(None,66,3)	910
Max_pool	(None,56,3)	0

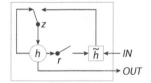

Figure 9.31 Structure of GRU.

The working of GRU-SVM is shown in Figure 9.32 and the decision function is formulated as shown in Eq. 9.10.

$$f(x) = \sin(wx + b) \qquad (9.10)$$

where x is the input
b is the bias.

Here the GRU solves the "vanishing" or "exploding" gradient problems and the SVM provide a stable results and trains faster, while softmax recalculates and includes the influence of other classes while making decision. In this topic, feature extraction and classification [20] have been carried out as a single process using the proposed C-GRU-SVM deep learning model.

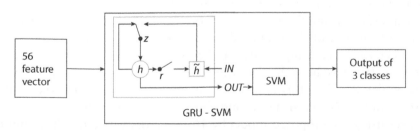

Figure 9.32 Working of GRU-SVM.

The features have been extracted based on the frequency component of the augmented input by using the convolution layer and those extracted feature maps have been classified using GRU-SVM. This proposed model has been analyzed by comparing it with the existing CNN and GRU deep learning models which are explained in-detail in the next topic.

9.6   Performance Analysis

The absence seizure pattern has been detected using the proposed C-GRU-SVM deep learning model with input as raw EEG to obtain an output of three categories, namely normal, abnormal, and absence classes by classification. From the literature it was observed that most of the work was done by pre-processing [21] the input for feature extraction and classification. But with the help of deep learning models the proposed work has been done without preprocessing an input for feature extraction and classification. Also, in this work, the two distinct works (feature extraction and classification) have been combined to detect an absence seizure pattern. In this topic, the result of the proposed work have been compared with those of the existing CNN and GRU deep learning models which have been discussed in detail with the performance metrics.

Confusion Matrix - A confusion matrix is a classification evaluator which has been widely used by the researchers. But it is not a metric; it describes the performance of a model with tabular visualization of test data with known true values. The row and the column in a tabular visualization [22] represent the instances of predicted class and actual class. In that table, True Positive (TP) belongs to the class and is correctly classified. True Negative (TN) does not belong to class and it is correctly classified. Misclassified cases include False Positive (FP) and False Negative (FN). FP, which does not belong to class but is classified by the classifier as positive (i.e., belongs to a class). FN, which belongs to the class but is classified by the classifier as negative (i.e., does not belong to a class). Apart from confusion matrices, the most used evaluation metrics for classification model are Accuracy, Precision, Recall, and F1 Score. With the help of these metrics, the performance of the proposed modal along with the CNN and GRU has been evaluated using the five-fold cross validation [23]. The 30 signals of each class have been divided into 20% for testing and 80% for training the model. Based on this evaluation we obtain a confusion matrix for the proposed C-GRU-SVM model and the accuracies are validated for three classes using the proposed model by 10-fold cross validation. The confusion matrices have been used to compute the performance metrics for the

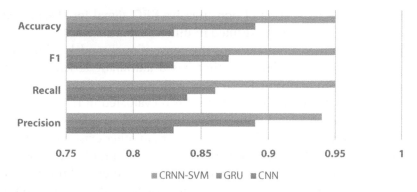

Figure 9.33 Performance of the classifiers.

proposed C-GRU-SVM model as well as GRU and CNN models and the values are depicted in Figure 9.33.

In this topic, with the help of statistical analysis (p-value) [24] it has been observed that the proposed C-GRU-SVM model is different from the other two classification models and the proposed model has been found to outperform the other two conventional models with 95% accuracy. Thus in this work, the performance of the classifier has been analyzed using performance metrics as well as tested with statistical analysis.

A novel idea has been presented in this research for the better detection of absence seizure. Decades ago it was difficult to study bio-electric signals but now a days these problems have been solved by technological improvements and many hardware devices. Even then lots of research is needed to process bio-electric signals. Enormous efforts have been taken in this research area. The combination of multiple techniques has been used for extracting features and classification. The processing of bio-signals is essential for disease diagnosis or monitoring or care tacking of patients.

9.7   Summary

In early day's medicine, seizures frequencies were counted for diagnosis and analysis. This process is tedious and generates many observational errors. For diagnosis only experienced clinicians can handle these signals. But now a days, taking care of patients out of medical set-up with the help of portable EEG recording systems is in practice which has not helped to record the satisfactory level of signals as found from clinical set-up. This task has been made easy with an automatic detection model. This work has focused on pre-processing (channel selection), augmentation, feature extraction, and classification of non-invasive EEG signal for absence sei-zure detection and has been executed in different levels.

The proposed model outperforms the conventional models. Thus from the proposed work, the deep learning based automatic absence seizure detection has been performed well even with no-removal pre-processing strategy. Finally, the proposed work has been evaluated in terms of accu-racy and has been validated statistically using paired sample t-test. Hence, the C-GRU-SVM model has better accuracy than other existing model. In this research work the major constraint has been found to be collecting real time data from the patients. As this requires an expertise knowledge of machinery, it is genuinely a difficult task to collect the data similar to that one's collected using medical machinery. To tackle this constraint the data have been collected from a neuroclinic database with the proper guidance of clinicians. This constrain could be addressed with a real time data accu-mulation process.

Further, this research work has classified normal, abnormal, and absence seizure subjects using the proposed task specific deep learning model that is useful for non-clinicians. Apart from these classes other seizure types could be included in an input and the proposed model could be used to classify and verify the results. This research work has used combinations of layers from CNN, GRU deep learning algorithm, and SVM machine learn-ing algorithm for absence seizure detection with normal, abnormal, and absence seizure data. Other algorithms could be applied for absence seizure detection and classification. Also, in this research work, with respect to the parameters of performance analysis paramount importance has been given to the accuracy of classification. Other parameters could be considered, and the proposed model could be analyzed to verify with results.

References

1. Rabbi, A.F. and Rezai, R.F., A fuzzy logic system for seizure onset detection in intracranial EEG. *Comput. Intell. Neurosci.*, 10, 1–13, 2012.
2. Gotman, J., Automatic recognition of epileptic seizure in the EEG. *Electroencephalogr. Clin. Neurophysiol.*, 54, 5, 530, 1982.
3. Walter, C., Cierniak, G., Gerjets, P., Rosenstiel, W., Bogdan, M., Classifying mental states with machine learning algorithms using alpha activity decline. *European Symposium on Artificial Neural Networks, Computational Intelligence and Machine Learning*, pp. 405–410, 2011.
4. Siuly, Li, Y., Wen, P., Clustering technique-based least square support vector machine for EEG signal classification. *Comput. Methods Programs Biomed. Elsevier Sci.*, 104, 3, 358–372, 2008.

5. Velu, P.D. and de Sa, V.R., Single-trial classification of gait and point movement preparation from human EEG. *Front. Neurosci.*, 7, 84, 2013.
6. Johal, P.K. and Jain, N., Artifact removal from EEG: A comparison of techniques, in: *Proceedings of International Conference on Electrical, Electronics,
   and Optimization Techniques*, Chennai, Indian, 2016.
7. Urigüen, J.A. and Garciazapirain, B., EEG artifact removal - state-of-the-art
   and guidelines. *J. Neural Eng.*, 3, 3–12, 2015.
8. Teplan, M., Fundamentals of EEG measurement. *Meas. Sci. Rev.*, 2, 2, 1–11, 2002.
9. Delorme, A., Sejnowski, T., Makeig, S., Enhanced detection of artifacts in
   EEG data using higher-order statistics and independent component analysis.
   J. Neural Eng., 9, 16–26, 2019.
10. Kline, J.E., Huang, H.J., Snyder, K.L., Ferris, D.P., Isolating gait-related move-
    ment artifacts in electroencephalography during human walking. *J. Neural
    Eng.*, 12, 741–1751, 2015.
11. Nathan, K. and Contreras-Vidal, J.L., Negligible motion artifacts in scalp
    electroencephalography (EEG) during treadmill walking. *Front. Hum.
    Neurosci.*, 9, 1–12, 2016.
12. Kilicarslan, A., Grossman R, G., Contreras-Vidal, J.L., A robust adaptive
    denoising framework for real-time artifact removal in scalp EEG measure-
    ments. *J. Neural Eng.*, 3, 13, 13–23, 2016.
13. Flumeri, G.D., Aricó, P., Borghini, G., Colosimo, A., Babiloni, F., A new
    regression-based method for the eye blinks artifacts correction in the EEG
    Signal, without using any EOG channel, in: *Proceedings of the 2016 38th
    Annual International Conference of the IEEE Engineering in Medicine and
    Biology Society (EMBC)*, Orlando, FL, USA, pp. 16–20, 2016.
14. Mahajan, R. and Morshed, B.I., Unsupervised eye blink artifact denois-
    ing of EEG data with modified multiscale sample entropy, kurtosis, and
    wavelet-ICA. *IEEE*, 19, 158–165, 2015.
15. Albuja, A.C. and Murphy, P.B., *Absence Seizure*, StatPearls Publishing, Treasure
    Island (FL), 2020.
16. Chavez, M., Grosselin, F., Bussalb, A., Fallani, F.D.V., Navarro-Sune, X.,
    Surrogate-based artifact removal from single channel EEG. *IEEE Trans.
    Neural Syst. Rehabil. Eng.*, 26, 540–550, 2018.
17. Somers, B., Francart, T., Bertrand, A., A generic EEG artifact removal algo-
    rithm based on the multi-channel Wiener filter. *J. Neural Eng.*, 15, 36–47,
    2018.
18. Basha, N.K. and Wahab, A.B., Single channel EEG signal for automatic
    detection of absence seizure using convolutional neural network. *Recent Adv.
    Comput. Sci. Commun. (Formerly: Recent Pat. Comput. Sci.)*, 13, 21–30, 2020.
19. Basha, N.K. and Wahab, A.B., Automatic absence seizure detection and early
    detection system using CRNN-SVM. *Int. J. Reasoning based Intell. Syst.*, 11,
    4–12, 2019. Inderscience.
20. Basha, N.K. and Wahab, A.B., Wavelet-based convolutional recurrent neural
    network for the automatic detection of absence seizure, in: *Lecture Notes in*

Computational Vision and Biomechanics, vol. 30, Springer, Berlin, Germany, 2018.

21. Basha, N.K. and Wahab, A.B., Analysis of single channel EEG features for epilepsy detection. *Int. J. Pure Appl. Math.*, 20, 118–128, 2018.
22. Basha, N.K. and Wahab, A.B., Brain signal processing: Technologies, analysis and application. *IEEE Conference*, 2016.
23. Basha, N.K. and Wahab, A.B., *Deep learning algorithms for a spike and wave pattern detection using electroencephalography (EEG) signal*, A Hand Book on Intelligent Health Care Analytics, Wiley-Scrivener, Hoboken, New Jersey, U.S, 2021.
24. Basha, N.K. and A.B. Wahab, System and method for the detection of absence seizure. IN Patent 202041047632, 2021.

10

Conclusion

10.1 Introduction

In this chapter, a detailed discussion of new trends in deep learning, challenges in its direction, and prospects along with a practical case study are shown with working proofs. Some of the notable works highlighted in this chapter are given below from different domains, such as semantic intelligence, quantum AI, deep learning in cyber security domain, working of the LAMSTAR system, epilepsy seizure onset prediction, image processing for cancer detection, processing images from 2D images to 3D, image analysis for scene classification, fingerprint recognition, face recognition, butterfly species classification, leaf classification, traffic sign recognition, data classification from transcribed spoken conversation, speech recognition, music genre classification, credit card fraud detection, test drills to predict where to drill for oil, prediction of forest fires, price movement prediction in market microstructure and finally fault diagnosis via acoustic emission.

10.2 Future Research Direction and Prospects

Semantic Intelligence
A key topic in computer science is semantics, which offers a set of guidelines for deciphering various data kinds and enabling machines to comprehend the relationships and meanings of data. The immense volumes of data produced by the current world, including online data, databases, emails, images, videos, satellites, sensors, and smartphones, are dealt with by real semantic AI.

Classic primitive types and non-primitive composite data types are the two categories into which data types in programming are split. Character, integer, floating point, fixed point, Boolean, and reference are examples of traditional primitive types. Non-primitive types include string, arrays, objects, and classes, or data structures [1]. The meaning of a data type, its

Niha Kamal Basha, Surbhi Bhatia Khan, Abhishek Kumar and Arwa Mashat (eds.) Deep Learning and Its Applications Using Python, (205–238) © 2023 Scrivener Publishing LLC

syntactic operations that can be applied to it, and the methods by which values or instructions of that kind can be stored are all defined by its semantics. A data type tells the compiler or interpreter how to use the data and gives a set of values from which an expression may derive its values.

AI virtually expands the reach and size of semantic data analytics to include all conceivable data types, data models, and data structures [2]. Semantic analysis is the automatic discovery of data relationships through the use of computer algorithms processing the data for discovery and invention, learning, insights and knowledge, predictions and forecasting, causal regularities and classifications into different categories, decision-making and problem-solving, and informed actions. Semantic analysis is referred to as Integrated Machine Intelligence and Learning (IMIL) in real AI, ML, and DL.

Applying pattern-matching string-searching methods to locate regular expressions is a part of syntactic analysis in the IMIL. Various text editors, word processors, search engines, text processing tools, and libraries for many programming languages all integrate it in their search functionality. When comparing results to a search query, lexical search engines could only examine the precise wording of the search phrase.

Semantic AI in business intelligence focuses on both numerical and unstructured data. Unstructured data is either poorly organized or lacks a pre-defined data model. Books, journals, articles, metadata, medical records, music, video, analogue data, photographs, files, e-mails, Web pages, and word processing documents are examples of unstructured data. By 2025, there will be 163 zettabytes of data in the world, and enterprises may have more than 70% to 80% of their data that is unstructured. Building global data types frameworks as master algorithms to effectively process any unstructured data is the goal of real AI, ML, and DL semantics.

In conclusion, semantics is a crucial area of research in computer science that offers the guidelines for deciphering various data kinds, enabling computers to comprehend the significance of individual pieces of data and the links between them. Real semantic AI uses computer algorithms to automatically find data relationships while working with enormous amounts of data, including unstructured data. Applying pattern-matching string-searching methods to locate regular expressions is a step in the syntactic analysis process. Building global data types frameworks as master algorithms to effectively process any unstructured data is the goal of real AI, ML, and DL semantics.

Semantic search: The perfect search engine should understand precisely and exactly what you mean to return precisely and exactly what you want.

In the web search, semantics relates to the relationships between a search query, the words and phrases related to it, and content on webpages.

Knowledge Graph:
The Knowledge Graph is supposed to "represent things, not strings", a "graph"—that understands real-world entities and their relationships to one another. It is realized as a database of facts about things in the world and the relationships between them.

Hummingbird and Rank Brain search algorithms:
Now, search algorithms may incorporate semantic search principles when ranking content. Google uses a machine-learning system called "RankBrain" to help sort through its search results.

Semantic web SE: Semantic query, from Wiki article
The semantic web [3] technology stack of the W3C is offering SPARQL to formulate semantic queries in a syntax similar to SQL. Semantic queries are used in triplestores, graph databases, semantic wikis, natural language and AI systems. The semantic AI model, promising to fuse Machine Learning and Knowledge Graphs, combining some methods, techniques and algorithms derived from symbolic AI and statistical AI. Last, not least. data is subjected to all sorts and kinds of treatment, as pictured below, except its prime operation and basic processing, deep understanding of data semantics.

Conceptual Abstraction and Learning by Analogy
The human abilities to learn, reason, and adapt the knowledge to altogether innovative fields are what defines as Conceptual abstraction and analogy-making aspects. Although there has been significant information and research on developing these AI systems with such abilities, still no AI system can actually compete of formulating decisions or analogies abstraction as close to humans be in machine to humanoid construction, robots or any other entity [4].

The problem is that for current AI systems like Deep Learning needs training on many instances. This does not comply with the concept of abstraction, rather it justifies when machine will learn on a very small number of examples.

The interesting topic gaining attractiveness is Abstraction and Reasoning Corpus (ARC), a rather difficult learning aspect with few-shot learning task built around "core knowledge" that humans are essentially born with [5].

Quantum AI

In order to create quantum algorithms for AI tasks, the discipline of quantum artificial intelligence (QAI) combines quantum computing and artificial intelligence (AI). Subatomic particles are used in quantum computing to carry out calculations, and it makes advantage of the superposition and entanglement principles to carry out some operations more quickly than using conventional methods. QAI intends to improve AI algorithms and address complicated issues that are now outside the scope of classical computing by utilizing the computational capability of quantum computing.

Drone applications are one application for QAI. Drones are being utilized more often for a range of tasks, including delivery, surveillance, and humanitarian help. By utilizing methods and technologies like quantum finite automata (QFA), a mathematical model based on quantum systems with finite memory, QAI can assist improve drone performance. In some cases, QFAs have proven to perform better than their conventional equivalents by providing solid solutions with less complex methods.

One advantage of QFA is that it can tackle space-efficiently tasks like promise fulfilment and language recognition even if the quantum state of such an automaton is always finite-dimensional. This makes it simpler to describe the group of languages that QCFAs can identify. QFA theory is useful for simulations in hospital applications, capital investment decision evaluations, network simulators, and working models of systems that enable management to comprehend performance drivers in diagnostics because it can even be used to small devices [6].

In addition, the relationship between algebra and QFA models, such as 1-way QFAs and Latvian QFAs, can be used to promote the requirements with drone applications in terms of a number of parameters, including computational power, closure properties, comparison, and inclusive relation with the models used in QFAs. This methodology mainly concentrates on quantum-enhanced AI algorithms, which are applied in conceptual research domains at the moment. Although putting these ideas into practice in the lab is difficult, some major corporations, including IBM and Google, are investing extensively in quantum research and have reported making great strides with the technology [7].

In conclusion, QAI has the potential to fundamentally alter how we use artificial intelligence in drone applications and other fields by utilizing the computational power of quantum computing to improve AI algorithms and resolve complex problems that are presently beyond the scope of classical computing. Although this sector is still developing, the progress gained so far is encouraging, and it is possible that we will witness substantial developments in the upcoming years.

Deep Learning in Cyber Security

Businesses must employ cutting-edge solutions in the modern world where cyber attacks are getting more common and complex in order to protect their data and networks. Technology like deep learning has a lot of promise for use in the cyber security industry. In order to examine data and find patterns that are challenging for humans to see, it uses machine learning algorithms. This enables it to recognize and stop cyber attacks before they harm the network [8].

Deep learning systems can be trained to recognize novel malware strains and flag threat alarms. Over time, they can develop the ability to identify patterns in typical network behavior and spot any departures from those patterns. Deep learning systems can enhance network security and keep ahead of cybercriminals who are continually coming up with new ways to get around conventional security measures by learning and updating on the fly.

Deep learning has several advantages for cyber security. The ability to automate the monitoring of massive volumes of data and traffic, which is impossible for humans to handle on their own, is one of its main advantages. This allows security specialists in businesses to concentrate on other crucial activities like researching and addressing risks.

Deep learning also has the benefit of assisting businesses in prioritizing their security-related duties by identifying and thwarting various varieties of threats, including phishing, denial-of-service, and ransomware. This is crucial because cyber attacks are growing more sophisticated and can originate from numerous sources simultaneously. Businesses can respond to these challenges more swiftly and successfully with the aid of deep learning.

Deep learning can also assist businesses in lowering their risk of cyber attacks and data breaches. Deep learning can save businesses from suffering major financial losses or reputational damage by identifying threats early and stopping them at the start [9].

Although deep learning in the context of cyber security is still a relatively new technology, it has already demonstrated enormous promise. Many large corporations are making significant investments in this technology to bolster their security framework and safeguard their networks and data. Deep learning is positioned to become the ultimate cyber security solution for businesses in the years to come because to its capacity to learn and adapt to evolving threats.

Tiny AI using deep learning

A new model of AI makes use of compressed algorithms to minimize the use of voluminous data and computational power using different deep learning techniques. The main aim of tiny AI is to reduce the size of artificial intelligence algorithms especially the ones that caters to voice or speech recognition. Smart use of data is an initial step towards efficient AI systems. AI assisted data processing, compression strategies such as network pruning, unsupervised learning methods such as GAN and LSTM and data reduction techniques such as surrogate modeling, advances in nanotechnology and newer architectures and materials, new edge learning methodologies (distributed and joint learning) are some of the issues being researched upon to usher in the era of tiny AI [10].

10.3   Research Challenges in Deep Learning

Besides, the conventional topics in ML the following upcoming areas look quite promising since they are guided by real practical challenges.

1. Model Explanability/Interpretability. This is vital for any ML algorithm that has to be put into practice.
2. Differential Privacy. Using informative data from individuals and yet without disclosing their identity.
3. Few shot learning. Learning from a few data points can be a challenging task. Since in many applications, struggling to get some real data is difficult.
4. Learning to reason possibly using varied knowledge sources. Humans learn from variety of information sources such as how objects interact in the real world, speech, text etc. The development of these systems that can learn to link above and reason about how things work can be a challenge to be considered.
5. Causal Inference: Attention and memory augmented deep architectures, generative models, specifically variants of Generative Adversarial Networks.

10.4   Practical Deep Learning Case Studies

Deep learning can help with comprehension in real-world situations. One may consider deep learning to be a subset of machine learning.

The only way for this subject to learn and develop on its own is by studying computer algorithms. Machine learning makes use of more straightforward concepts whereas deep learning makes use of artificial neural networks designed to replicate how individuals think and learn.

Up until recently, neural network complexity [11] was limited by available computing power. But advances in big data analytics have made it feasible to construct more intricate neural networks, giving computers the capacity to observe, learn from, and react to complex situations more swiftly than people.

Deep learning can be employed to automatically solve any pattern identification problem, including those involving image classification, language translation, and audio recognition.

How then does deep learning function?

Analytics has in the past used supplied data to derive new variables and develop new features. After the data has been analyzed, an analytical model is selected.

This strategy can result in a reliable prediction system, although it is not very generic. It is employed inside parameters or unknowns to form a model.

This suggests that the model might not be precise or comprehensive enough to account for factors like recent knowledge. Instead, you need to start the process over. This approach is improved by deep learning. The definition and formulation of the model are replaced by layers, or hierarchical features. These layers have the ability to learn, which enables them to differentiate between specific traits of the imputed data set that distinguish them from established regularities. Humans may need hours or even years to go through this type of unstructured material and find the relevant information.

By swiftly identifying, analyzing, and presenting the data in a useful way, Deep Learning Systems [12] can deal with unstructured data.

Machine learning is the most widely used technique for processing enormous amounts of data, as opposed to deep learning.

Numerous deep learning applications can be employed in practical settings. One such application uses deep learning to identify and recognize faces. Now, it is possible to identify anything with a high degree of accuracy using just one photograph and an algorithm, as opposed to hundreds or even thousands of images in the past.

This kind of technique has also been used to identify nudity in photographs and propose appropriate content for social media posts, despite concerns from some academics about the potential misuse of this information.

Deep learning is widely used in classification tasks, which entail developing computer algorithms that can ascertain the meaning of each thing based on samples of that same object or notion.

To recognize both objects and activities in a visual scene, deep learning is employed in the field of computer vision. This might be employed, for example, in social robots, where a robot could learn how to help around the house by recognizing everyday items like dishes or clothing while exploring its environment on its own.

Deep learning is frequently linked to the human and animal brains.

However, recent research has revealed that artificial neural networks, the main component of deep learning models, are less adaptable, flexible, and efficient than their biological counterparts.

Future predictions made by AI experts include that deep learning models would be able to learn with little to no help from humans, be flexible enough to alter with their surroundings, and be able to solve a wide range of reflexive and cognitive problem.

LAMSTAR

Introduction

A deep learning neural network model called LAMSTAR (Enormous Memory Storage and Retrieval) is created to efficiently store and recover large volumes of data. In terms of pattern [13] storage and retrieval, as well as the steps for forgetting and recalling sensory observations, it is designed very similarly to the human central nervous system (CNS). Because of this, it is a fantastic tool for handling issues involving enormous volumes of data and intricate patterns.

To store and retrieve data, the LAMSTAR network combines Winner-Take-All and Self-Organizing-Map based layers. These layers are intended to locate patterns in the data fast and effectively, then store them for future use. The network employs weights in a unique way. It distinguishes between storage weights, which are essentially Associative Memory weights (AM), and inter-cortex link weights, which serve as its learning engine and enable deep learning by integrating as many co-processors as may be required for a particular task [14].

The "Verbindungen" or "Interconnections" that Kant developed in his well-known "Critique of Pure Reason" provide the foundation for the Link Weights (LW) in the LAMSTAR network. The two fundamental concepts on which the understanding process is founded are these connections between memory elements, which are frequently referred to as "objects" or "atoms of memory," and memory components themselves. The LAMSTAR NN is more transparent than other ANNs since the LWs are presented in a totally Hebbian and even Pavlovian fashion [15].

The basic Hebbian laws are followed by the link weights of the LAMSTAR network. Functional MRI studies and the principles of the Pavlovian Dog experiment from 1901 have demonstrated that the link weights do in fact meet these criteria. Furthermore, machine learning was recommended as a viable application, are matched by the connection weights. Since lack of transparency is one of the main criticisms levelled against ANNs, the LAMSTAR network uses Link-Weights to make itself more transparent than other ANNs [16].

The inhibitory feature and forgetting feature, which are biological pre-requisites for learning in non-stationary situations, are also included in the LAMSTAR network. It also doesn't react negatively to initial issues, and maybe most importantly, it never ceases learning new information and duplicating the CNS. The aforementioned characteristics, particularly for-getting and never-ending learning, assist the network in avoiding overfitting.

The LAMSTAR network's ability to effectively store and retrieve enor-mous amounts of data is one of its main features. It is therefore the perfect instrument for dealing with issues involving enormous volumes of data and intricate patterns. Its design is also quite similar to the human central nervous system, making it a great tool for modelling and comprehending how the brain functions.

The LAMSTAR network's capacity to learn and adjust over time is an additional benefit. This is due to the fact that it contains the blocking and forgetting characteristics that are crucial for learning under non-stationary conditions. It also never stops learning new ideas and replicating the CNS, which enables it to continuously adapt to changing conditions.

The LAMSTAR network is capable of being used in a variety of ways. It might be applied, for instance, to find patterns in massive data sets, model intricate biological processes, or create more sophisticated artificial intel-ligence systems. It could also be applied to enhance already-existing tech-nologies like speech recognition, image recognition, and natural language processing.

As a deep learning neural network model, the LAMSTAR network is created to effectively store and retrieve vast volumes of data.

Versions of LAMSTAR

The LAMSTAR neural network model has two variants - LAMSTAR-1 and LAMSTAR-2 (also known as Modified LAMSTAR). While the fun-damental ideas of both versions are the same, the Modified LAMSTAR has some minor differences and is often referred to as LAMSTAR-2 in the literature after 2008. However, both versions are examined independently and included in this article. LNN-1 and LNN-2 are alternate names for the two versions of LAMSTAR. It's worth noting that the performance of the Modified LAMSTAR is almost always the same or better than the original LAMSTAR, but the latter is still frequently referred to as LAMSTAR-1 in earlier literature [17].

Basic principles of the LAMSTAR neural network
For analytical and non-analytical problems with multi-category, multi-vector data [18], where some categories may be absent entirely or partially, where data are both exact and fuzzy, and where the sheer volume of data necessitates very quick algorithms, the LAMSTAR network [19] is an ideal solution. Data loss does not necessitate reprogramming or a halt in service. These qualities are uncommon in neural networks as a whole, but especially uncommon when combined.

Because of this, there is no need to make any changes to the code or suspend operation in the event of data loss. These characteristics, especially when coupled, are rare in other types of neural networks.

The ease with which any external co-input processors, such as analytical, mathematical, or other sorts of processors, can be integrated and ranked into the LAMSTAR's input-layer array contributes significantly to the system's deep learning computing capabilities, as was previously indicated. Therefore, the network has been able to solve a wide range of decision, diagnostic, and identification problems across many different domains.

For the sake of this analysis, the LAMSTAR network is split into two subsets: LAMSTAR-2, which was released in 2008 The two variants of the LAMSTAR neural network were created specifically for use in, prediction, and decision-making issues that cover a very broad range of categories. By combining Kohonen's SOM-based network modules with statistical decision-making tools

The LAMSTAR network [20] is perfectly suited to handle analytical and non-analytical problems with data of many different categories and vector dimensions, where some categories may occasionally be absent entirely or partially, where data are both exact and fuzzy, and where the sheer volume of data necessitates very quick algorithms When there is missing data, there is no need for programming modifications or service interruptions. When combined, these characteristics are rare in other neural networks.

The LAMSTAR network is perfectly suited to handle analytical and non-analytical problems with data of many different categories and vector dimensions, where some categories may occasionally be absent entirely or partially, where data are both exact and fuzzy, and where the sheer volume of data necessitates very quick algorithms. When there is missing data, there is no need for programming modifications or service interruptions. These features are unusual in other neural networks, particularly when combined.

As was already mentioned, the LAMSTAR's deep learning computing capabilities is largely attributable to how simple it is to integrate and rank any external co-input processors, whether they be analytical, mathematical, or other types of processors into its input-layer array. As a result, a variety of decision, diagnostic, and identification challenges in a variety of fields have been successfully addressed by the network.

LAMSTAR network is categorized and studied into two groups here, i.e. as of 2008 [21], LAMSTAR-2 has replaced LNN-1, the first iteration of LAMSTAR, and LNN-2, the version from 1996.

CASE STUDIES
In the case studies that follow, we put a lot of emphasis on real-time applications used in various business world features. The number of training and testing data sets used in this method is the same for all neural networks considered in a single case study.

By combining Kohonen's SOM (Self Organizing Map)-based network modules [22] with statistical decision-making tools, the resulting LAMSTAR neural network [23], is designed to store and retrieve patterns in a computationally efficient manner.

The Use of Case Studies
The following case studies place a strong emphasis on real-time applications utilized in a variety of business world settings. Every neural network in a single study uses the same number of training and testing data sets.

Identification of Human Activities
Using CNN, LNN-1, and LNN-2 to apply to the objective of identifying human behaviors, this Case Study evaluates the efficiency of these three deep learning neural networks [22] and their individual computation durations. The input data and pre-processing used by all three of the networks taken into consideration in this study were the same. Additionally, results are contrasted from 18 additional recently published studies on the same subject that used the same database (see the Results tabulations of the present study, below).

600 different postures were used for evaluation and 7590 were used for training in these 6 activities. In this study, five of the 18 activities that CAD-60 participants engaged in—brushing teeth, using a phone, drinking water, chopping food, and using a computer—were chosen (brushing teeth, using the phone, drinking water, cutting food, and using a computer).

PREPROCESSING: A 3D graphic representation of our data is shown. As a result, we must consider the 20 joints' 3D Euclidean coordinates (see Figure 10.1), specifically the hip center, the spine. In this case study, the neural networks [24] under consideration will receive an input consisting of a 1 64 input vector that has been structured into an 8 x 8 input matrix by adding zeros. We acquire 60 coordinates from 20 body-joints for each frame (position of human activity) using normalized data from the aforementioned.

COMPUTATION: An 8 x 8 input vector of the aforementioned coordinate picture is sent to the CNN network. The DeepLearnToolbox for CNN developed in MATLAB was utilized as the CNN software in this investigation.

RESULTS: Table 10.1a compares the study's worst three performers for positions taken from the MRSDaily database, whereas Table 10.1b does the same for stances taken from the CD-60 database. Take note of the LNN-2's flawless recognition in Table 10.1c's findings.

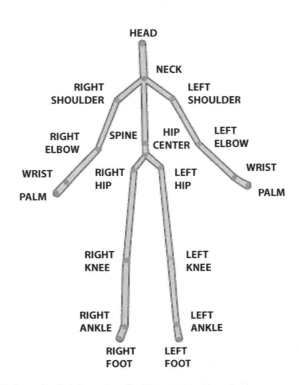

Figure 10.1 Skeleton body joints given by Kincet.

Table 10.1a Human activity categorization findings on the MRSDaily database: precision and recall.

Method	Accuracy (%)
LOP [Wang J, 2012]	42.5
Depth motion maps [Yang X, 2012]	43.13
Joint position [Wang J, 2012]	68
Moving pose [Zanfir, 2013	73.8
Local HOV 4D [Oreifej, 2013]	80
Actionlet ensemble [Wang J, 2012]	85.75
SNV [Yang X, 2014]	86.25
HDMM+3ConvNets [Wang P, 2015]	81.88
CNN (present study)	93
LNN-1 (present study)	95.33
LNN-2 (present study)	99.67

Table 10.1b Classification of human activity results from the CD-60 database, with regard to precision and memory.

Method	Precision	Recall
MEMM [Sung, 2011], [Sung, 2012]	67.9	55.5
SSVM [Koppula, 2013]	80.8	71.4
Structure-Motion Features [Zhang C, 2012]	86	84
NBNN [Yang X, 2013]	71.9	66.6
Image Fusion [Ni B, 2013]	75.9	69.5
Spatial-based Clustering [Gupta R, 2013]	78.1	75.4
K-means Clustering+SVM+HMM [Gaglio, 2014]	77.3	76.7
S-ONI [Parisi, 2015]	91.9	90.2
SI Point Feature [Zhu Y, 2014]	93.2	84.6
Pose Kinetic Energy [Shan J, 2014]	93.8	94.5
CNN (present study)	92.33	93
LNN-1 (present study)	96.67	95.33
LNN-2 (present study)	100	100

Table 10.1c Comparison in brief classification of human activities in the MRSDaily database.

Parameter	CNN	LAMSTAR-I	LAMSTAR-II
Training time (sec)	507.30*	378.63[†]	429.425[†]
Training accuracy (%)	94.33[‡]	98.67[‡]	100[‡]
Tasting time (sec)	172.36[§]	151.23[§]	153.365[§]

*Training time of 7590 training samples for 50 epochs
[†]Training time of 7590 training samples for threshold 0.9999
[‡]Testing with the same input used as training set
[§]Testing time of 600 test samples on trained network
[¶]For a trained CNN for 50 epochs
[Δ]For a trained LAMSTAR/LAMSTAR II with threshold 0.9999

Human Activity — Codes (A Bose)

Part 1: CNN
1. Code_CNN.m

```
clearall; close all; clc;
load (activity_dataset.mat');
[tsR, tsC] = size(testdata);
[trR, trC] = size(traindata);
fori=1:tsR
testdata(i,3:62) = normalizeData(testdata(i,3:62));
end
fori=1:trR
traindata(i,3:62) = normalizeData(traindata(i,3:62));
end
testdata = double(reshape(testdata',8,8,tsR));
traindata = double(reshape(traindata',8,8,trR));
testlabel = double(testlabel');
trainlabel = double(trainlabel');
rand('state',o)
ttr =[];
fori=1:50
cnn=[];
cnnlayers = {
cnn.layers = {
struct('type', 'i') %input layer
struct('type', 'c', 'outputmaps', 24, 'kernelsize', 5) 9%convolution layer
```

```
struct('type', 's', 'scale', 2) %sub sampling layer
};
opts.numepochs = i;
opts.alpha = 0.85;
opts.batchsize = 30;
cnn = cnnsetup(cnn, traindata, trainlabel);
[enn, ttr(i)] = cnntrain(cnn, traindata, trainlabel, opts);
disp([Total training time:' nume2str(ttr()));
tic;
[er(i), correct(i), decision{i}] = cnntest(cnn, testdata, testlabel);
tts = toc;
disp('--------------');
savettrttr;
saveerer;
save correct correct;
save decision decision;
generateConfusionMatrix(decision{50}');
figure; plot(er(1:50), 'LineWidth', 2);
xlabel(Number of epoch');
ylabel('Bit error (%)');
figure; plot(ttr(1:50), 'LineWidth', 2);
xlabel('Number of epoch');
ylabel('Training time (sec)');
figure; plot(correct(1:50)/600*100, 'LineWidth', 2);
('Number of epoch');
ylabel('Recognition rate (%)');
```

10.4.1   Medicine: Epilepsy Seizure Onset Prediction

In this case study, we compare the efficiency and accuracy of three different deep learning neural networks—one trained with Back Propagation, one with Long Short-Term Memory [25] and one with LNN-2.

The ictal phase lasts only a few minutes, but the preceding 20-30 minute Pre-ictal (pre-seizure) phase is used to forecast seizures by comparing it to the inter-ictal interval (without seizures), which can last for days or weeks. And, without considering the possibility of convulsions, speedy calculations are just as important as accurate forecasts (oncoming seizures being missed). The dataset used in this study can be available at https://www.kaggle.com/c/seizure-prediction/data [26]. The data segments, which included both the pre- and post-ictal phases, lasted for a total of 10 minutes (10 minutes). The data collected before to the onset of seizures occurred between

Table 10.2 Comparison of results — Seizure prediction.

Method	Accuracy	Training time	Testing time
CNN	70%	170 sec	3 sec
LNN-1	81.25%	< 1 sec	< 1 sec
LNN-2	81.25%	< 1 sec	< 1 sec

15 and 5 minutes beforehand. Each data window has a 30 second interval. A random sample was taken of all available interictal data at intervals of at least one week before and after a seizure.

The input data for LNN-1 and LNN-2 comprise the dominant frequency of in each one-second time window, which is used for preprocessing.

Check out Table 10.2 for the final tally. According to [26], CNN was able to achieve a sensitivity of 71% despite using a different data source (University of Freiburg, Germany) and a different pre-processing strategy.

Medicine: Image Processing: Cancer Detection
The goal of this case study is to use mass spectrometry data to develop a classifier that can distinguish between cancer patients and control individuals. The "High-Resolution SELDI-TOF Study Sets" section of the FDA-NCI Clinical Proteomics Program Databank is where the data used in this study was sourced from. The collection includes 95.txt files describing average people and 121.txt files describing cancer patients.

The strategy utilized in this work is to pick a small number of measurements, or "features," that can help a classifier tell cancer patients from control patients. The OvarianCancerQAQCdataset.mat file was made using software #3, MSSEQPROCESSING [27], which extracts the raw mass-spectrometry data. Three parameters are present in this file: "grp," a matrix with the labels "cancer" or "normal," "MZ," a matrix with 15000 by 1 values for mass-charge, and "Y," a matrix with 15000 by 216 values for ion intensity levels for each of the connected 15000 Mass-Charge values of MZ.

A feature vector of 100 points was chosen from a total of 15000 points using the Ranking Key Feature of the MSSEQPROCESSING programme, creating a matrix of 100 216 points. LAMSTAR and CNN inputted this final 100 216 matrix, or 100 feature points for every 216 patients. The 216 patients' 100 feature points were however transformed using CNN into a 10 10 matrix.

The ConvNet for CNN tools from MATLAB/Octave were used to create the Convolution Neural Network (CNN). The pre-processing portion from the preceding sentence corresponds to its input of 100 216. In LAMSTAR, the features obtained from the previous pre-processing are represented using 100 layers altogether. The computation was done using the MATLAB Toolbox.

In the preprocessing method, a limited number of measurements, or "features," that can help distinguish between cancer patients and control patients were chosen. The 100 feature points for every one of the 216 patients were used to construct the LAMSTAR and CNN classifiers [28]. ConvNet for CNN tools from MATLAB/Octave were used to build the CNN, and a total of 100 layers of LAMSTAR were used to represent the features obtained from earlier preprocessing.

BOTTOM LINE: Look at Table 10.3 below.

Image Processing: From 2D Images to 3D
In this case study, deep learning neural networks are used to extract depth information from 2D photographs. The study examines the individual processing rates of three distinct networks, including CNN and LNN-1, and assesses each network's performance. The Berkeley 3-D Object [29] Dataset, which includes RGB images taken with the Microsoft Kinect depth camera and ground truth depth maps, serves as the same source of input data for all three networks. Prior to pre-processing, the images are divided into super-pixels, the depth data is quantized and log-scaled, and a patch is drawn around the super-centroid pixel. The entire training set consists of 319,200 unique patches that have been labelled at granularities ranging from 1 to 18. Five convolutional layers and four completely linked layers are included in the CNN programme CONVNET, which is used for scripting. The decision layer of the LNN-1 network has 18 output neurons,

Table 10.3 Comparison between efficiency and effectiveness computation time — Cancer detection.

Parameter	BP	CNN	LAMSTAR-I	LAMSTAR-II
Training time (sec)	3.984	4.1190	0.8019	0.7998
Training accuracy (%)	88.8	86.768	98.67	100
Testing time (sec)	1.728	0.7068	0.142	0.1605
Recognition rate (%)	84.4	88	92.00	94.00

and there are 22 SOM levels. The outcomes of the study are contrasted with two other studies that were written on the same subject. In conclusion, the study offers useful information about the use of deep learning neural networks to the extraction of depth information from 2D images.

Comparisons are made between the results obtained using CNN by [30] and those obtained using RMF (Random Markov Field) by the Make3D method are presented in Table 10.4 [31].

Table 10.4 Comparison of performance (RMS error) – 3D from 2D image.

	RMSE train	RMSE test
CNN	19.14%	21.82%
LNN-1	15.83%	22.46%
Eigen *et al.* – CNN-based	17.51%	24.92%
Make3D – RMF-based	20.06%	26.73%

Image Analysis: Scene Classification

In order to solve the Scene Classification problem, this case study compares the performance of three deep learning neural networks, CNN, LNN-1, and LNN-2, using the Places2 ILSVRC2015 mini-place-focused dataset. The Mini-Places dataset has 400 different scene types, although the study is only interested in 100 of them. Each image has 128x128 RGB pixels. The preprocessing stage comprises resampling the image resolution to 64x64. The Keras framework is used to code the CNN network, which has 128x128x3 inputs and 100x100 outputs. The network consists of three completely linked layers, five Max-Pooling layers, and ten convolution layers with three-by-three filters. The study also looks at how quickly each network computers. Overall, the study offers insightful information about the efficiency and effectiveness of deep learning neural networks for the Scene Classification problem. The training and testing time along with its accuracy for CNN, LNN-1 and LNN-2 are presented in Table 10.5a and Table 10.5b respectively.

Table 10.5a Computation time — Scene classification.

Network	Train time (128 x 128) min	Test time (10,000 images) min.
CNN	954 (30 epochs)	5.83
LNN-1	734.6 (27 epochs)	62.5
LNN-2	581.7 (21 epochs)	64.17

Table 10.5b Comparison of performance - Scene classification.

Network	Accuracy (128 x 128)	Accuracy (64 x 64)
CNN	69.24%	47.53%
LNN-1	71.04%	49.54%
LNN-2	73.04%	47.23%

Be warned that the training period is substantially longer than the testing time, even for 10.000 images. LNN-1 and LNN-2 have fewer epochs than CNN owing of their rapid convergence. Also note that utilizing 30 parallel processors, one for each category, and only 2 neurons in the decision layer for LLN parallel computing will accelerate testing for each of the LNN networks.

Image Recognition: Fingerprint Recognition
This case study compares the performance and computing times of three deep learning neural networks, CNN, LNN-1, and LNN-2, for fingerprint identification. The study uses a dataset based on the fingerprint dataset, which includes eight black-and-white fingerprints from different individuals, with six fingerprints collected from each person, two of which are used for testing.

METHOD: Three ridge patterns—Arch, Loop, and Whorl—are chosen as the fundamental patterns in the current fingerprint identification investigation (Figure 10.2a).

PREPROCESSING: Minutiae are very distinctive characteristics of the patterns. Ridge terminations and bifurcations are the primary minutiae of fingerprint ridges (Figure 10.2.b). Using the Matlab algorithm from [Matlab, Fingerprint Minutiae], these minutiae are extracted during a pre-processing

In a fingerprint deep learning case study, pre-processing software including thinning, ridge-end fining, and bifurcation detecting features was applied. Pre-processing, a neural network (NN), two layers of linear neural networks (LNN-1 and LNN-2), and the CNN method were all employed in the calculation. The CNN algorithm was implemented using Python's Theano.tensor module. A Table 10.6 contains a summary of the findings.

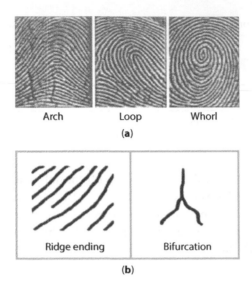

Figure 10.2 (a) Fingerprint ridge patterns. (b) The fingerprint details the three components of the pre-processing software are thinning, ridge-end fining, and bifurcation finding.

Table 10.6 Summary of results—Fingerprint recognition.

Network	Success-rate	Computation time
CNN	90%	1.3 sec
LNN-1	92%	0.9 sec
LNN-2	96.3%	0.7sec

Image Recognition: Fingerprint Recognition

In this case study, three deep learning neural networks for fingerprint recognition were tested for efficiency and performance. The CASIA Fingerprint Image Database Version 5.0, which includes 20,000 fingerprint pictures from 500 individuals, was used in the investigation. Each fingerprint has five photographs of the eight fingers, totaling 40 photos. The pre-processing method comprised thinning, feature extraction, picture enhancement, and binarization. By deleting false information, the backpropagation method was employed to enhance the BP software. Lasagna was used to implement the CNN code, and usage instructions are supplied. LNN-2 and BP were used in this case study in contrast to earlier work to handle minutiae. (http://lasagne.readthedocs.org/en/latest/user/installation.html). A Table 10.7a and Table 10.7b contains a summary of the findings.

RESULTS:

Table 10.7a Lists the outcomes.

Method	Accuracy	Computation time
BP	92.2%	38.6 sec
BP (with postprocessing)	94.5%	28.9 sec (faster convergence)
CNN	92.3%	2.4 sec
LNN-1	95.1%	1.1 sec

Table 10.7b Comparison of results - Fingerprint recognition.

Method	Accuracy	Computation time
BP	92.2%	38.6 sec
BP (with postprocessing)	94.5%	28.9 sec (faster convergence)
CNN	92.3%	2.4 sec
LNN-1	95.1%	1.1 sec

Face Recognition

The objective of this case study is to apply three deep learning neural networks, CNN, LNN-1, and LNN-2, to the problem of face recognition and evaluate their performance and computing speed. The Yale University Face Database was used to pull 45 RGB face photos from 15 individuals. The pre-processing of the data involved feature extraction using PCA, cropping, binarization, and conversion of RGB to grayscale. The 20 eigenvectors produced by PCA for each face, corresponding to the unique characteristics of a face, were fed into LNN-1 and LNN-2. CNN used Python's PIL image package to incorporate PCA pre-processing into the network's input. The computation involved the use of the CaffeeNetConv code for CNN, with components including Convolution Layer 1, Max Pool Layer 1, Convolution Layer 2, Max Pool 2 Layer, ReLu Layer, and Output Layer (using Python Softmax Regression with 15 output neurons). The pre-processing and input data were the same for all three networks in this study.

RESULTS: See Table 10.8 below:

Table 10.8 Performance comparison - Face recognition.

	Success rate	Computational time
LAMSTAR-2	97.78%	0.914a
LAMSTAR-1	95.56%	1.286a
CNN	91.12%	1.405a

Image Recognition - Butterfly Species Classification

The objective of this case study is to use deep learning neural networks, including CNN, LNN-1, and LNN-2, to classify different butterfly species into subgroups and evaluate their processing speeds. The Leeds Butterfly Dataset was used, containing 832 RGB photos categorized by the scientific names of 10 butterfly species. The dataset was split into 80% for training and 20% for evaluation. Preprocessing operations were performed, including background removal, grayscale conversion, noise reduction, segmented mask with contours, and feature extraction, which involved establishing color, shape, and texture vectors. The CNN network used Theano code, operating on a raw image of 150x150 pixels. LNN-1 and LNN-2 had 16-layer architectures and took the pre-processing algorithm as an input. The results are summarized in Table 10.9, where it's worth noting that CNN does not perform any pre-processing, which may affect its accuracy and calculation time compared to LNN-1 and LNN-2. This study provides insights into the effectiveness and processing speeds of different deep learning neural networks for butterfly classification.

Table 10.9 Comparing training performance—Butterfly classification.

Network	Accuracy	Training time (sec)
CNN (1 epoch)	91.2%	20.3
LAMSTAR-1	92.1%	2.1
LAMSTAR-2	94.4%	1.07
State of the art-MPL-BP	81.57%	
State of the art (3-layer feed forward) BP	86%	

Image Recognition: Leaf Classification
In this case study, the identical input data are used to apply CNN, LNN-1, and LNN-2 neural networks to a problem of image categorization. There are 50 greyscale photos in the dataset representing 32 different plant species, and feature extraction is used to create 11 feature vectors for each image. While LNN-1 and LNN-2 need a pre-processing method as input, CNN uses Theano code and works with 200 x 200 pixel pictures.

Table 10.10 shows the results. Though CNN conducts the aforementioned pre-processing, keep in mind that CNN uses the raw data. This could affect performance.

Image Recognition: Traffic Sign Recognition
This case study explores the application of CNN, LNN-1, LNN-2, and SVM to a text classification problem for data visualization, with a focus on identifying traffic signs. The goal is to compare the performance of these three networks and their individual compute times. All three networks and SVMs use the same input data and pre-processing techniques to enable a fair comparison.

Table 10.10 Performance comparison: Leaf classification (CNN doesn't pre-process data).

Network	Accuracy	Training time (sec)
CNN	91.7%	100.3
LAMSTAR-1	92.5%	5.6
LAMSTAR-2	94.2%	3.48
State of the art using (MPL) BP	90%	

The dataset used for this study is obtained from the benchmark.ini.rub. de website, which provides information on the German Traffic Sign Recognition Benchmark (GTSRB) dataset. The dataset includes traffic sign images in PPM format, with sizes ranging from 45x45 to 250x250 pixels.

Due to the various colors, shapes, and sizes of traffic signs, pre-processing is crucial. The pre-processing techniques used in this study include grayscale conversion, noise filtering, thresholding, region hole filling, boundary recognition, and sign cropping and scaling.

The LNN codes in this study consist of 20 input layers and 10 neurons per layer, with the core code being followed by the LNN code. The CNN

code uses the MatConvLibrary and employs Softmax regression for classification, with two convolutional layers. The actual code is not included in
this content.

RESULTS: The results are given in Table 10.11 below.

Table 10.11 Comparison of results — Traffic sign recognition.

Method	Success rate	Computation time
CNN	94.23%	12.64 sec
LNN-1	86.93%	18.54 sec
LNN-2	92.23%	15.29 sec

Information Retrieval: Programming Language Classification (E Wolfson)
This case study focuses on classifying programming languages using
deep learning neural networks with back propagation (BP), LNN-1, and
LNN-2. The collection is made up of bits of code produced by a genera-
tor in many computer languages, including C, Python, and Ruby. Object-
oriented functions, local variables, arguments, and returned variables are
all included in each piece of code. Each snippet of code is 600 bytes in size
and is presented in ASCII format. Each value is multiplied by 0.015873
during preprocessing in order to create vectors with lengths appropriate
for LNNs and LNNa. In this study, programming language classification
performance and processing speeds of these three networks are compared.
    COMPUTING: The back propagation network employs the Matlab BP
Library code, whereas the LAMSTAR coding follows the Core Code of
Chapter 6.

RESULTS: Table 10.12 provides a comparison of performance and computational time.

Table 10.12 Comparison of results - Programming language classification.

Method	Accuracy	Training time	Test time
BP	44.6%	1.34-11.11 sec	0.036-0.038 sec
LNN-1	72.76%	0.34-1.25 sec	0.35-0.46 sec
LNN-2	83.15%	0.13-0.975 sec	0.27-0.525 sec

Information Retrieval: Data Classification from Transcribed Spoken Conversation

In this case study, transcribed natural language conversations were classified for data visualization using CNN, LNN-1, LNN-2, and SVM. The objective was to create cutting-edge data visualizations, update current ones, or relocate visualizations in response to user requests. For training and testing, the study employed 40 and 60 user requests, respectively. The same input data and pre-processing processes were used for all three networks and SVM in this study to ensure accuracy and consistency. The types of crime data and preprocessing steps are shown in Table 10.13a and Table 10.13b.

Preprocessing was required to get rid of superfluous terms from every user request. The preprocessing techniques utilized included lemmatization, part-of-speech recognition, and stop-word elimination. Lemmatization and part-of-speech recognition were carried out using the Stanford Parser and the OpenNLP library, respectively. On the other hand, since the stop-word removal just entailed eliminating terms from a list of stop-words, no specific API was needed.

To ascertain which network produced the best outcomes in terms of accuracy and speed, the performances and individual processing times of the three networks and SVM were evaluated. The goal of the study was to shed light on the most effective network for categorizing natural language conversations for data visualization.

Table 10.13a Types of Chicago crime data.

Crime types		
Homicide	Criminal damage	Criminal trespass
Theft	Battery	Deceptive Practice
Location types		
Alley	Apartment	Street
Gas Station	Parking Lot	Residence
Small Retail Store	Restaurant	Grocery Food Store
Time types		
Day of Month	Day of Year	Month of Year
Time of Day	Year	Month of Year

Table 10.13b Preprocessing steps.

Stop-word Removal	Remove common words ("the", "because", "for", …).
Lemmetization	Provide lemma of each word ("meet" is lemma of "meeting")
Part-of-Speech	Remove word if not noun, Verb, or adjective

RESULTS: See Table 10.13c.

Table 10.13c Comparison of performances — Natural language text classification.

Method	Accuracy	Computation time
BP	60%	1268 m sec
SVM	67%	345 m sec
LNN-1	78%	322 m sec
LNN-2	78%	680 m sec

Speech Recognition

This case study investigates how well CNN, LNN-1, and LNN-2 neural networks function and how quickly they interpret spoken words. The study employed five untrained sets of 10 words each as the testing dataset, and a collection of 10 different words spoken by 20 different speakers as the training dataset. Pre-Emphasis, Frame Blocking, Windowing, and MFCC were the preprocessing phases. 20 frames with 12 coefficients each made up each word. Theano. tensor was used to create the CNN (LeNet), which has 20 levels and 12 neurons in each layer in LNN-1 and LNN-2.

OBSERVATIONS: See Table 10.14.

Table 10.14 Performance comparisons — Speech recognition.

Network	Success rate	Computation time
CNN	94%	1.4 sec
LNN-1	96%	1.0 sec
LNN-2	98%	0.93 sec

Music Genre Classification [32]
Y Fan's team analyzed the effectiveness and speed of CNN and BP networks for categorizing musical genres in a case study. 500 songs from the Chinese, pop, rock, folk, and other musical genres are included in the dataset. The data is transformed into a 2D spectrogram in order to get it ready for CNN processing. The CNN algorithm's single convolutional layer and the Matlab BP code are used to calculate the BP network. Table 10.15a's results reveal that, with CNN trained for 100 epochs, BP and CNN networks perform similarly. The training duration for each network is also shown in the table.

Table 10.15a Comparison of results — Music genre classification.

Method	Accuracy	Computation time
BP	81.91%	35.66 sec
CNN	92.52%	9.46 sec

C Deshpande carried out a similar Case Study [33]. only had three types (classical, rock, jazz). The dataset that was used was the Marsyas GTZAN dataset, which may be downloaded from marsyasweb.appspot.com/data sets. There was coverage of CNN, LNN-i, and LNN-2. The Python setup code for the CNN code, which was required as input, was built using Marsyas Software (http://marsyas.info/), which was used to acquire the image-like spectrograms. The results are displayed in Table 10.15b below:

Table 10.15b Comparison of results — Music genre classification.

Method	Accuracy	Computation time
CNN	90%	5.33 sec (train), 3.87 sec (test)
LNN-1	93.3%	4.965 sec (train), 2.11 sec (test)
LNN-2	96%	3.17 sec (train), 1.85 sec (test)

Security/Finance: Credit Card Fraud Detection
The processing speed and performance of the BP, LNN-1, LNN-2, and SVM networks are examined in this Case Study [34] to determine the likelihood of credit card fraud.

DATASET: The German Credit dataset was used for this Case Study. Each of the 1000 users in this database is assigned a good or bad credit risk assessment.

Table 10.16 Comparison of results — Credit card fraud detection.

Method	Success rate
BP	65.3%
LNN-1	70%
LNN-2	70%
SVM	68.6%

The credit dataset in Germany has 30 features. The total number of attributes is 20, including seven numerical and thirteen categorical. Age, credit limit, monthly payment amount, and other numerical requirements are examples of numerical criteria. Credit history, purpose, savings account/ bond status, and the state of an existing checking account are among the elements that comprise the categories. There are several categories and designations for qualitative traits. For example, credit history is divided into five categories: no credit taken or all credit paid back in full; all credit at this bank paid back in full; existing credits paid back in full up to this point; past payment delays; and critical account/other current credits (in other banks). Twenty dataset variables were preprocessed to create 28 features and sub-words that will be used across all networks.

COMPUTATION: The BP code is a conventional Matlab programme with 24 inputs and 1 hidden unit of 20 neurons. The LAMSTAR networks generally made from a combination of 24 SOM input layers, which correspond to the 24 qualities stated above. The SVM (support "Vector Machine") algorithm is contained in the Toolbox Statistics Package function fitesvm, which itself is utilized in this research.

RESULTS: See Table 10.16.

10.4.2 Using Data from Test Drills to Predict where to Drill for Oil

In the current Case Study, data augmentation neural networks are used to evaluate the potential oil production locations using permeability data from expensive test drill well logs. The output is built on these few samples [35] and reliable cost projections. Deep learning neural networks can be utilized to solve the challenging nonlinear permeability problem mathematically. This study compares and contrasts BP, LNN-1, and LNN-2 for this application [36].

The dataset for this case study was 396 core [37] well log data points from actual well log data from a reservoir location. The data comprised calliper jog (CALI — inches), neutron porosity (NPHI — fraction), total porosity (PHIT — fraction), bulk density (RHOB — gm/cc), density (DRHO — gm/cc), un-flushed zone saturation (SWT — fraction), and true formation conductivity (CT — fraction).

PREPROCESSING: Logio [37] was used to conduct correlation study on the information relating to the permeability of the core and the individual logs using CT and MSFL. The inclusion of correlation coefficients considerably enhanced the results.

In the Octave BP code, the output layer is the sole one of two hidden layers [38], each of which has five neurons. The network's input, as indicated in the Preprocessor section of this Case Study, comprises of a large number of well logs that are fed into the single SOM input neurons in the Octave.

RESULTS: See Table 10.17.

Table 10.17 Comparison of results — Drill site prediction.

Method	Success rate	Computation time (sec)
BP	50%	57.8 sec (to converging)
LNN-1	69.79%	0.865 sec
LNN-2	73.03%	0.8445 sec

Prediction of Forest Fires
By contrasting the functionality and processing speed of CNN, LNN-1, LNN-2, and SVM deep learning neural networks [39], this case study aims to predict forest fires.

Predicting Price Movement in Market Microstructure (X Shi)
The specifics [42] of this Case Study were given in (Graupe, 2013). The purpose of this study was to forecast price changes in the market infrastructure, where 90% of trade now takes place and where many equities see over 100,000 price changes each day. LNN-1 (LAMSTAR), BP, SVM, and RBF were used in the Case Study (Radial Basis Function).

DATABASE: HFT (High Frequency Trading) data is public domain (Nasdaq HFT ete,
PREPROCESSING: See in [31] for details, PROGRAMMING: See in [39, 40].

RESULTS: See Table 10.18 below.

Table 10.18 Comparison of performances — Market microstructure.

Method	Accuracy	Computation time
RBF	72.2%	126 sec
SVM	73.15%	206 sec
BP	73.15%	127 sec
LNN-1	73.35%	92 sec

Fault Detection: Bearing Fault Diagnosis via Acoustic Emission (M He)
Based on the information provided, it appears that the Case Study aimed to identify machine bearing issues using acoustic emission (AE) data by comparing the performance and processing times of three deep learning neural networks: Back Propagation (BP), LNN-1, and LNN-2. The AE measurement data used in the study was provided by [41] at the University of Illinois in Chicago's MIE Department, and the type 6025 complete ceramic bearings from the Boca Bearings Company were utilized in the AE [42] tests.

The AE signal's preprocessing using the Hilbert-Huang (HHT) [43] transform produced several intrinsic mode functions (IMFs), and in this Case Study, the three IMF functions RMS, Kurtosis, and Peak-to-Peak were used as features for the LAMSTAR [44, 45] network and as inputs for the BP network.

The results of the study were presented in Table 10.19, which contained entries expressed in terms of accuracy while training time was expressed in seconds. The time indicated in the table corresponds to the point at

Table 10.19 Comparison of performance — Fault detection.

	BP	LNN-1	LNN-2
Inner race	93.75	95.89	98.78
Outer race	100.00	100.00	100.00
Case	78.57	93.23	99.89
Bal	94.12	96.89	100.00
Healthy	100.00	100.00	99.14
Overall	93.75	97.20	99.56
Training time	254	98	133

which performance reaches the maximum accuracy shown in the table. According to the information provided, LNN-2's detection was almost perfect with an accuracy of 99.566.

10.5 Summary

This chapter has discussed main future direction, concerns and practical case studies in the context of deep learning and its applications. Various techniques are exploited to present the exceptional features of present techniques with systematic review and enlisting the advantages and disadvantages of all in this chapter. Moreover, the interdependence of social being with smart bionetworks, which goes well beyond technical limitations and requires inter-disciplinary algorithm with the aim to also address all types of societal and ethical enforcing issues is the central issue of research in this domain.

The variety of critical concerns also ascend, comprising of like developing for significant humanoid control over machines, safeguarding smart systems' clearness and efficiency, and accounting for intelligent machines intrinsic imperviousness and irregularity by employing deep learning in many practical aspects. The standards of choice is that the chosen procedure should own most of the desired features of constrained environment, including a reckless and well-organized data treating and handling capability, lesser requirement of storage, high compression proportion as well as high image fidelity. Centered on the investigation of the evidence concise and wide-ranging collected works studies, it is observed that emphasis on the exploring the contents and features of different techniques can be used in various domains.

Intercepting the discussed concerns and inspecting the developing study problems necessitate collaborative efforts underneath a wide-ranging inter-disciplinary space. The collaborated research to be done by interconnecting elements globally and internationally.

References

1. Mitchell, M., Abstraction and analogy-making in artificial intelligence. *Artificial Intelligence,* arXiv, 10, 21–29, 2021. https://www.quantamagazine.org/melanie-mitchell-trains-ai-to-think-with-analogies- 20210714.
2. Sgarbas, K.N., The Road to Quantum Artificial Intelligence, in: *Current Trends in Informatics,* vol. A, Papatheodorou, T.S., Christodoulakis, D.N., Karanikolas, N.N. (Eds.), pp. 469–477, 2007.

3. *Cornell Activity Datasets: CAD-60 & CAD-120*, Copyright (c) Cornell University, Robot Learning Lab, Ithaca, NY, 2009.

4. Gaglio, S., Lo Re, G., Morana, M., Human activity recognition process using 3-D posture data. *IEEE Trans. Human-Machine Syst.*, 41, 1471, 2014.

5. Gupta, R., Chia, A.Y.S., Rajan, D., Human activities recognition using depth images, in: *Proc. of the 21st ACM International Conference on Multimedia*, 2013.

6. Koppula, H.S., Gupta, R., Saxena, A., Learning human activities and object affordances from RGB-D videos. *arXiv*, 12, 1207, 2013.

7. Ni, B., Pei, Y., Moulin, P., Yan, S., Multilevel depth and image fusion for human activity detection. *IEEE Trans. Cybern.*, 14, 1371, 2013.

8. Oreifej, O. and Liu, Z., Hon4d: Histogram of oriented 4d normals for activity recognition from depth sequences, in: *CVPR*, 2013.

9. Parisi, G., II, Weber, C., Wermter, S., Self-organizing neural integration of pose-motion features for human action recognition. *Front. Neurobot.*, 10, 33–43, 2015.

10. Shan, J. and Akella, S., 3D Human action segmentation and recognition using pose kinetic energy, in: *IEEE Workshop on Advanced Robotics and its Social Impacts (ARSO)*, 2014.

11. Sung, J., Ponce, C., Selman, B., Saxena, A., Human activity detection from RGBD images, in: *Proc. AAAI Workshop on Pattern, Activity and Intent Recognition (PAIR)*, 2011.

12. Sung, J., Ponce, C., Selman, B., Saxena, A., Unstructured human activity detection from RGBD images, in: *Proc. ICRA*, 2012.

13. Wang, J., Liu, Z., Wu, Y., Yuan, J., Mining action let ensemble for action recognition with depth cameras, in: *Proc. CVPR, Providence*, Rhode Island, June 16–21, 2012.

14. Wang, P., Li, W., Gao, Z., Zhang, J., Tang, C., Ogunbona, P., Deep convolutional neural networks for action recognition using depth map sequences. *arXiv*, 15, 4686, 2015.

15. Yang, X., Zhang, C., Tian, Y., Recognizing actions using depth motion maps-based histograms of oriented gradient, in: *ACMMM*, 2014.

16. Yang, X. and Tian, Y., Effective 3D action recognition using EigenJoints. *J. Visual Commun. Image Representation*, 25, 2–11, 2013.

17. Yang, X. and Tian, Y., Super normal vector for activity recognition using depth sequences, in: *CVPR*, 2014.

18. Zanfir, M., Leordeanu, M., Sminchisescu, C., The moving pose: An efficient 3D kinematics descriptor for low-latency action recognition and detection. *Proceedings of the IEEE International Conference on Computer Vision (ICCV)*, pp. 2752–2759, 2013.

19. Zhang, C. and Tian, Y., RGB-D camera-based daily living activity recognition. *J. Comput. Vision Image Process.*, 4, 4–15, 2012.

20. Zhu, Y., Chen, W., Guo, G., Evaluating spatiotemporal interest point features for depth-based action recognition, in: *Image and Vision Computing. American Epilepsy Society Seizure Prediction Challenge*, 2014.

21. Mirowski, P., Madhavan, D., LeCun, Y., Kuzniecky, R., Classification of patterns of EEG synchronization for seizure prediction. *Clin. Neurophysiol.*, 120, 11, 1927–1940, 2009.

22. Saxena, A., Sun, M., Ng, A.Y., Make3d: Learning 3d scene structure from a single still image. *IEEE Trans. Pattern Anal. Mach. Intell. (PAMI)*, 30, 5, 824–840, 2009.

23. Eigen, D., Puhrsch, C., Fergus, R., Depth map prediction from a single image using a multi-scale deep network. *CoRR*, 14, 2283, 2014.

24. Russakovsky, O., ImageNet large scale visual recognition challenge. *Int. J. Comput. Vis.*, 115, 211–252, 2015.

25. Murphy, J., 2nd Fingerprint Verification Competition (FVC), 16th ICPR (International Conference on Pattern Recognition), University of Bologna, Bologna, 2002. bias.csr.unibo.it/fvc2002/databases.asp.https://www.microway. com/hpc-tech-tips/keras-theano-deep-learning-frameworks.

26. Kaur, M., Singh, M., Girdhar, A., Sandhu, P.S., Fingerprint verification system using minutiae extraction technique. *Int. J. Computer, Electrical, Automation, Control Inf. Eng.*, 2, 10–19, 2008.

27. Belhumeur, P., Hespanha, J., Kriegman, D., Eigenfaces vs. fisherfaces: Recognition using class specific linear projection. *IEEE Transactions on Pattern Analysis and Machine Intelligence*, July, pp. 711–720, 1997.

28. Siddique, S., *A wavelet based technique for analysis and classification of texture images*, vol. 70, p. 593, Carleton University, Ottawa, Canada, Proj. Rep, April, 2022.

29. Keras 0.1.0, Python Software Foundation, . https://testpypi.python.org/pypi/ Keras/0.1.0.

30. Wang, O., Markert, K., and Everingham, M., Learning models for object recognition from natural language descriptions. In *Proceedings of the 20th British Machine Vision Conference (BMVC2009)*, September 2009.

31. Models for object recognition from natural language descriptions. *Proceedings 20th British Machine Vision Conference*, http://www.comp.leeds. ac.uk/scs6jwks/dataset/leedsbutterfl.

32. Flavia Database, nttp:/flavia-plant-leaf-recognition-systemsoftss2.com/.

33. Chaki, Parekh, Chakt, J., Parekh, R., Plant leaf recognition using shape based features and neural network classifiers. *Int. J. Adv. Comput. Sci. Appl.*, 44, 1256, 2011.

34. Lasagne, Python - https://pypi.python.org/pypi/Lasagne, Stanford Parser Java API used for Lemmatization Pre-processing - http://nlp.stanford.edu/ software/lex-parser.shtml. Apache OpenNLP Java API used for part-of-speech pre-processing - https://opennlp.apache.org/. deep learning, lenet - http://deeplearning.net/tutorial /lenet.html.

35. Blake, C., Keogh, E., and Merz, C.J., UCI Repository of Machine Learning Databases. University of California, Irvine, 1998.

36. Garcia, V., Sanchez, J.S., Mollineda, R.A., Alejo, R., Sotoca, J.M., The class imbalance in Pattern Classification and Learning, in: *Cong Espanol de Informatica*, F.J. Ferrer-Troyano (Ed.), pp. 283–291, 2007.

37. Niedermeyer, E. and Lopes da Silva, F., *Electroencephalography: Basic principles, clinical applications and related Fields*, Press, Oxford University, Great Clarendon St, United Kingdom, 2017, ISBN 9780190228484.

38. Webster, J.G. and Eren, H., *Measurement, instrumentation, and sensors handbook: Electromagnetic, optical, radiation, chemical, and biomedical measurement*, 2nd Edition, CRC Press, Boca Raton, Florida, United States, 2017, ISBN 9781138072183.

39. Sanei, S. and Chambers, J.A., *EEG signal processing*, Wiley Publications, Hoboken, New Jersey, 2017, ISBN: 978-0-470-02581-9.

40. Teplan, M., Fundamentals of EEG Measurement. *Measurement Sci. Rev.*, 2, 2, 1–11, 2002.

41. Fisch, B., *Fisch and Spehlmann's, EEG Primer*, 3rd Ed, Elsevier, Amsterdam, Netherlands, 1999, ISBN: 9780444821485.

42. Rabbi, A.F. and Rezai, R.F., A Fuzzy logic system for seizure onset detection in intracranial EEG. *Comput. Intell. Neurosci.*, 12, 1–13, 2012.

43. Gotman., J., Automatic recognition of epileptic seizure in the EEG. *Electroencephalogram Clin. Neurophysiol.*, 54, 5, 530–540, 1982.

44. Walter, C., Cierniak, G., Gerjets, P., Rosenstiel, W., Bogdan, M., Classifying mental states with machine learning algorithms using alpha activity decline, European Symposium on Artificial Neural Networks, in: *Computational Intelligence and Machine Learning* pp. 405–410, 2011.

45. Siuly, Li, Y., Wen, P., Clustering technique-based least square support vector machine for EEG signal classification. *Comput. Methods Prog. Biomed. Elsevier Sci.*, 104, 3, 358–372, 2008.

Index

Printed and bound by CPI Group (UK) Ltd, Croydon, CR0 4YY

27/10/2024

14580177-0001